THE QUEST FOR THE GOOD LIFE IN PRECARIOUS TIMES

ETHNOGRAPHIC PERSPECTIVES ON THE DOMESTIC MORAL ECONOMY

THE QUEST FOR THE GOOD LIFE IN PRECARIOUS TIMES

ETHNOGRAPHIC PERSPECTIVES ON THE DOMESTIC MORAL ECONOMY

EDITED BY CHRIS GREGORY AND JON ALTMAN

MONOGRAPHS IN ANTHROPOLOGY SERIES

PRESS

Published by ANU Press
The Australian National University
Acton ACT 2601, Australia
Email: anupress@anu.edu.au
This title is also available online at press.anu.edu.au

A catalogue record for this book is available from the National Library of Australia

ISBN(s): 9781760462000 (print)
9781760462017 (eBook)

Cover design and layout by ANU Press

Contents

List of Figures

List of Tables

List of Abbreviations

AHED	Arnhem Human Enterprise Development
ATSIC	Aboriginal and Torres Strait Islander Commission
BAC	Bawinanga Aboriginal Corporation
BJP	Bharatiya Janata Party
CAEPR	Centre for Aboriginal Economic Policy Research
CDEP	Community Development Employment Projects
CPO	Chief Police Officer
ESRC	Economic and Social Research Council
GRA	Gazelle Restoration Authority
MAC	Maningrida Arts and Culture
OBC	Other Backward Castes
PNG	Papua New Guinea
RSE	Recognised Seasonal Employer
SC	Scheduled Castes
ST	Scheduled Tribe
TCU	Traditional Credit Union

Contributors

Jon Altman is a research professor at the Alfred Deakin Institute for Citizenship and Globalisation at Deakin University in Melbourne and an emeritus professor with the School of Regulation and Global Governance at The Australian National University (ANU), Canberra. Altman has a disciplinary background in economics and anthropology and has been institutionally embedded at ANU since 1978, including a period between 1990 and 2010 when he was the foundation director of the Centre for Aboriginal Economic Policy Research (CAEPR) in which he sought to refine his ability to combine sound scholarship with progressive policy advocacy. Since 1979, Altman has worked with Kuninjku-speaking people in western Arnhem Land, advocating for their right to maintain their distinct life ways and to live on their ancestral lands. In 2011, he joined the UK Economic and Social Research Council (ESRC) 'Domestic Moral Economy in the Asia–Pacific' project, first as a Hallsworth Visiting Professor at the University of Manchester and then as the International Visitor for the duration of the project.

Matti Eräsaari is an Academy of Finland Postdoctoral Researcher in social anthropology at the University of Helsinki. His research interests span time and value, food and drink, ceremonial exchange, money and the early contact period in Fiji. He has carried out field research in Fiji since 2003. Eräsaari earned his PhD in social and cultural anthropology at the University of Helsinki in 2013. He is the author of '*We Are the Originals*': *A Study of Value in Fiji* (2013), and co-editor of *Ruoan kulttuuri* (2016), a Finnish-language volume on the anthropology of food. Eräsaari worked as a Newton International Fellow in social anthropology at the University of Manchester in 2015–17, before returning to Helsinki. His current research deals with the comparative valuations of time in Fiji and Finland.

Chris Gregory has been a member of the Anthropology Department at ANU since 1983 and was a visiting professor of Political and Economic Anthropology at the University of Manchester from 2008–15. He has been conducting fieldwork on the economy and culture of rice cultivation in Bastar District, India, periodically since 1982. He lived and worked in Papua New Guinea (PNG) for three years (1973–75) and Fiji for four years (2008–12). His books include *Gifts and Commodities* (2nd ed., 2015), *Observing the Economy* (with Jon Altman, 1989), *Savage Money* (1997) and *Lachmi Jagar* (with Harihar Vaishnav, 2003).

Rodolfo Maggio is a social anthropologist currently working as a postdoctoral researcher at the University of Oxford. He leads 'Mothers: Early Intervention Ethics', an empirical research study into the social, political and ethical dimensions of early intervention in maternal health and child development. He has conducted ethnographic research in a variety of cultural settings, including the metropolitan areas of Dublin, Rome and Prague, the suburbs of London and the Asia–Pacific region. As part of his doctoral research, he conducted 13 months of fieldwork in an illegal settlement on the outskirts of Honiara, the capital of Solomon Islands. Residing with local families, he closely observed the concretion of ordinary ethics in their everyday dealing with moral dilemmas, confrontations and tensions over the meaning and significance of their values. This gave him an empirical understanding of how people construct, negotiate and defend their sense of belonging, identity and life trajectory.

Fiona Magowan is professor of anthropology and a fellow of the Senator George J. Mitchell Institute for Security, Peace and Justice, Queen's University, Belfast. Her research interests span religion, ritual and value in the domestic moral economy, music, sound and movement, and art, emotion and the senses. She has conducted fieldwork among Yolngu of the Northern Territory, Australia, at different times since 1990, and has also worked with stolen generations artists in South Australia (2010–12). Her publications include *Christianity, Conflict, and Renewal in Australia and the Pacific* (with Carolyn Schwarz, 2016), *Performing Gender, Place and Emotion in Music: Global Perspectives* (with Louise Wrazen, 2013) and *Melodies of Mourning: Music and Emotion in northern Australia* (2007).

Keir Martin is associate professor in social anthropology at the University of Oslo. He completed his PhD in 2006 after two years of fieldwork in East New Britain Province, PNG, working among the Matupi community in the aftermath of the volcanic eruptions of 1994. He is the author of *The Death of the Big Men and the Rise of the Big Shots* (2013) and articles covering issues of contested transactions, social movements, land tenure, tourism and possessive individualism.

Rachel E. Smith is a postdoctoral fellow at Stanford University working on a comparative project focused on the theory of mind and religious experience. She received her PhD in social anthropology at the University of Manchester in 2016. Her thesis was based on 16 months of ethnographic fieldwork at Lamen island and Lamen Bay, Epi, in central Vanuatu, a rural community with a high degree of engagement in New Zealand and Australia's Pacific seasonal-worker programs. The thesis examined Li-Lamenu people's moral reasoning about their motivations for working overseas, and the intended and unintended consequences of this in terms of socioeconomic change. The aspiration for a durable, modern 'good house' concretises the Li-Lamenu vision of heightened moral and material standards of living. However, this quest for a material good life produces a number of tensions and contradictions that seasonal workers and their kin must negotiate to 'live together well'.

Karen Sykes is professor of anthropology at the University of Manchester. She has undertaken numerous periods of fieldwork in PNG since 1990, accumulating over four years residence there. She has researched and published on intergenerationality, education, funerary rituals and cultural property at the intersection of kinship and state politics. Research for the chapter in the present collection was funded by the UK ESRC and carried out during 2012 and again in late 2014, when she conducted fieldwork in far North Queensland and extended that research to other cities and towns in Australia. Her newest research is funded by the Australian Research Council and enquires into how PNG households in Australia plan for ageing and later life, including the funerals and burials of their members in distant locations.

Preface

The chapters in this collection were among papers presented at a conference held at the University of Manchester, 24–26 March 2015, entitled 'The Quest for the Good Life in Precarious Times: Grassroots Perspectives on the Value Question in the 21st Century'. The conference marked the end of a UK Economic and Social Research Council (ESRC)–funded project entitled 'Domestic Moral Economy: An Ethnographic Study of Value in the Asia–Pacific Region', which was administered from Manchester by Karen Sykes. It provided PhD scholarships—successfully completed—to Rodolfo Maggio and Rachel Smith, and funds for Karen Sykes, Chris Gregory, Fiona Magowan and Jon Altman to return to the sites of their long-term fieldwork in Papua New Guinea (PNG), India and Australia, respectively, and, in the case of Sykes and Gregory, to investigate transnational familial links between PNG and North Queensland and between India and Fiji, respectively.

The main focus of the project—'domestic moral economy'—defined its scope and limits, and the subtitle—'an Ethnographic Study of Value in the Asia–Pacific region'—the need for a method that privileged twenty-first century accounts of the 'native point of view' and for historically informed comparative analyses of such data.

Workshops and conferences held in Manchester (2011, 2015), Canberra (2012), Belfast (2013) and Edinburgh (2014) provided a forum to test our ideas among colleagues who had not only done fieldwork in the Asia–Pacific region, but had worked on the general problem of moral economy in Africa and Europe. Needless to say, the papers and the general discussion that followed were invaluable in enabling us to grasp the comparative, historical and theoretical significance of our own material. This volume includes chapters by the above-named senior and junior participants of the ESRC grant, plus two Manchester-based Oceanists, Keir Martin and Matti Eräsaari, who were closely involved with the project over a number of years.

The aim of the work in this volume is to provoke debate and pose new questions for analysis. The term 'domestic moral economy', as mentioned above, is used to define the scope and limits of our approach, not to suggest the conceptual framework for a new general theory of moral economy. Economy, as classically understood, has reduced the value question to that of the determinants of market prices. Scholars from other disciplines, such as historians, sociologists, philosophers and anthropologists who have worked under the general umbrella of 'moral economy', have striven to extend the narrow focus of economists by introducing other values of a religious, sociological, moral and familial kind. The literature on moral economy in this interdisciplinary sense is now vast. Our use of the adjective 'domestic' is intended to narrow the focus of our studies to something ethnographically possible, while retaining the focus on the complex interplay of market values (e.g. exchange value/use value) with religious values (e.g. pollution/purity and sacred/profane), moral values (e.g. virtues/vice) and domestic values (e.g. familial love/respect). Values everywhere seem to be informed by the logical principle of thesis/antithesis, but their concrete realisation is invariably complex, as people practise the difficult art of trying to live together well using some notion of 'the good'. Values are mere instruments in the hands of valuers in the definition of the good. A study of values, then, must examine the social relations of the valuers and note the differences between points of view and moral environments. Women's morality is not men's morality, the morality of the old is not that of the young and the morality of the wealthy elite is not that of the poor subaltern. Mauss (2007) outlined these dictums in his *Manual of Ethnography* and provided the methodological principles that have informed the research behind our domestic moral economy project in general, and the chapters in this volume, in particular.

The authors are collectively indebted to the ESRC for the generous funding of the project, and to the many colleagues from different parts of the world who participated in the workshops and conferences and offered valuable hints and suggestions. The final conference in Manchester brought together participants from four other research projects dealing with closely related themes: 'Popular Economies and Citizen Expectations in South Africa', led by Deborah James of the London School of Economics; 'Grassroots Economics: Meaning, Project and Practice in the Pursuit of Livelihood', led by Susana Narotzky of the University of Barcelona; 'Globalization, Sports and the Precarity of Masculinity', led by Niko Besnier of the University of Amsterdam; and 'Realising Eurasia: Moral Economy and Civilisational Pluralism in the 21st Century', led by Chris Hann of the Max Planck Institute at Halle in Germany. We are grateful to the team members of these projects for their contributions and critiques.

Support staff at the University of Manchester, Queen's University Belfast, the Academy of Social Sciences in Australia and The Australian National University provided invaluable assistance at various stages of the five-year project. The editors of this volume, who bear equal responsibility for it, as in past collaborations, are grateful to the Alfred Deakin Institute for Citizenship and Globalisation at Deakin University in Melbourne (where Jon Altman is currently located) for financial assistance as we edged towards completion. Thanks also to Alison Caddick from Arena Publications who assisted us with her subediting skills and standardisation of the essays in this volume prior to final copyediting by Capstone Editing.

We are grateful to The Australian National University's Emeritus Faculty, ANU Pacific Institute and ANU Press for assistance with publication costs.

Chris Gregory, Canberra
Jon Altman, Melbourne
September 2017

References

Mauss, M. (2007). *Manual of Ethnography*. London, England: Berghahn.

1

Introduction

Chris Gregory

The study of the quest for the good life and the theoretical questions about morality and value it presupposes is not new. To the contrary, it is an ancient issue; its intellectual history can be traced back to Aristotle and beyond. In anthropology, the study of morality and value has been a central concern from the beginning of the discipline, despite the claim of some scholars who see the recent upsurge of interest in questions of morality and value as new. What *is* novel is the present historical context in which scholars in many disciplines are posing the question of value in new ways, again. The rise in the popularity of morality as an academic interest, it seems, is in inverse proportion to the decline in morality in society as a whole. The popular evidence for this hypothesis seems to grow by the day, as Hollywood films such as *The Wolf of Wall Street*, reports of ever-increasing multi–million dollar bonuses given to CEOs and official investigations into firms such as Enron and others reveal the corruption and greed that inform business as usual in the twenty-first century.

The merits of this popular hypothesis aside, what is beyond dispute is that the world has undergone profound social, economic and political change over the past five decades, and this has had equally profound effects on anthropological thought. We anthropologists like to think that our inquiries are contributing to the analysis of the new problems of morality and value that are being posed; however, if we are honest, we must consider the possibility that those inquiries are part of the problem rather than the solution. Understanding the present is a task that is beyond us all and a certain humility is needed given the difficulty of the task at hand. We are all in the dark; the torch that the anthropologist carries casts a useful, but very narrow, light—not one that illuminates the whole. Trying to understand the present requires the efforts of scholars from many disciplines in the social sciences—history, geography and sociology—as well as those in ecology and other natural sciences, as global warming becomes an ever-greater concern.

Many anthropologists take their bearings on this new world order via the lens of the 'global/local' distinction. This reduces the anthropologist's quest for the 'native point of view' to that of understanding the process of the 'globalisation of the local' and the 'localisation of the global'. For instance, indigenous agency is celebrated formulaically as the 'indigenisation of modernity'. This is a noble hypothesis, but the question arises as to whether this formulaic approach to a complex historical conjuncture tells us more about the point of view of members of the academy than it does about those outside it. The trend in current anthropological thought has been away from a study of the social lives of people towards the study of the social lives of things, and away from a concrete study of the 'becoming' of power towards the metaphysical study of being. For example, the rise of globalisation theory takes our attention away from what used to be called 'imperialism' precisely at a time when inter-imperialist rivalries between nation-states are becoming a crucial issue. The rise of China and the economic and political challenge it poses to the US everyday becomes a more urgent issue, one that has its origins in the gradual deindustrialisation of the Euro-American economic bloc and the industrialisation of Asia, developments that have been in process for many decades.

A focus on the 'global' as a conceptual category of analysis also diverts our attention away from class, an ancient sociological category that has acquired new historical forms in the era of so-called globalisation. The new grassroots language of the '1 per cent' versus the '99 per cent', and the more academic language of the 'plutonomy' and the 'precariat' (Chomsky, 2012), reference this new social phenomenon. Its origin is to be found in the rapidly widening economic inequalities that have arisen in recent years; its contradictory consequences are to be found in the increasing bipolarisation of political movements, as the recent rise of Donald Trump and Bernie Sanders in the US exemplifies. People everywhere are confused by the world they find themselves in, as opportunistic politicians from the extreme left and extreme right strive to give voice to the grievances of the precariat by claiming to seize the moral high ground.

Piketty's (2014) classic work succeeds in capturing the economic paradox that lies at the heart of recent developments in the world economy. His statistical analysis of the metamorphosis of capital in Europe over the past 300 years shows that Europe has gone from being an agrarian society ruled by capital owned by a patrimonial landlord class, to an *urban* society in which capital, in the form of *residential land* (rather than industrial capital), is the most important form of wealth. Patrimonial capitalism, Piketty asserted, is back, but in a totally new form. As Polanyi (1944) argued, land is a 'fictitious' commodity because, as something that is a 'gift of nature' rather than the product of labour, its price is 'fictitious'. By this logic, the reality of capitalism today is that *it* is 'fictitious', which is another way of saying that we do not really understand much about the 'fictitious' people who control it; this is because, unlike the landlords of yesteryear, the familial relations of this new patrimonial class are largely unknown. One reason for this is the concealment that goes under the guise of 'commercial in confidence'—the name of the economic game today. What is clear is the rapid growth of cities, booms in land prices here and busts there and the emergence of palaces in the gated communities of those members of the new rich who choose to spend their new-found wealth conspicuously in the age-old quest for fame. This is happening in cities everywhere, including those in the Pacific area, where many political and business leaders eagerly embrace the new global warming language of the Anthropocene and exploit it for their own commercial advantage.

The reality of the new world order today, in which all people are forced to participate, poses many political, moral and theoretical questions, but the central question the essays in this collection address is: how do relatively poor people in selected areas of the Australia–Pacific region survive in these precarious times? From here, we ask how they cope with the moral issues that confront them today, and about the values that inform their quest for the good life. Authors in this volume were asked to privilege the values and concepts of their interlocutors rather than those of the currently fashionable high priests of the academy. We do not seek to revise anthropological theories of globalisation, but we do hope that the essays here make some small contribution to reformulating our understanding of the present conjuncture. We are motivated by the belief that a disciplined approach to anthropology, grounded as it is in a radical empirical critique of received ideas based on intensive fieldwork, has something to offer those seeking to grasp the bigger picture.

Some of the essays presented in this book were delivered at the conference 'The Quest for the Good Life in Precarious Times: Grassroots Perspectives on the Value Question in the 21st Century', held at Manchester in 2015. This was the final event of a UK Economic and Social Research Council (ESRC)–funded project called 'Domestic Moral Economy: An Ethnographic Study of Values in the Asia–Pacific Region'. Four of the essays are based on fieldwork in the Pacific—Matti Eräsaari in Fiji, Keir Martin in Papua New Guinea (PNG), Rachel Smith in Vanuatu and Rodolfo Maggio in Solomon Islands; three are based on fieldwork in northern Australia—Karen Sykes, Jon Altman and Fiona Magowan; and one on fieldwork in India—Chris Gregory. The aim of the conference was to assemble grassroots perspectives on the value question in general, using ethnographic data from the Australia–Pacific region. The geographical focus was chosen simply to limit the scope of the analysis and not to suggest that the region constitutes a 'cultural area'. While the main interest of the collection lies in the concrete descriptive accounts of people located in different sociocultural settings and their struggles to cope with the dilemmas of life in the twenty-first century, three general themes emerged.

The first emerged in the process of trying to classify the essays by either the 'rural' or the 'urban' location of the fieldwork. Demographic data the world over reveals a definite trend towards urbanisation; however, from the perspective of the values of the people involved, the situation is much more complex. For a start, the expansive growth of cities means that the city now sometimes comes to the country and urbanises rural villages, as the essays by Gregory in Sargipalpara, India and Maggio in Honiara, Solomon Islands, illustrate. Land tenure in the Pacific is notoriously complex but, as Maggio's essay shows, the growing demand for urban land and soaring land prices in prime areas have complicated the situation even further as landowner, settler and the state negotiate the politics of the new moral, ethical and legal relationships that have arisen. Not only is rural land being urbanised, new forms of migration have arisen to blur the distinction between rural and urban dweller, creating new intercultural forms. Karen Sykes's essay is based on fieldwork in the city of Cairns, Far North Queensland, with transnational PNG migrants who have houses in both countries. These migrants have created new kin networks of two kinds: those that bind some PNG women with non-PNG men from Australia and elsewhere; and those that bind most PNG men with PNG women from different PNG regions and, hence, different language groups. Rachel Smith's essay describes how the New Zealand seasonal-worker program has created new money-earning opportunities for village-based men (and some women) in Vanuatu who spend a few months each year overseas. This official form of migration is the latest in a long line of state-sponsored programs developed by the Australian and New Zealand governments, who view the Pacific islands as a pool of cheap labour. Long gone are the exploitative practices of the 'blackbirders' of the late nineteenth century; what persists is the expatriation of the worker at the end of his contract replete with newly won wealth. The bags and boxes of yesteryear that carried such wealth in the form of steel axes, clothes and other consumer items have been replaced by a cheque that enables returnees to build a 'good house'. This has created new tensions in the village, as the durable brick houses that migrant workers build create long-lasting claims to disputed land of a type that bush-material houses did not.

Matti Eräsaari's essay is based on fieldwork in a village near Suva that is considered 'home' by a population who resides, for the most part, in Fiji's major urban centres and overseas, but who gather in the village for funerals and other ritual activities. This coming and going of people has seen traditional respect for the chiefly hierarchy decline and commoners' egalitarian values flourish. Keir Martin's essay illustrates how the movement of people is sometimes a one-way movement from town to country. Such movements are exceptional; in this case, the consequence of a volcanic eruption that destroyed the town. Martin shows how the event enabled the local government to overcome a problem of urban overcrowding by resettling people on virgin land, a move that enabled some to try and escape *kastom*—the customary ties that bind and obligate—as others sought to enforce it. The customary values of the Bininj and Yolngu people of Arnhem Land, whom Altman and Magowan discuss, have also proved resilient, but Aboriginal people have always been mobile and their customary values have different implications. To take one example, the new neighbourhoods that have been established in urban centres are referred to using the language of 'camps'. Houses in these urban 'camps' are filled to overflowing with people, their number of occupants varying daily as people continually move from outstation to town, and from one camp to another, to participate in life cycle rituals—mostly funerals—or to go on fishing or hunting expeditions for livelihood.

The implication of the above is that 'place' means one thing for the state and its functionaries and another for the people who occupy places within that state and beyond it; that is, place has a complex affective value informed by *kastom* as well as an exchange value as private property. This is not to deny the importance of official conceptions of place, but it does highlight the need to understand the unofficial concepts and the tensions and dilemmas that arise as a consequence of this difference. For residents in a 'strong' state, such as Australia, the sudden twists and turns of government policy profoundly affect the lives and morale of a precariat like Indigenous Australians. Karen Sykes, in her essay on a PNG transnational family in Cairns, begins by noting that these policies are informed by concepts and data that make questionable assumptions about the structure of migrant households. She also notes the paradoxical fact that migrants, who use the idiom of 'working other gardens' to refer to their residence in Australia, are increasingly finding that they are estranged from their traditional lands in PNG. For residents of 'weak' states, such as Solomon Islands, PNG and elsewhere, laws are something to be dodged and negotiated. Rodolfo Maggio's essay is a case study of how a 'hybrid' court dealt with a land problem involving a death that was rumoured to be caused by witchcraft. His close analysis of his recording of the proceedings reveals that a dispute between sisters was at the heart of the problem. Martin reminds us that there is 'nothing necessarily geographically Melanesian about the "Melanesian city"' when it comes to the actions of the modern welfare state. He draws a thought-provoking comparison with Young and Willmott's (1964) famous study, *Family and Kinship in East London*, which showed, as his own work does, that kinship networks provide forms of social solidarity that can grow stronger, rather than weaker, with the growth and development of a market economy.

A second general theme is that of differing valuations of time. Householders everywhere measure time by generations: the past with reference to one's parents and grandparents, the future with reference to one's children and grandchildren, and the present with reference to oneself. Where householders live in kinship-intensive neighbourhoods, this familial way of talking about time informs thoughts and actions. In Melanesian cultures, the language of *kastom* is used to value the past as either good or bad depending upon who is speaking. The title of Martin's essay, 'This Custom from the Past Is No Good', expresses the sentiments of one interlocutor about the values of his ancestors. These sentiments are not shared by everyone of course, and their expression signals the emergence of new social tensions and new social categories as the language of the 'big man' is replaced by the language of the 'big shot'. The latter expression is considered disrespectful behaviour of the kind that should not characterise familial relations. The people of Epi island in Vanuatu with whom Smith worked do not, as yet, use the language of the 'big shot', but they experience the same tensions between senior and junior generations, as her essay illustrates.

Matti Eräsaari's essay charts an analogous generational change in values occurring in the Fijian village of Naloto. This village is in the heartland of chiefly Fiji, an area where hierarchy was classically expressed through the exchange of whale's teeth. Unlike the classic agonistic exchange of shell valuables between competing equals for which PNG is famous, the giving of whale's teeth ritually celebrated hierarchy. A giver would kneel on one knee and literally present the valuable upwards to a chief. A ritual speech, heavily laden with honorifics, would accompany the presentation, which was usually a submissive request of some kind and never a claim to superior or equal status. The rise of egalitarian exchanges of whale's teeth between commoners at funerals, which Eräsaari describes, signals a profound shift that is permeating all levels of indigenous Fijian society, from village household to parliament. The decision of the current prime minister, leader of the 2006 military coup, to abolish the Great Council of Chiefs is but one of the many signs of this transformation.

These changing valuations of time and place provide the background to the various ways in which the inhabitants of these places pursue their quest for the good life. Like people everywhere, this involves, among other things, the quest for fame and fortune. The central theme of Smith's essay, the quest for the 'good house' in Vanuatu, is also a theme in Gregory's essay on a market town in India. In both cases, it is the relatively wealthy migrant who is able to build the good house, which, in both cases, is the sign of a newly emerging economic class. The big difference between these examples is that, in the Indian case, class difference divides unrelated people, whereas in Vanuatu, it divides friends, neighbours and relatives. The 'big shots' of PNG have been very successful at exploiting the economic opportunities presented by the twenty-first century; so too have Aboriginal artists in Arnhem Land who have benefited from a booming art market and access to large flows of cash. However, the quest for a good house has little meaning in the 'mobile' Aboriginal value system in which access to good transport is the supreme value. As such, successful artists used their new-found wealth to purchase vehicles—for the benefit of all, not for their exclusive use; only their fame as an artist of renown was theirs alone. For some, this renown was international, as Altman's essay shows. While fame can survive the fluctuations of prices in the market, money wealth cannot. People everywhere are the victims of price fluctuations of this kind and Aboriginal artists in Arnhem Land, whose livelihood has been shattered by a collapsing art market, would trade their fame for a vehicle if that were possible.

While the quest for money is part and parcel of the quest for the good life, it by no means defines it. The notion of wealth epitomised by the Hindu goddess Lakshmi, which gives equal if not greater weight to human values such as abundant progeny, good friends, good neighbours, good health and longevity, is shared by people across many faiths, as the essays in this volume illustrate; apart from Gregory's, they all examine Christian communities. These values, which concern right conduct and good fellowship, define the moral basis of most religions. What divides people are the culturally specific forms of 'true beliefs' and the ritual and poetic expressions of them. These values are intimately related to familial values of respect and familial love. The idiom of kinship is often used to express these religious values. Kinship, for its part, is often defined as a form of 'good fellowship' because estrangement of kin is an ever-present danger, as Maggio's chapter illustrates. The importance of familial values in the quest for the good life is found in all the essays in this book. In Maggio's example, the emphasis is on the pragmatics of kinship, not the semantics of kin terms—that is, with how people use familial values for their own ends rather than blindly following 'marriage rules'. This broad conception of wealth is the third general theme that emerges from this work; like the other themes, it is informed by familial values anchored in culturally specific ways of life, death and reproduction.

Bruno Latour's (2004) article, 'Why Has Critique Run Out of Steam? From Matters of Fact to Matters of Concern', raised an important question:

> Wars. So many wars. Wars outside and wars inside. Cultural wars, science wars, and wars against terrorism. Wars against poverty and wars against the poor. Wars against ignorance and wars out of ignorance. My question is simple: should we be at war, too, we, the scholars, the intellectuals? Is it really our duty to add fresh ruins to fields of ruins? Is it really the task of the humanities to add deconstruction to destruction? More iconoclasm to iconoclasm? What has become of the critical spirit? Has it run out of steam?

Latour's answer, that we should move from a debate about matters of fact to a debate about matters of concern to people living in the twenty-first century, has much to recommend it, but he sends anthropology down the wrong track with his ontological turn. 'The solution', he asserted, 'lies in this promising word gathering that Heidegger had introduced to account for the "thingness of the thing"' (p. 245). While it is important to study the thought of celebrated European academic philosophers, and while it is important to study the metaphysics of being, the fact remains, as Hegel (1969) showed, that 'being' without 'becoming' is 'nothingness'. Anthropology has its origins in the concrete study of the voice of the uncelebrated, non-European, non-academic, colonised subject; in the study of the rising and passing away of mere mortals as they cope with the necessity of finding food for the belly and food for imaginative thought; and in the study of morality, that ancient art of trying to live together well.

Anthropology is a child of imperialism, as Gough (1968) famously claimed, but it also provided the basis of a radical empirical critique of received ideas. What has become of this critical spirit? Has it run out of steam? Why is the primacy of critical ethnographic research being challenged by the ontological turners (Ingold, 2008)? This is a matter of concern for us, as we live in a world that is entering an era of inter-imperialist rivalry of a fundamentally new historical kind. There are no new formulae in this collection to replace 'the localisation of the global' or the 'indigenisation of modernity'; however, we hope to have raised some matters of concern by highlighting some of the moral dilemmas and paradoxes faced by some people in the twenty-first century: those who find themselves to be land-rich and dirt-poor; who seek the good life by participating in rituals about good deaths; who value kin highly but are faced with the reality of estrangement; or those other, less fortunate members of the precariat in the Pacific, such as the stateless, 'illegal' refugees imprisoned on Nauru by the Australian Government, whose quest for the good life is caught in the horns of much more vicious dilemmas than those experienced by the people discussed in these essays.

References

Chomsky, N. (2012, 8 July). Plutonomy and the precariat: On the history of the U.S. economy in decline. *Huffpost.* Retrieved from www.huffingtonpost.com/noam-chomsky/plutonomy-and-the-precari_b_1499246.html

Gough, K. (1968). Anthropology and imperialism. *Monthly Review, 19*(11). doi.org/10.14452/mr-019-11-1968-04_2

Hegel, G. W. F. (1969). *Hegel's science of logic* (A. V. Miller, Trans.). Atlantic Highlands, NJ: Humanities Press.

Ingold, T. (2008). Anthropology is not ethnography. *Proceedings of the British Academy, 154*, 69–92. doi.org/10.5871/bacad/9780197264355.003.0003

Latour, B. (2004). Why has critique run out of steam? From matters of fact to matters of concern. *Critical Inquiry, 30*(Winter), 225–48. doi.org/10.1086/421123

Piketty, T. (2014). *Capital in the twenty-first century.* Cambridge, MA: Harvard University Press. doi.org/10.4159/9780674369542

Polanyi, K. (1944). *The great transformation: The political and economic origins of our time.* New York, NY: Rinehart.

Young, M. & Willmott, P. (1964). *Family and kinship in East London.* Harmondsworth, UK: Penguin. doi.org/10.4324/9780203802342

2

The Good Death? Paying Equal Respects in Fijian Funerals

Matti Eräsaari

Introduction

The 'good life' is an equivocal idea. It is routinely evoked in reference to one's material circumstances and abstract ideals, to signify future hopes ('I want the good life') and to critique a faulty present ('not a life worth living'). It also acts as a stamp of approval on present achievement ('this is the good life') and as an evaluation of a past life ('she lived a good life'). Therefore, to talk of the good life is to pick a viewpoint from among a range of possibilities.

In Fiji, people commonly portray a village-based lifestyle as the already accomplished good life. I have been told countless times by people who want to show that life in Fiji's villages amounts to an affluent paradise that 'everything is already here'. Yet, the majority of people born to a village end up living most of their lives elsewhere, and even those who remain in their home villages often express a preference for an urban life. In the village of Naloto, Verata, just outside Fiji's main metropolitan area, the preference for urban careers is most often seen in terms of necessity, due to the better schools and other opportunities available outside the village; however, the money from tourist resorts, or careers in civil service, also has a pull beyond the merely pragmatic. 'Some people dream about a good job in town; others dream of getting respect by drinking *yaqona*

[kava]', a Naloto village man in his early 30s told me. This is a starting point that epitomises two key positions in an ongoing discourse on the good life. What the village man was telling me was that one can either seek the esteem of fellow villagers by maintaining a presence in front of the village community or one can seek success outside the village.

In this chapter, I adopt a village-centric viewpoint in which the home village acts as a centre and organising principle for the greater village community, which includes the village residents and its emigrants alike. Most indigenous Fijians are registered as members of the landowning groups in their village at birth; it is to the village that most seek to retire at the end of their careers, and it is the village of their birth, or the one they married into, where they are eventually buried. Indeed, it is specifically by looking into funerals that I seek to foreground what it means to be respected by the community. In short, my starting point is the posthumous recognition of a good life.

In Metcalf and Huntington's (1999, p. 24) words, 'the issue of death throws into relief the most important cultural values by which people live their lives and evaluate their experiences'. As far as the elaboration of shared values is concerned, it seems safe to say that indigenous Fijian culture gives considerably more attention to funerals than other rituals, such as weddings. Funerals are big, public affairs, the preparations, exchanges and distributions of which involve entire villages. This is also to say that the issue of death is not shunned or brushed aside; when death occurs, local and international extended kin networks are called quickly into action. Funerals concern people on a wide scale, and even though weddings are currently growing in size, the ideal, typical wedding remains a relatively small-scale affair conducted largely between two families. Even the large-scale rituals held to legitimise the now prevalent elopement marriages, which in Naloto are routinely combined with the presentation of children to their maternal kin (see Eräsaari, 2013, pp. 172–76; Pauwels, 2015; Williksen-Bakker, 1986), always have to give precedence to funerals. This may be partly because a death, unlike a marriage celebration, cannot be rescheduled; however, it also reflects the wider scope and general sense of obligation that a death stands for. Such a sense of obligation is perhaps best conceptualised by Barraud, De Coppet, Iteanu and Jamous's (1994) notion of 'life credit' and its closure or 'summation' at funerals (pp. 35–39). The funeral acts as a public acknowledgement and repayment of debts to the deceased.

Fijian funerals, at least implicitly, embrace a parallel idea wherein the number of groups attending is seen as recognition that the deceased had previously come to the aid of others. During my fieldwork in Naloto village in 2007–08, I often heard people talking about this in the context of past funerals; they generally sought to estimate the number of groups that had arrived to pay their final respects. This, in the final analysis, was the indicator that someone had lived a good life. The number of arrivals is the key data recorded at funerals. The anthropologist, Tuomas Tammisto, who conducted fieldwork among the Mengen of New Britain, once told me about a moment during fieldwork when he realised that the participants of ceremonial exchanges were not only producing multiple lists of the things exchanged, but that their lists were more accurate than the ones he had compiled. I was similarly preoccupied with listing things given and received on ritual occasions during my fieldwork, and my lists were occasionally even used by the organisers—not to ascertain the quantities that I had carefully documented and my hosts marked out in generics, but to make sure that the participating groups were all accounted for.

A funeral sums up a person's life: the times they did their duty towards others and when they came to others' aid in times of need. Being socially active in life is acknowledged in the number of groups that come to pay their final respects to the family of the deceased. However, a focus on the groups that arrive at funerals calls further attention to *how* they pay their respects, and here we are faced with a significant change in comparison to what has generally been reported in Fiji in the past. For instead of expressing a pre-established difference between the groups involved, the funeral gifts in Naloto that I witnessed established the similarity, even equality, between the parties participating in the funeral exchanges; in doing so, they revealed the degree to which a funeral might be regarded as an index of the relatively equal relations one has had in one's lifetime. This represents a major departure from the traditional values of chiefly East Fiji, a difference that is highly salient for understanding not only death, but the good life too.

By pursuing the meaning of the good life in death rituals, my aim is to highlight an emergent ideology that informs not only the ceremonial life, but also the lifetime ambitions—'career choices'—of the people I worked with. Rather than saying that Nalotans place high value on dying, or that their life ambitions are geared towards funerals, I want to show that Nalotan funerals have come to be social occasions that reveal a significant change in the types of relations people consider relevant. I will be arguing that these funerals display a shift, from a pattern of differentiating exchanges between people marked out by pre-existing hierarchical difference, to exchanges characterised by symmetrical reciprocity. This chapter tries to point out how such a pattern, found in a place often regarded as the home of the major chiefly families in Fiji—a heartland of Fijian chieftaincy—reflects wider changes that have occurred in Fiji gradually over a number of decades. I present my argument by first contextualising Naloto village, then describing Nalotan funeral exchange, before focusing on the most visible part of funeral gifts: the whales' teeth. I then highlight the significance of Nalotan funeral practice in contrast to Tongan concerns with rank and differentiation. This will allow me to comment, in conclusion, on the limits of the emergent ideology expressed through the funeral rites—that is, the extent of the egalitarianism and the new spaces of distinction it carves out.

Naloto Village: Historical and Ethnographic Context

Naloto is one of the seven villages that make up the chiefdom of Verata on the east coast of Viti Levu island, roughly an hour's drive north from Nausori town. Just outside Fiji's main metropolitan area—the so-called Suva–Nausori urban corridor—Naloto offers no daily access to urban Fiji: it is too deep in the forest, the gravel road does not support buses and there are no cars in the village. On most days, a lorry goes from Naloto or the neighbouring villages to Korovou town, Nausori or Suva; however, it is neither regular nor fast enough for a job in town. Most village households sell their produce at the Nausori or Suva marketplaces on weekends, but this is considered supplementary income; people in the village maintain a semi-subsistent lifestyle, getting most of their daily food by farming, fishing and gathering wild produce.

Farmland is abundant in the village; even the kin groups who hold the least agricultural land per capita (see Eräsaari, 2013, pp. 18–39) have enough to subsist on. For the majority of villagers, life in the village represents an ideal—a lifestyle based on neighbourly sharing, subsisting on the land and, most importantly, having no need for money. From this highly idealised point of view, the 'good life' is a reality for indigenous Fijians living in their native villages.

However, although rich in land and food, the village lacks easy access to money and market goods, ranging from necessities such as clothing and building materials, to consumables such as DVDs and instant noodles. Raising money in the village is hard. Young families that need to accumulate the essentials of an independent household frequently move away from the village to work in the urban market, often in the hope of putting their children in good schools as well. In fact, while Naloto village—the largest of the seven Verata villages—boasts a population of around 300 people, the number registered as Nalotan landowners (but not living in the village) is roughly 600.[1] Especially for young villagers, moving to town for work is practically a life cycle expectation, just as most expect to retire back to the village with enough earnings to set up a house and lead a comfortable village life. However, for those who never attain urban employment, the village may become synonymous with failure: 'the last place', as one villager phrased it. In other words, there are two conflicting views on village life; it is either a paradise of fulfilled needs or a bare-bones existence without development or 'moving forward' (*toso*).

Naloto is the focal point of an extensive network of emigrant villagers living in urban centres or working in tourist resorts, with many more living overseas on other Pacific islands or in Australia, the US or even Europe. These emigrant Nalotans participate in the life of the village by supporting their close village kin with money and gifts, in communal development projects through fundraisers and by taking part in village events when they are able.[2] Absentee villagers remain affiliated with Naloto and the encompassing chiefdom of Verata even after residing elsewhere for generations. Access to village land is an inalienable right that is usually passed down from father to children; however, one's home village is also a source of identification that predetermines certain collective relationships between villages, chiefdoms and precolonial 'confederations'.

The protocol associated with one's home village combines traditional categories for classifying relations between places—such as *bati* (warrior ally), *tauvu* (common origin), *veitabani* (descendants of cross-cousins) and so forth—with a system of ranking among the chiefdoms of Fiji. Regardless of whether one has ever even visited one's home village, a place

1 Both figures are from 2008. The number of village residents is from the administrative headman's (*turaga ni koro*) records; the number of people of Nalotan descent comes from the register of native landowners (*Vola ni Kawa Bula*).

2 It is typical to try and organise big fundraisers and 'pre-arrangeable' life cycle events during public holidays to make it possible for the emigrant villagers to participate as well.

of origin determines the terms of address and appropriate behaviour in certain relationships, as it does one's place in the order of precedence applicable in formal meetings, kava drinking and so on. The chiefdom of Verata occupies a unique place in the national mythology; it is one of the most widely agreed upon origin places for the chiefly families of Fiji—a heartland of Fijian chieftaincy, which stands for seniority and gravitas. While there are high chieftaincies that outrank Verata in power and prestige, Verata is nonetheless commonly recognised as the original home of the chiefly houses of East Fiji, a status to which other chiefdoms also pay homage. For example, in the aftermath of the December 2006 military coup, Nalotans reported circulating prophecies foretelling the arrival of peace and wellbeing for the nation accompanying the rise of a true leader from Verata.

However, while the symbolic status of Verata and its chiefs remains high, chiefly authority does not. This has been accentuated in Fijian politics since the 2006 coup, wherein chiefly politics has been challenged more generally; the interim government's power struggle with Fiji's Great Council of Chiefs finally resulted in the council's formal disestablishment in 2012. Coup leader Bainimarama's sustained campaign against the constitutional role of chieftaincy in Fiji has been carried over to his post-election politics as prime minister.

The political campaign against the official status of chieftaincy has been prefaced by significant shifts in the political, economic and even cosmological underpinnings of chieftaincy. Not only have the chiefs lost their status as superhuman others ('stranger kings'), they have also lost their standing as landless 'guests' distinct from common people, a distinction elaborated in traditional chiefly installations (cf. Eräsaari, 2015; Hocart, 1929; Sahlins, 1985). In 2008, it was estimated that over 80 per cent of chiefs in Fiji had not been traditionally installed (Vunileba, 2008), a figure including paramount chiefs such as the *Vunivalu* of Bau or the *Ratu* of Verata.

The same applies to the Naloto hereditary chieftaincy, the *Komai Naloto* title. The title is one of numerous chiefly titles that have foregone the traditional installation ceremonies and reverted to hereditary succession. Naloto has effectively abandoned the ritual of installing—'making' (*buli*)—the chief, wherein a 'kingmaker' clan elects the new chief who is installed in office by a group of specialists. Neither of these specialist groups are part of the chiefly clan; rather, they represent a typical Fijian ritual arrangement into opposed sides that recurrently create a whole community out of two dichotomous halves, sides or ritual moieties. Installed chiefs, I was told, bore the title of *Ratu*, whereas the current hereditary titleholders are 'just *komais*', as a Naloto woman put it: holders of an inferior title.

Indeed, the *komai* title is not a very coveted one in Naloto. Before it was bestowed upon the current incumbent, it was apparently refused by another, and possibly several senior members of his lineage, just as in the previous generation the title was handed over to another lineage because no one in the chiefly lineage wanted it. Many in Naloto claim that the rightful heir to the chieftaincy actually lives on another island, in a village now blessed with prosperity, while, in Naloto, left for generations with a junior lineage, things are changing for the worse. This is another way of saying that the villagers, despite feeling let-down by their own chiefs, still yearn for a powerful, authoritative chief like the chiefs of old (cf. Tomlinson 2009).

The diminished title is paralleled by the respect and authority awarded the chief. The *Komai Naloto* may be acknowledged as the head of the village, but is often ignored in actual decision-making and disobeyed when giving commands. The old chief responds by refusing to play the chief's part in church services or formal events. The head of the Naloto 'sea people' (*Na Tunidau*) fares somewhat better, though, like the village paramount, also carries little authority. Indeed, in 2008, the sea chief became so infuriated by the lack of respect shown to him by his people that he moved to the capital. Rather than apologising or requesting his return, most of the people in the sea moiety found this amusing.

In 2008, Nalotans had various opinions as to why their chiefs commanded less respect than they used to. Some urban Nalotans thought it was their village-based relatives' tendency to put on airs that resulted in the belittling of the chief. 'Today, everybody wants to be the chief, to drink first', a Naloto man based in the Western Province explained with reference to the hierarchical order of serving kava. Others blamed the kava itself, claiming that the village elders were unable to give commands; they 'stay up too late and wake up late', one of the village-based youths put it, again with reference to kava drinking. Some blamed the division of labour in the village, pointing to the failure of the chief's 'constabulary' (*bati lekaleka*) to make sure that his commands were obeyed. Still others blamed food; a few claimed that the Fijian people were deteriorating as a consequence of eating too much bread and noodles and were generally less commanding than their ancestors. Others thought that the problem was the large-scale discontinuation of food taboos separating 'nobles' from 'commoners' in Naloto. Predictably, money and individualism acted as the most popular scapegoats, even if no one could pinpoint, specifically, what it was they did.

While the villagers could not agree on the causes of weak leadership in the village, their own actions revealed its wider structural underpinnings. The funeral rituals discussed below justify such an opinion, for while they obviously give expression to key ideas of mutual aid and communal obligation, the formal features observed during these events throw into relief the absence of hierarchical markers in Nalotan funerals. In this sense, the 'enumeration' of final respects not only sums up a life, it also gradually undermines traditional ideas of rank.

Egalitarian Ideology in Funeral Rituals

Veratan death rituals span from the time of death to 100 nights after the burial. Here I focus on two key stages: the time reserved for paying final respects before the burial and the closing feast afterwards. It is during these stages that the hosting group welcomes the numerous groups of guests that arrive to pay their final respects to the deceased, gradually subsuming them before 'releasing' them to go their way after the burial. The exchanges that take place during these stages can be seen both as a summative index of the deceased's life achievement and an affirmation of the relationship between the groups that participate in a funeral.[3]

In Verata, the time of paying final respects—*gauna ni reguregu* (approximately, 'time for kissing goodbye')—is usually on the evening before burial. This is when numerous kin groups come to convey their condolences to the family of the deceased, each group presenting *reguregu* (from *regu*, kiss) gifts to the hosts in turn. The smallest funeral I witnessed in Fiji hosted only a half-dozen groups of guests; however, this funeral of an adolescent who had not yet accumulated social connections beyond the village community was a rare exception. The largest funerals I took part in involved more than 20 groups of guests, each presenting their funeral contributions one after the other.

3 For a description of Nalotan funerals, see Eräsaari (2013, pp. 176–79).

The proceedings always follow a fixed protocol. The funeral guests begin by presenting their *sevusevu* (bundle of kava roots), which are offered in greeting to the hosts. After accepting this, the hosts, in turn, offer a *sevusevu*. It is customary for a group hosting a funeral to have a cardboard box of kava bundles standing by so they constantly have a number of appropriate items ready. In most of the cases I saw, the guests' spokesperson quickly gestures that they wish to forgo the bundle received in reciprocation, which the hosts' spokesperson usually accepts with a respectful hand clap (*cobo*) (see Arno, 2005). After this initial exchange, the visiting group's spokesperson offers their *reguregu*, a condolence gift brought to the family of the deceased. This usually comprises woven mats and a bark cloth accompanied by items of food: taro or cassava and some variety of meat—predominantly beef—or, alternatively, purchased items such as biscuits, bread and milk. All of these are represented by a whale's tooth (*tabua*) presented by the guests' spokesperson; this handheld token stands for the bark cloth, the mats, the roots and the meat—in ceremonial speech, it is 'the valuable with its wealth, its food, its relish'. The hosts reciprocate with a whale's tooth of their own to thank their guests for the gifts received, after which the arrivals take their place as part of the ever-expanding group of hosts as the next group arrives to present its condolences.

The group entrusted with the task of bringing the coffin home (*weka ni mate*) should be the last to arrive (although, in practice, latecomers may arrive even during the church service or burial on the following day). The *weka ni mate* are the guests of honour in the funeral and their arrival is accompanied by heightened formality. They are presented with a whale's tooth immediately on their arrival; this item, known as *vakasobu* (from *sobu*, to exit a vehicle, canoe etc.) is presented outdoors, often with car headlights lighting the event. Only a small group of the deceased's close kin go out to meet them while others wait in the meeting hall or under a canopy constructed for the event. Once they are all back indoors, the *weka ni mate* present the coffin to the hosts with one whale's tooth, known as *yago ni mate* ('body of the deceased'), and offer their condolence gift of mats, bark cloth and food with another whale's tooth, before receiving a tooth that stands for some taro and sometimes a pig, as well as the food prepared by the hosts for all the condolers. Once the coffin has been carried from the hall, the *weka ni mate* collect the mats upon which the coffin has temporarily been resting and roll them into a bundle, which they take away with them.

The day of the burial completes the sequence. However, whereas the eve of the burial is marked by the repetitious arrival of gifts and establishing the funeral communion, the following day is about fission, albeit notably less ceremoniously. After a church service and the burial itself—in which many of the funeral guests do not actually participate—the hosts present the funeral feast, embodied by yet another whale's tooth, to all the guests. The feast comprises large quantities of tubers baked in an earth oven, beef '*soposui*' (chop suey) and stew. Bigger funeral feasts often also have pork cooked in an earth oven. Sometimes there is fish too, but it is neither a compulsory core item nor reserved for particular groups of guests.

The whale's tooth used for offering the feast food sometimes also stands for a separate gift of raw meat known as '*burua*', an offering in which the hosting group distributes a slaughtered bull among the visiting groups. If they wish to single out a group of eminent guests who have arrived from afar, they may sometimes also present pork, but this is quite rare. As a rule, the *burua* involves very little elaboration; there are no speeches beyond a spokesperson brusquely calling out which portion is for which group of guests. There are no reception speeches by senior men; youths simply carry away the portions for subsequent—equally unceremonious—redistribution among the visiting groups. Most adult men then continue the funeral by drinking kava until a senior guest, such as the leader of the *weka ni mate*, requests permission to leave. He does so on behalf of all the funeral guests by presenting the hosts with a whale's tooth; the hosts reciprocate with a whale's tooth if they have one left, or with kava roots if not. Afterwards, the hosts distribute the mats and bark cloth among the assisting groups, before taking what is left themselves. In turn, the assisting and visiting groups divide their portions among their members.[4]

The funeral exchanges are conducted almost solely using a limited range of exchange media: kava, whale's teeth, bark cloth, mats, tubers, beef, pork and certain purchased foods, such as breakfast crackers, bread, milk and the like. This marks a departure from previous ethnographic descriptions of mortuary exchange in the area (Hocart, 1924; Ravuvu, 2005; Sahlins, 1976; Toren, 1988, p. 716, fn. 8), in which the focus has been on exchange between two kinds of people, both marking their relationship to the other by the use of relationship-specific exchange goods.

4 Final distribution is typically carried out by women, while the various stages of pooling preceding and during the funerals are supervised and conducted by senior men.

The paradigmatic example of such relationship-specific exchange media is in funeral exchanges between groups designated as 'chiefly' *(turaga)* and 'warriors' (*bati*). These designations largely overlap with a division into 'sea people' and 'land people' found throughout indigenous Fiji. I have discussed these in greater detail elsewhere (see Eräsaari, 2013); here I will merely point out that this binary classification has traditionally been connected with the institution of landless foreigner chiefs and their landowning subjects. It also connotes ritual moieties, occupational specialisation in sea- and land-based produce, as well as a more general dichotomy of hosts (*taukei*) and guests (*vulagi*). The host–guest dichotomy retains an association with local land ownership vis-a-vis immigrating affines; however, the 'guest' category now commonly refers to recently arrived wives, or to the islands' devalued ethnic others, rather than the foreigner chiefs for which Fijian ethnography is better known. Hocart (1924, p. 186) perceived the relationship between 'warrior' and 'chiefly' groups as characterised by irreversible, differentiated obligations and privileges that were highlighted in food exchanges and eating prohibitions: the land people (Hocart's 'hill tribes') should provide pork to the sea people (Hocart's 'nobles') and abstain from eating it in the presence of the latter; the sea people should provide fish to the land people and abstain from eating it in their presence. These prescriptions were particularly associated with funerals, in which predetermined relations between groups were thereby perpetuated.

Hocart (1924) showed how these relations were superscribed on the map of north-eastern Viti Levu island, so that inland polities were 'land people' in relation to the people seaward of them, but were 'sea people' for the people landward of them. Hence, it is possible to read the traditional polities of the area as a sequence of land–sea relations bounded by the Kauvadra range in the interior and the coastal chiefly polities on the seashore. Within this scheme, Naloto is not only a coastal village, it is also part of the chiefdom of Verata, whose chiefly house is reckoned senior among Fiji's chiefly families. In many ways, Verata is 'as sea as can be', just as the Vatukaloko people living by the Kauvadra range can be said to represent the other extreme, ultimate land (see Kaplan, 1995). Adding to this, the people I lived with during my fieldwork, the Naloto sea moiety, represent 'sea' in the intra-village version of the dichotomy—sea within sea, so to speak. When asked to explain what being 'sea people' means, most resort to the food exchanges and eating prohibitions: 'we are sea people, we don't eat fish with the land people'.

Yet, the exchange items classified as 'sea'—fish and other saltwater produce—were almost completely absent from the exchanges between land and sea people during my fieldwork, not only in the intra-village funeral exchanges between the Naloto chief's local land warriors (*bati lekaleka*) and sea people (*kai wai*) but also, notably, from the much more formal inter-chiefdom relations between the Veratans and their traditional allies (*bati balavu*) in the chiefdom of Vugalei.[5] In both instances, instead of exchanging fish and pork, the two sides exchanged beef for beef—slaughtered bulls for stew (*stiu*), beef chop suey (*soposui*) and raw meat (*burua*). To be more precise, pork, the ceremonial due of chiefs, still persists as something with which a special guest of honour may be honoured. However, fish, the sea people's contribution, has virtually disappeared from traditional exchange, along with the accompanying eating prohibitions.[6]

People may go to great lengths to avoid putting themselves in the marked position of noble/guest/sea people; for example, some sell fish in town to convert it into other types of food. Even outside the funeral context, the sea people's ceremonial presentations are never made, as protocol requires; although the Naloto *bati* have repeatedly requested gifts of fish that the landsmen would reciprocate with whale's teeth (*bati ni ika*), the sea people take no heed of such requests. Tellingly, on a day when the prescribed chiefly 'sea' offering actually was taken to a funeral in Vugalei, the Naloto man responsible for the funeral gift was too ashamed to speak when offered a whale's tooth in reciprocation. It was as if presenting things 'downwards' from a 'chiefly' position was no longer considered appropriate, while whale's teeth, which are ceremonially always presented 'up' to the gentleman (*turaga*) overseeing the proceedings, seem to abound.

Exchanging Whale's Teeth

Whale's teeth are sometimes known as *ulu ni yau*, the 'head of valuables'. The expression indicates their singular status as the highest ranking of traditional Fijian wealth items. The ceremonial language used in Naloto

5 The traditional chiefdom and coinciding administrative district of Verata comprises seven villages of which Naloto is one. Verata's inland neighbour, the chiefdom/district of Vugalei, comprises nine villages.

6 Although everyone in Naloto knows of the eating prohibitions, only a few people follow them. Nalotans are aware of the fact that in more traditional places in Vugalei the eating prohibitions are still observed.

classifies all valuables into six categories. *Kamunaga* (valuable) is only used for a whale's tooth during a ritual event. *Yau* (wealth) is used in reference to kava, bark cloth, mats and certain items associated with a particular region, as well as a limited range of store items, from print cloth and kerosene to washing powder and soap bars; it is also used for money on the rare occasion that money enters the ceremonial sphere. *Magiti* (feast food) refers to the tubers or plantains that are part of most ceremonial presentations and sometimes refers to purchased chop suey ingredients, such as carrots, onions or pak choi. *I coi* (relish) refers to the meat given as part of the presentation. Nalotans are familiar with more specific terms for the meat items discussed above—*wai tui* (saltwater) for fish and *uro* (fat) for pork; however, these are used only rarely and people say they are in the process of being replaced by the more general *i coi* (cf. Eräsaari, 2013, pp. 169–70, fn. 63). In addition, the category *wai katakata* (hot water) may be used in reference to tea, milk, bread, butter, crackers, sugar and flour. For small, informal occasions, *kamikamica* (sweet) may be used for snacks brought along as an accompaniment to kava.

A typical Naloto funeral gift (*reguregu*) consists of a whale's tooth, kava, bark cloth, pandanus mats, taro, cassava and beef. This reflects the fact that ceremonial gifts are given by groups rather than individuals; the items are pooled together in events known as *vakasoso yau* (from *soso*, 'to exchange', 'to replace' and *yau*, 'wealth') that are organised separately by each participating group before the more formal funeral rites. In these events, each group—usually a clan, sometimes a moiety or representatives of an entire village—brings together men's wealth (kava, whale's teeth and usually the food items) and women's wealth (bark cloth and pandanus mats) to combine the parts into a gift that represents the whole group. Regardless of the pre-existing relations between the two groups—the hosts and the guests—the contributions are always the same.

Not only that, over the course of the funeral proceedings, gifts tend to be reciprocated in kind. I mentioned the initial identical exchange of kava bundles preceding the presentation of *reguregu* at funerals; I also showed how the distinction between proteins classified as 'fat' and 'saltwater' has been levelled to mere 'relish'.[7] Moreover, although the exchange of identical bundles of pandanus mats is not customary in Naloto,

7 The distinction between raw and cooked food does not appear to be particularly significant in Naloto.

as is the case among their neighbours in Vugalei, funerals nonetheless see participants giving and receiving identical media: mats, bark cloth and tubers in addition to the above mentioned items. Further, the language of ceremonial presentations not only uses generic categories for the kinds of things presented, it also employs indistinct units of accounting—sets and bundles—and participants make full use of every opportunity to belittle their own offerings. One consequence of this is that there may be genuine uncertainty about what a gift actually consists of, with most participants sitting on the ground hearing simply that the gift includes a 'valuable', some 'wealth', 'feast food' and 'relish'; the muddy or bloody foodstuffs often remain outside the ceremonial space, while the mats and bark cloth are rolled into bundles that are only opened after the funeral. The focal point of the ceremony—the one object explicitly displayed—is the 'head of the valuables': the whale's tooth.

Tabua are different from all other exchange items; they outrank everything else in prestige. A *tabua* has executive power unlike any other. A *tabua* is always presented for a nominated purpose—to propose or finalise a marriage, to ask forgiveness, to pay final respects and so forth—and, once accepted, it effects that purpose. Hence, the presentation and, especially, the reception of whale's teeth follows a protocol that is more formal and complicated than in other ceremonial exchanges.

A *tabua* is presented by the gift-givers' spokesperson who lists the traditional titles present in the event and states the purpose of the object, before handing the object over and returning to their place. The object is then conveyed to the head of the receiving party who accepts (*ciqoma*) it with a few words. The acceptance is followed by an elaborated pronouncement (*kacivi*) from the receiving party's spokesperson who again lists the titles in attendance and announces the accepted object's effect. Indeed, in idiomatic Fiji English, one does not 'give' or 'exchange' a *tabua*—one 'does' a *tabua*. The performative power of whale's teeth comes out at the final exclamation ending the proclamation of acceptance, '*Mana! E dina*' ('Effective. It is true'), the last words chanted in unison by everyone in attendance as the object takes effect.

This is why a *tabua* always has to be accepted by a chief. Whale's teeth are the only objects personally received by a senior titleholder in the receiving party; when a presentation does not include a *tabua*, it is received by the chief's spokesperson. Whale's teeth are the only objects that are accepted 'twice': by a chief of the receiving party and by their spokesperson. This means that the receiver of a *tabua* is always a chief. Whether the head of a household or sub-clan, or the senior representative of the chiefly lineage, the receiver will always assume a title and be the chief in attendance. The entire process of 'doing' a *tabua* is geared towards the reception—right from the ritual cry (*tama*) made to introduce the valuable, down to the honorific terms of address used for the recipient. Indeed, it has been pointed out that the presentation of a *tabua* elevates the recipient above the giver; it is the supreme honour, but also the ultimate expression of loyalty and even submission, that a group can make (see Hooper, 2013, p. 106). The presenter of a *tabua* is, quite literally, paying respects to the recipient.

It is here, at the point at which both the prestige and ritual elaboration of the exchanges are at their highest, that the like-for-like pattern of exchange also becomes the most pronounced. I described above how every *tabua* received as a condolence gift in a Naloto funeral is immediately reciprocated with another, similar object, usually labelled simply *vakavinaka na yau* ('in thanks for the wealth'). While the guests of honour are obliged to present two whale's teeth—one accompanying the casket, the other their *reguregu* gift—they also receive two teeth: one upon arrival, the other in thanks for the gift. At the end of the funeral, when it is time to break-up the funeral communion, the leader of the guests presents a *tabua* when requesting permission to leave (*tatau*) and this, too, is reciprocated with a *tabua*, simply labelled *vakatale* ('likewise' or 'return'). If I were to lay out examples of marriage exchanges, it would become obvious how much manipulation may be involved in keeping the number of *tabua* given and received equal: when to give two objects, when to perform two in succession or when to give none (see Eräsaari, 2013, pp. 137–49). However, in a funeral, when the average group presents its gift with a single *tabua*, they also receive one, or, if they present their gift without one (in which case a bundle of kava roots will act as the focal point), they also receive none in return.

In the historical literature, the reciprocation of *tabua* with *tabua* seems to exist only in the practice of cancelling (*dirika*) one *tabua* with another. A whale's tooth presented as a *dirika* carries no cause or purpose except to cancel the effect of one *tabua* by giving another. It is a practice known in Naloto; however, to my knowledge, it is restricted to the sole situation where a man has left behind a widow. On such an occasion, the woman's kin, in offering to take her back to her natal family, present a *tabua* during the funeral. It is customary in Naloto to *dirika* such an offer. Although it sometimes occurs that an unpopular wife or woman with no offspring may be allowed to return, it is such a rare and marked practice that it merely serves to illustrate how very untypical it is in Naloto to not reciprocate whale's teeth.

I am not saying that every traditional event ends up being even. 'You might not get a *tabua* back', I was sometimes reminded regarding the risks involved in ceremonial exchange. However, that, too, ultimately highlights the assumption that one is very much expected to get as good as one gives. Compare this with Hooper's (2013) account of tabua use in the Lau group in Fiji in the 1970s. Hooper was explicitly told that presenting whale's teeth in combination with other categories of exchange items (such as food), and the undiscriminating reciprocation of tabua with tabua, regardless of context, went against received protocol (pp. 122, 129). Yet Hooper also pointed out that it is members of chiefly clans who should present and receive *tabua* (p. 110). Conversely, in Naloto, it is said that every man should be in possession of a *tabua* in case he might need one; by the same token, every man is said to be a chief in his own house.

Equal and Unequal Exchange

This is where I finally pick up the topic of the good life by way of pointing out what a strange thing it is to be spending one's resources on the equal exchange of things of the same class or of identical things. These, Forge (1972, p. 534) once argued, can be viewed as 'the principal mechanism by which equality is maintained'. Joel Robbins, developing Forge's idea in his 1994 essay on 'equality as a value', likewise regarded equal exchange to be 'the mechanism which produces value' on the condition that 'what Melanesians value in exchange is equality' (Robbins, 1994, p. 39). Naloto funerals, too, express and reproduce balance and equality rather than hierarchy and distinction. I have elsewhere argued that in Naloto the appearance of egalitarian exchange corresponds with the disappearance of a binary distinction between autochthones and strangers (see Eräsaari, 2013, 2015). Here I want to go further, pointing out how the lack of interest in quantitative valuation produces relatively egalitarian relations among exchange partners.

Let me give a comparative example. Douaire-Marsaudon's (2008) analysis of the exchange of food (*kai*—i.e. pork and tubers) and wealth (*koloa*—i.e. mats, bark cloth and coconut oil) in Tonga and Wallis drew on, and thereby highlighted, an astounding degree of attention paid to the quantification of exchange goods. From the early nineteenth-century material onwards, Douaire-Marsaudon was able to comfortably list staggering amounts of food used in ceremonial exchange—14 tonnes in the three instances discussed. What made such precise quantification possible was that all contributions were carefully enumerated during the ceremonies, and people paid close attention to this. 'Piling up, distributing and destroying food', Douaire-Marsaudon explained:

> Are also designed to make clear to everyone who is who: in effect, a chief accumulates and distributes more than an ordinary man. His wealth and his liberality are measured first of all in food … from the bottom to the top of the Tongan social pyramid: each must make gifts to his hierarchical superior, and first of all gifts of food, if he wants to *maintain his rank* [emphasis added]. (p. 211)

The same happens with traditional wealth. 'The amount of cloth and mats collected are indications of the wealth and station of the families', to which end 'gifts are solemnly enumerated and counted before being distributed' (p. 215). Even today, despite what Douaire-Marsaudon regarded as the equalising influence of Christianity, events that include the presentation of ceremonial wealth can become highly competitive. All of this is indicative of the way that power is realised in Tonga and Wallis 'in terms of "wealth"' (p. 217). Gifts of food and wealth are a powerful medium for competition among relative equals who need to make explicit their status differences, and for maintaining pre-established differences among unequals.

Douaire-Marsaudon (2008) demonstrated that this mattered to onlookers as well. People expect the chiefly redistributions to match the original contributions; in this way, the enumeration can be seen as a form of accountability. Money contributions are not particularly problematic in Tongan and Wallisian ceremonial exchange, as quantification is an inherently important aspect of traditional exchange. However, the custom of placing money contributions in envelopes is problematic. Presenting money in an envelope, hidden from sight, places it beyond the usual social controls; thus, it may be put in the bank and kept for personal use instead of being redistributed (p. 223). In short, the ceremonial preoccupation with quantities in Tonga and Wallis serves the purposes of status competition while simultaneously providing a measure for redistribution.

In Naloto, cash envelopes are part of ceremonial exchange on the rare occasion that money is used in such exchange. Rather than standing in opposition to established custom, they reflect the prevailing Nalotan preference for non-quantification and undifferentiation (cf. Autio, 2010) among participants. Yet, the assertion of egalitarian practices in which chiefly prestige has traditionally been displayed does not make all Nalotans equal—it simply means that rituals of status verification take place elsewhere.

In Naloto village, such a context can be found in the abundant fundraisers that form the basis of public welfare. The school, community hall, water pump and other common utilities are made and maintained through public fundraisers, which the villagers, as a rule, treat similarly to ceremonial exchange: participants meet a preordained sum precisely, everyone making identical donations. Hence, the fundraisers, as events, tend to be similar to traditional ceremonies in the sense that both are time-consuming affairs in which people take turns making similar or identical presentations. However, the fundraiser format pays particular attention to quantity (see Eräsaari, 2013, pp. 194–207). By publicly listing and announcing the precise quantities presented by individuals rather than groups, fundraisers favour emigrant villagers who have easier access to money and who do not participate in village fundraisers on a weekly basis. In other words, they provide an occasion for the transient visitor to make an impression.

Conclusion: 'A Good Job in Town'

I have briefly evoked the fundraisers here to highlight the contrast with funerals. The funerals discussed in this chapter show that Nalotans have adopted a form of exchange that practically counters the chiefly system for which the whole polity of Verata is famous. As employed during funeral rites, these exchanges act as an evaluation of a life lived, providing a summative account of the merit due to the deceased and his or her kin group. Hence, these ceremonial exchanges make the 'worth' of a person's accomplishments known to posterity—a clear indication that the ancestors still comprise an important part of the Fijian kinship system, as has recently been argued (e.g. Hulkenberg, 2015; Cayrol, 2015). However, for the living, what is given and what is received are too closely matched to act as a medium of status rivalry among the participating groups.

Yet, this does not mean that we ought to limit our final analysis of equal exchange to a mechanical functioning of gifts and counter gifts or the annulment of gift debt and hierarchical relations. For although Fijian equal exchange does not produce the verifiable status differences described in Douaire-Marsaudon's (2008) Tongan and Wallisean examples, one should not assume that an egalitarian form of exchange produces 'equality' per se. Gregory (2014) took up this topic in his Anthony Forge Memorial Lecture, in which he called for more attention to the historically situated realities of egalitarian or 'democratic' ideals in postcolonial settings such as Fiji and Papua New Guinea.

In Fiji, such historical circumstances include the often-significant quantities of agricultural land available to indigenous landowning clans. In areas such as Tailevu province, of which Naloto is a part, the availability of land results in a lifestyle in which the village offers a safe backdrop or 'safety net' that can be counted on for the provision of the basic necessities of life. However, these egalitarian conditions also give rise to the choice that young men, in particular, face: 'some dream about a good job in town, others dream of getting respect by drinking *yaqona*', as my friend phrased it.

From a village-centric viewpoint, the choice may indeed be concretised as kava drinking versus urban employment: sitting still with others versus paid employment away from the village. However, the exchanges accompanying the kava drinking reveal a set of egalitarian, rather than chiefly, practices at the ceremonial core of village life, in which one would assume chiefly hierarchy to preside. Still, the absence of a marked hierarchy in this one (albeit traditionally very significant) sphere, does not pre-empt the possibility of status distinction in other contexts or spheres. This should be particularly evident in a time when the constitutional underpinnings of chiefly power have been discontinued (Bainimarama, 2012) and the use of chiefly titles in parliament have been banned; even the senior title-holding member of parliament makes nothing of it, because, in her words, 'we are all equal' (Swami, 2015).

The withdrawal of chiefly influence in national politics demonstrates how reputations are made with money donations and other non-traditional gifts. This was evident to me from the beginning of my fieldwork in Naloto in May 2007; making a voluntary contribution at a school fundraiser led villagers—so I was later told—to view me as a decent person who recognised their need. The same fundraiser gave a well-known politician, a member of the pre-coup government, access to the village. After donating hundreds of dollars, instead of the required FJD65, he was garlanded and treated to a place at the top of the kava ring, from which he addressed first one-half, then later the entire village, on the political situation following the 2006 coup. Subsequently, the villagers were keen to point out what a good and generous man he was; by coming to their aid and speaking words of encouragement in troubled times, he made a lasting impression on the village. Some months later, he led the villagers on a political mission that was not only an open show of support for the ousted government, but also a dangerous show of dissent against the military rule at that time.

There is a very strong ideology of what constitutes the good life in Naloto village. Although commonly expressed in terms of self-subsistence and sharing, the egalitarian implications accompanying the subsistence-based ideal come through on ceremonial occasions in a way that reveals the more wide-reaching notion of an undifferentiated village of similars. However, this extended village community of moneyed emigrants cannot be contained by the ideal model any further than the strict formalities of exchange. It is the latter that provides grounds for differentiating the village chieftains and the political leaders of Fiji, just as the egalitarian practices exemplified by funerals pave the way for new ways of signifying distinction.

References

Arno, A. (2005). Cobo and Tabua in Fiji: Two forms of cultural currency in an economy of sentiment. *American Ethnologist, 32*(1), 46–62. doi.org/10.1525/ae.2005.32.1.46

Autio, P. (2010). *Hard custom, hard dance: Social organisation, (un) differentiation and notions of power in a Tabiteuean community, southern Kiribati*. Helsinki, Finland: University of Helsinki. Retrieved from urn.fi/URN:ISBN:978-952-10-6151-6

Bainimarama, J. V. (2012, 14 March). *Remarks by the Prime Minister on the Great Council of Chiefs*. Retrieved from www.scoop.co.nz/stories/WO1203/S00245/bainimarama-on-de-establishing-great-council-of-chiefs.htm

Barraud, C., de Coppet, D., Iteanu, A. & Jamous, R. (1994). *Of relations and the dead: Four societies viewed from the angle of their exchanges.* Oxford, England: Berg.

Cayrol, F. (2015). How would we have got here if our paternal grandmother had not existed? Relations of locality, blood, life and name in Nasau, Fiji. In C. Toren & S. Pauwels (Eds), *Living kinship in the Pacific* (pp. 207–41). New York, NY: Berghahn.

Douaire-Marsaudon, F. (2008). Food and wealth: Ceremonial objects as signs of identity in Tonga and in Wallis. In S. Tcherkezoff and F. Douaire-Marsaudon (Eds), *The changing South Pacific: Identities and transformations* (2nd ed.) (pp. 207–29). Canberra, ACT: ANU E Press. Retrieved from press-files.anu.edu.au/downloads/press/p90711/pdf/ch10.pdf

Eräsaari, M. (2013). *'We are the originals': A study of value in Fiji* . University of Helsinki, Finland. Retrieved from hdl.handle.net/10138/40203

Eräsaari, M. (2015). The iTaukei chief: Value and alterity in Verata. *Journal de la Société des Océanistes, 141*, 239–54. doi.org/10.4000/jso.7407

Forge, A. (1972). The golden gleece. *Man, 7*(4), 527–40. doi.org/10.2307/2799947

Gregory, C. (2014). Unequal egalitarianism: Reflections on Forge's paradox. *The Asia Pacific Journal of Anthropology, 15*(3), 197–217. doi.org/10.1080/14442213.2014.916342

Hocart, A. M. (1924). Maternal relations in Melanesian ritual. *Man, 24*(132), 185–86. doi.org/10.2307/2787616

Hocart, A. M. (1929). *Lau Islands, Fij*. Honolulu, HI: Bernice P. Bishop Museum.

Hooper, S. (2013). 'Supreme among our valuables': Whale teeth tabua, chiefship and power in eastern Fiji. *Journal of the Polynesian Society, 122*(2), 161–210.

Hulkenberg, J. (2015). Fijian kinship: Exchange and migration. In C. Toren and S. Pauwels (Eds), *Living kinship in the Pacific* (pp. 60–86). New York, NY: Berghahn.

Kaplan, M. (1995). *Neither cargo nor cult: Ritual politics and the colonial imagination in Fiji*. Durham, NC: Duke University Press.

Metcalf, P. & Huntington, R. (1999). *Celebrations of death: The anthropology of mortuary ritual* (2nd ed.). Cambridge, England: Cambridge University Press.

Pauwels, S. (2015). The Vasu position and the sister's mana. The case of Lau, Fiji. In C. Toren & S. Pauwels (Eds), *Living kinship in the Pacific* (pp. 143–64). New York, NY: Berghahn.

Ravuvu, A. (2005). *Vaka i taukei: The Fijian way of life*. Suva, Fiji: University of the South Pacific, Institute of Pacific Studies.

Robbins, J. (1994). Equality as a value: Ideology in Dumont, Melanesia and the West. *Social Analysis, 36,* 21–70.

Sahlins, M. (1976). *Culture and practical reason*. Chicago, IL: University of Chicago Press.

Sahlins, M. (1985). *Islands of history*. Chicago, IL: University of Chicago Press.

Swami, N. (2015, 11 February). PM: Out with insults in Parliament. *Fiji Times*. Retrieved from www.fijitimes.com/story.aspx?id=294671

Tomlinson, M. (2009). *In God's image: The metaculture of Fijian Christianity*. Berkeley, CA: University of California Press.

Toren, Christina (1988). Making the present, revealing the past: The mutability and continuity of tradition as process. *Man* (new series) *23*(4), 696–717.

Vunileba, A. (2008, 1 April). Some chiefs not installed. *Fiji Times* (p. 4).

Williksen-Bakker, S. (1986). Ceremony and complication in an urban context. In C. Griffin & M. Monsell-Davis (Eds), *Fijians in town* (pp. 196–208). Suva, Fiji: Institute of Pacific Studies, University of the South Pacific.

3

Changing Standards of Living: The Paradoxes of Building a Good Life in Rural Vanuatu

Rachel E. Smith

Introduction

> There have been big changes—'good houses', solar lights—we no longer have the same living standards as before. (Seasonal worker)

> Before, in the 1970s and 1980s, life was totally different … We no longer have the 'good life' of before. (Father, school cook)

The construction of a 'good house' had become a preoccupation for seasonal-worker households in my fieldwork site of Lamen Bay on the island of Epi, and the small offshore Lamen island, by the time of my arrival in Vanuatu in November 2011. The day after I landed in Lamen Bay, my host mother, Mary,[1] took me on a tour along the dirt road that looped around the settlement, pointing out the many new houses and more under construction. An educated local woman, Mary acted as an administrative agent for the largest recruiter of seasonal workers from Epi in New Zealand's Recognised Seasonal Employer (RSE) temporary migration program. She told me later that she always urged the seasonal workers she recruited to build a 'good house', to install solar power and to prioritise their families with the money they earned overseas.

1 To protect the anonymity of my interlocuters, the personal names in this chapter are pseudonyms.

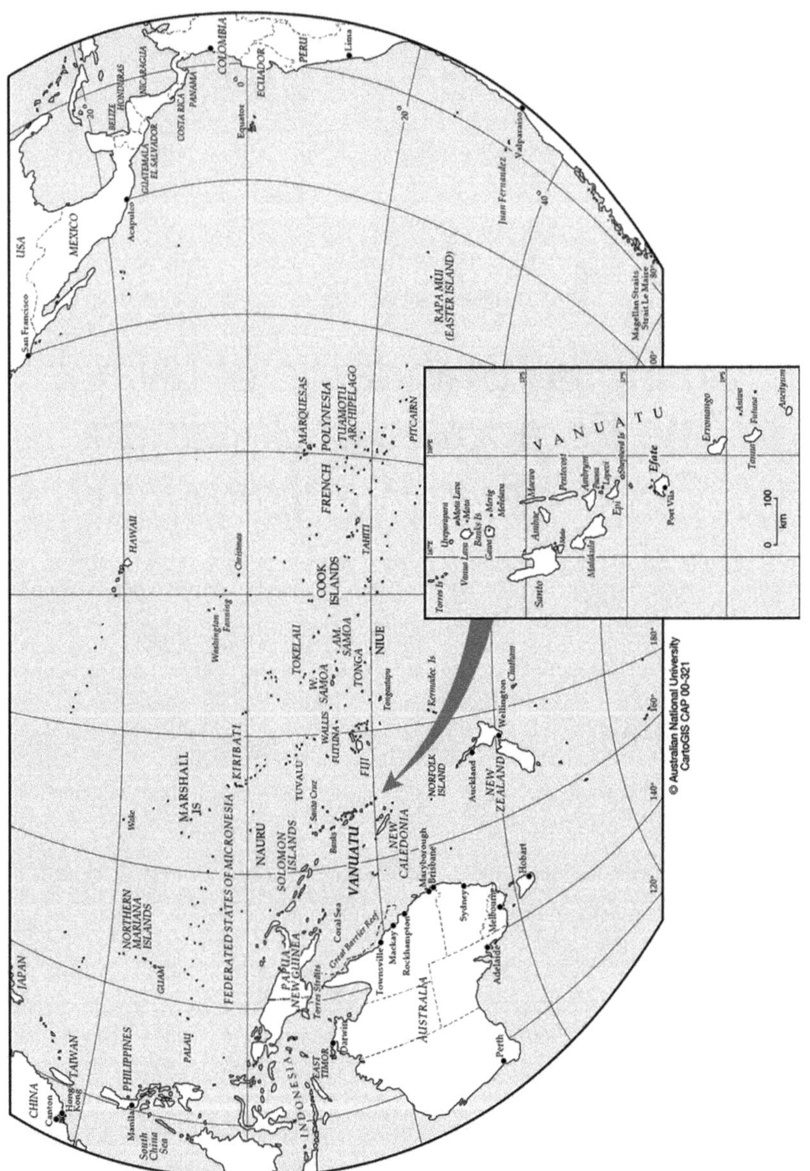

Figure 3.1: Vanuatu, South-West Pacific Ocean

Source: CartoGIS, College of Asia and the Pacific, The Australian National University.

Lamen Bay is located on the north-west coast of Epi island, central Vanuatu, so named after the small offshore Lamen island, whose inhabitants travel back and forth to the bay to cultivate gardens. Since around the 1960s, increasing numbers of Li-Lamenu[2] have been moving across to the mainland more permanently. Unlike Epi mainland to the south and east, Lamen island and Lamen Bay are densely populated and there are growing worries about future land shortages. Within Vanuatu, Lamen Bay and Lamen island are well known as communities with a high degree of engagement in New Zealand's horticultural seasonal-worker program. When New Zealand's RSE program was launched in 2008, two major employers began to recruit in the area and several others followed. By the time of my fieldwork (November 2011 – March 2013), seasonal work had become an important means of making a living for most families. A household survey I conducted in 2012 revealed that over two-thirds of all households (including those ineligible due to age) had had at least one member engage as a seasonal worker, many of whom were, by then, returning for their fourth or fifth season.

For Li-Lamenu seasonal workers, the construction of a 'good house' and the payment of school fees are the most common reasons for working overseas; this reflects a collective desire to improve standards of living and secure a future for the next generation in a wage economy. At a community council meeting a few days after my arrival in Epi, the chief and the chairperson led a discussion to thank the seasonal workers for the development they had brought. The chairperson stated, 'many thanks to those of you who have created development with your houses and the things in which we can see that now this place is developing'. The chief affirmed this sentiment, declaring that 'it is a good thing that we go and come and make … our homes. We have changed Lamen Bay: all the buildings'.

2 Just as the people whose ethnic origin is from Vanuatu are known by the demonym 'Ni-Vanuatu', I refer to people who identify as originating from Lamen island as Li-Lamenu, meaning 'people of Lamen' in their vernacular.

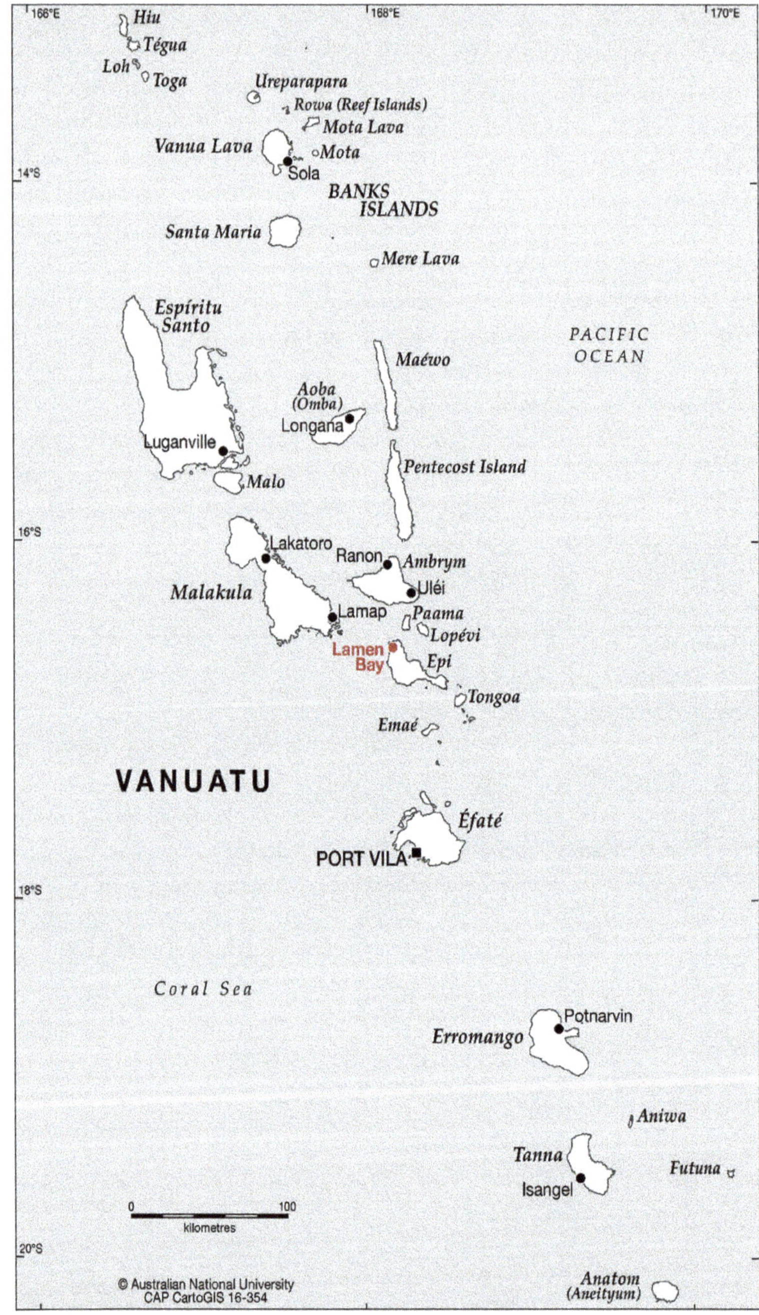

Figure 3.2: Map of North and Central Vanuatu, with Lamen Bay in Epi Marked

Source: CartoGIS, College of Asia and the Pacific, The Australian National University.

However, not all of the changes associated with seasonal migration were as welcome as the new housing. The actions of seasonal workers were often evaluated against moral as well as material standards, as being more or less conducive to living together well. Both the chief and the chairperson admonished seasonal workers for neglecting to contribute money and labour to community and church projects. The chief said, 'whose future is this for? It's for your own children's future. We should be glad about New Zealand … I want to see good things everywhere we go'. He advocated a selective approach to incorporating foreign attitudes and behaviours. For instance, although the workers had learned to follow rules in New Zealand, such as regulations on fishing, they often ignored the chiefs' rulings on reef prohibitions (*tabu*).[3] He added:

> We need to change ourselves in some ways. We shouldn't go just for money: we need to change our attitudes. Anything they have that is better, you bring it with you.

As the chief's statement suggests, Li-Lamenu do not indiscriminately welcome outside goods and practices. Rather, they seek to incorporate those actions and objects deemed moral 'goods' from outside, while maintaining traditional or autochthonous *kastom* (custom) practices and modes of relating that are seen as essential to living in peace and respect with kin. However, this envisioning of the 'good life' and 'good development' as some combination of *kastom* and material and social 'goods' from the 'outside' is open to deliberation and contestation.

Li-Lamenu conceptions of the moral life fit well with those of Mauss (2007) who observed that 'morality is the art of living together, and it can be recognised by the presence of the notion of the good' (p. 156). The trouble is that 'the good' is always subject to contest and change; thus, the quest for, or the question of, the good life requires 'moral reasoning, through the contrary and contradictory value standards of the good' (Sykes, 2012, p. 173). The quest for the good presents Li-Lamenu with a number of problems and dilemmas. For one, standards of the good are always subject to change, corresponding with economic, political and religious transformations. Second, the matter of the good is always subject to contestation; a good for one, or in one context, may be a bad for another. Third, the pursuit of the good can often lead, paradoxically, to the introduction of 'bads'.

3 Words in Bislama vernacular are in italics, while vernacular Lamen terms are also underlined.

Indeed, engagement in overseas seasonal work is repeatedly said by Li-Lamenu to have a 'good side' and a 'bad side'. Justifications for channelling money into houses, land and school fees revolve around securing a future for the household and community 'development'. However, this pursuit of standards of living gives rise to a number of contradictions including land disputes and scarcity, broken homes, withdrawal from community work and a perceived decline in respect and reciprocity. These different visions of the good life relate to different valuations of space and time, corresponding with idealised pasts and futures. A vision of the good life associated with the household's material success in a cash economy can come into tension with, or threaten, a conception of the good life associated with an ancestral past, in which the good life—'living together well' (Gregory, 2013, p. 137)—is understood as maintaining mutual relations of respect in line with customary expectations.

In this chapter, I discuss the ways in which Li-Lamenu negotiate the paradoxes of building a good life, and how they navigate contradictory values and changing standards of the good. First, I discuss how constructing a 'good house' is seen as a moral as well as a material 'good', standing for household security and prosperity in conditions of economic and environmental uncertainty. While a house is seen as a self-evident 'good', it gives rise to tensions and paradoxes concerning the possibilities for living together well with kin, as I describe in the second section. Workers are also investing in the education of their children to the end of secondary school, sometimes even into tertiary or higher education. In the third section, I discuss how workers aim to secure a place for their children in an increasingly wage-based economy and to improve or maintain their children's standards of living, thereby mitigating anxieties over land scarcity and environmental disasters. However, this vision of the 'good life' in terms of improving material standards of living for one's household as well as the next generation is often met with a counter narrative in which a good life, as founded on relations of respect, is in decline. In the final section, I discuss how, although material standards are changing, people are concerned to retain relations of respect as crucial to leading a good life and living together well.

Changing Standards of Living

The 'good house' is frequently associated with improvements in 'standards of living', an English phrase often incorporated into Li-Lamenu expressions of their desires. Standards of living are moral as well as material and ideas of the good are historically and socially particular. Over 25 years ago, Rodman's (1985a, p. 275) informants on the island of Ambae (Aoba in Figure 3.2), North Vanuatu, were distinguishing houses in terms of their 'goodness', concluding that 'for most people in Longana, a "good" house is a simple structure, perhaps 15 feet square, with a corrugated iron roof, cement floor, and walls of woven bamboo'. Li-Lamenu people today also aim for a 'good' house, but most would no longer be satisfied with the house Rodman described. For a New Zealand returnee, a 'good' house has, perhaps, three to six bedrooms, a separate 'sitting room' constructed entirely of durable materials, a corrugated metal (*kapa*) roof, walls of concrete or a combination of concrete and *kapa*, and a cement floor. Ideally, it also has a front veranda, one or two solar panels and a large rain tank.

Following the introduction of the RSE program in 2008, there was a rapid proliferation of 'good houses' in Lamen and Lamen Bay. My December 2012 household survey revealed a rapid transition to more durable imported housing materials on Lamen island. Between 2008 and 2012, 46 'good' houses were built, compared with just four in the five years prior. Houses often take at least three successive seasons to build; many were coming to completion during my fieldwork, while others were still under construction. A comparison with national census data (Vanuatu National Statistics Office, 2009) reveals that the use of traditional plant materials for walls and roofs was halved in the three years prior to my survey. There was an even more dramatic transformation in transition to electric light sources; kerosene lamp use dropped from 71 households in 2009 to just eight in late 2012. In the same period, solar lighting increased fourfold.

Household and residence patterns have taken shape together with changes in moral and material standards of living over the last 150 years. Changes in houses and domestic spatial patterns have materialised aspects of historical and social transformations and changing identities (Rodman, 1985a, pp. 269–72). In the colonial period, spatial and residential configurations made visible and tangible the conversion of people to a new moral temporal order (Mitchell, 2013, p. 292), which was brought about through the subdual of warfare, reduction in fear of sorcery and spirit attacks, and missionary influence. Prior to European trade and conversion to Christianity, people lived in small hamlets in clusters of between one and three clans. Encouraged by missionaries and colonial officers, pacification and a desire for trade, clans began to concentrate into adjacent yards (*rove*) nearer the sandy shoreline, divided by low dry-stone walls. Men were encouraged to leave men's houses (*nakamal, kumali*) and live with their wives as a conjugal unit, eating with their families and encouraging more household nucleation (Rodman, 1985a, p. 272). Pigs were fenced and older people today recall how community work parties kept shared spaces clean and tidy.

The household's form and function and its relationship with wider kin and community has changed over time as a result of outside influences, including the colonial promotion of nuclear family models and ideas about health, hygiene and economic transformations. The precolonial Li-Lamenu house (*kanayum̃a*) featured a low saddle roof that stretched to the ground on either side, with a small entrance door at one end, and a cooking fire inside. Missionaries and colonial officers arriving in Vanuatu from the mid-nineteenth century saw precolonial houses as dirty, dark and smoky; they enforced new 'civilising' moral and material standards that promoted hygiene, cleanliness, ventilation and light (Jolly, 1991, p. 39; Rodman, 1985a, p. 272). Gradually, during the late colonial period, *kanayum̃a* were replaced with upright houses with pitched sago (*natangura*) thatch panelled roofs and a more familiar, boxy European-style shape. The walls were made of woven bamboo or, more typically for Lamen, wild cane. They often had an A-framed house style, along with separate 'kitchen houses' and private drop toilets. Some people told me this transformation largely took place in the 1950s–60s, triggered by an infestation of small millipedes, known in Bislama as *kruked*. This may be true; however, this transition also took place on islands across Vanuatu and, it would seem, largely due to colonial and church influence. Many men would have become familiar with new technologies and materials during service in World War II and further changes were introduced by post-war health and development initiatives (Taylor, 2008, pp. 144–45).

People on Lamen also experienced new construction techniques and styles when a Presbyterian missionary and his family took up residence on the island in 1948. The missionary, Graham Horwell, soon began work on a large European-style lime house, for which he summoned an architect and a carpenter from New Zealand. When the new mission house was finished, a visitor described how it drew considerable attention from the Li-Lamenu congregants:

> A house is built for him that is necessarily large and airy for health reasons. The natives eye this mansion with envy … to them he appears to want for nothing … the natives try to sponge on him for all manner of things … He certainly sacrifices many things which we regard as essential to a comfortable life. (France, 1953, p. 110)

In the decades that followed, some Li-Lamenu men were trained as carpenters and employed by the district officer to construct buildings elsewhere in the district. Others had experience of construction in Noumea, New Caledonia, a popular destination for temporary migration in the 1960s and 1970s. When they returned, they often spent their money on housing materials, constructing European-style houses. Some of these houses were built from manufactured materials or lime. Moreover, they were built using styles and techniques that serve as testament both to the influence of the mission house and the increasing familiarity with urban and colonial architecture.

More than three decades after independence and the departure of foreign missionaries on Lamen, there remain strong associations of the 'good house' with moral and material development. The 'lighting up' of the good house seems to have assumed a particularly spiritual significance, recalling the transition between a common Melanesian Christian temporal idiom of the time of 'darkness', being the pre-Christian past, and the 'light' ushered in by the missionaries (Jolly, 1991; Tonkinson, 1982, p. 51). In fact, the opportunity to work overseas and to change one's living standards is often said by Li-Lamenu people to be a 'blessing', suggesting that they see it as part of God's plan. Many claim that the opportunity to participate in the seasonal work program is a legacy of the last missionary, as it was Horwell's relative who first recruited seasonal workers from Epi.

Many material changes are seen as self-evidently 'good' for their perceived convenient and pragmatic benefits. Solar panels and rain tanks are especially valued material outcomes of engagement in overseas work. Rainwater run-off from a metal roof can be collected in a tank; this is especially useful on Lamen island where access to potable drinking water is limited. People often comment that solar-powered electric lighting allows them to carry out activities at night that they could not have done when they relied on kerosene lamps. However, the transition is not advantageous in every respect of material comfort and practicality. Metal roofed houses, especially those with metal walls, are much hotter than the cool and airy houses built of natural materials. As such, people tend to avoid spending any length of time inside until they retire to bed, preferring to congregate outside in the shade, under a veranda or perhaps in a cool, thatched kitchen building.

Perhaps the most common reason people give for building a 'good house' is the durability and strength of imported materials, which are associated with security for one's family. A 'traditional' or 'local' thatch house might last only two years, whereas a 'permanent' or 'semi-permanent' house may last 20 years before the *kapa* roofing sheets have to be replaced. Additionally, 'permanent' houses are less likely to need maintenance during the period the seasonal worker is away. One married seasonal worker, who faced criticism for choosing to return to New Zealand when his wife was seriously ill, legitimated his decision by stressing his desire to complete the house, then under construction, as a means of demonstrating his care and nurture for his wife and children:

> Most of the workers that go over there, their goals are to build a house, light up a house. When you stay in a *kastom* house, it is a short time before you must build another … When you build a house—a 'good one'—you no longer worry about your family, your family has a good place to live when you are away.

As this statement articulates, seasonal workers often emphasised protection for their family when justifying their decisions. The most common reason for building a good house was to provide protection from cyclones, both for the household and for less well-off relatives. The following news item (Radio New Zealand, 2015), which is based on an interview with a Li-Lamenu nurse following a severe, category five cyclone, illustrates the value of safety from such disasters:

> If it were not for those who went to New Zealand and built these big buildings I can say [that] many people would have died because we would have been running from house to house and we would have been killed by the flying debris. But these big buildings that we have saved the lives of everyone on Lamen island.

Due to the prevalence of seasonal work opportunities in Lamen and Lamen Bay, cumulative household accomplishments have, generally, been welcomed as conducive to the development of the community and island in the form of material standards of living. Judged by material standards of living, the durable 'good house' has come to stand for a certain conception of the good life and the future wellbeing of its occupants; however, this can be contested against other standards of the 'good'.

Household Goods and Bads

While the durability and practical aspects of the good house are almost taken for granted as 'good', moral evaluations of their occupants are underpinned by whether their behaviour is deemed conducive to maintaining good social relations. In an interview, Chief Waiwo reiterated common reasons for the positive valuation of the 'good house', but also described how the house and the 'goods' it contained could become 'bads' when they were used in a way that was counter to living together well:

> Before there were few [good houses], but now there are many, which is good. Their families are safe. They carry solar, and do good things. But sometimes they use their solar in a bad way: they carry noisy things. When that happens, people no longer have respect: there's mourning, but there's music in another house. It means there's no respect for others. Then you find out they are trying to 'compete': who can carry the loudest? Some things are good, but some things are like that.

Household 'goods' are only considered 'good' when they appear to bring benefits without having negative effects on others. In this sense, the kinds of effects termed '(negative, consumption) externalities' by economists (and some cultural economists) (Callon, 1998, p. 246) can be seen as integral to value creation and realisation from the point of view of the domestic moral economy in which the moral grounds of value depend on respect, which is crucial to living together well.

Li-Lamenu frequently remarked that before the rise of the RSE program they could not have imagined having a 'good house' or electric lighting. Most workers only had basic education, and many perceived their access to previously unavailable amounts of money through remittances as akin to closing a gap between 'haves' and 'have-nots'. For them, New Zealand work meant that people who schooled to Class Six (primary level) could now build houses that, before, were mainly only achievable for educated teachers and government workers.

'Good houses' achieved through seasonal work are not necessarily markers of class distinction; yet, in reflecting regional disparities in work opportunities and a shift away from reciprocal patterns towards household accumulation, they may create foundations for further economic differentiation in the future. Spending on the house and land is a means to allocate remittances in such a way that it allows household accumulation without entailing the types of criticism reserved for individual consumption. However, it also limits the wide dispersal of remittances to kin networks (Gamburd, 2004, p. 180). This raises the more general question of whether the good house reflects a shift away from a kin-ordered morality towards a more nucleated household-centric moral order. Rodman (1997) identified a similar transition towards household nucleation in rural Vanuatu, noting:

> In the past, a house expressed connection to the community; now it expresses the importance of nurturing the nuclear family and of material success. A 'good provider' under these changed circumstances turns inward toward the household more than outward toward the larger social unit. (p. 227)

Changes in housing and residence can be seen as a concrete manifestation of changing social relations; the shift in emphasis of the distribution of time and resources from a deferred return in kind within kin networks, to more immediate and household-oriented transactions, can be seen in the construction of the fabric of the house itself. The construction of a thatched house is an event involving wide networks of kin and is tied up with acts of reciprocity of food and labour. When building a thatch house, the household gather together a wide circle of kin and neighbours whose collective efforts mean that the build can be completed in just one or two days. The women pre-prepare the materials and then get to work cooking food to feed all those who contribute; the helpers, in turn, can expect reciprocal assistance in the future. By contrast, permanent houses demand a certain level of technical expertise. Often a local carpenter, albeit usually a kinsman, is employed for a considerable fee. The demand for a 'good house' has provided impetus for the commoditisation and division of labour, which has undermined the principle of reciprocity of work. Today, people often complain that if you ask someone to come and help with a domestic task, they will expect payment.

Good houses are often built in secluded spots, away from the tightly packed yards where clan members have tended to live side-by-side. The desire for a 'good house' is leading to a spatial dispersal of households, as some households are identifying larger and more secluded areas of land on which to build a 'good house'. The attraction of proximity to roads and amenities, the convenience of not having to canoe or pay for boat rides, as well as more opportunities to obtain money, are leading many to move to Lamen Bay where the houses can be large and spaced far apart, suitable for creating secluded private yards with lawns and flower gardens. Further, there is an increasing quest for higher ground due to anxieties over climate change and natural disasters. These factors are contributing to the increasing turnover of land previously used for gardens or coconut plantations to residential land. This change in land use appears to be exacerbating the problem of land scarcity and food insecurity; on a recent return visit to Lamen, a pair of brothers told me that they were worried about the loss of garden land and would encourage their sons to build on the small island.

Across Vanuatu, the affective value of place (*ples*) is crucial to social identity; good houses can be seen as a long-term investment in remaining part of the community. Conversely, the 'good house' can become an object of social conflict and moral disapproval when the land identified for its foundations is disputed. Indeed, land disputes between kin[4] were said to be intensifying, and it was very often the earmarking of plots on which to build new houses that triggered these conflicts. During my fieldwork, there were at least two occasions of vandalism of property on disputed sites, and other planned houses left unbuilt or abandoned due to ongoing disputes. Perhaps the fact that the houses represent fixed investments that stake a long-term claim on the land means that they are more objectionable and contested than the more mobile and temporary houses of homegrown materials that could easily shift according to different circumstances, or shifting plots of garden land that were more shareable and short term?[5]

New spatial arrangements emerging through the founding of 'good houses' appear as a process of privatisation of land and space and a transition from communal shared 'yards' towards more private properties. Further, it appears that these spatial reconfigurations may be mapping changing kin relations and a shift from clan to household as the locus of economic concern. Ward and Kingdon (1995, pp. 1–2) suggested that settlement patterns changed as people's efforts became more directed at self-interest and the contracted nucleated family group, rather than extended kin and the wider community, and as economic relations, previously organised through reciprocal obligations, became increasingly mediated through money (cf. Martin, 2007, pp. 49–50; 2013, pp. 72–73). In Vanuatu, Jolly (1989, p. 230) reported that on Pentecost island, richer families tended to build isolated homesteads outside the village; she suggested that such a move could be a partial withdrawal from kin networks of generalised reciprocity.

4 For more on land tenure and disputes in Lamen Bay, see Smith (2017).

5 Use rights to land for making a garden or building a thatched house could be allocated to clan or kin members according to need and stages in the life cycle (Rodman, 1985b, p. 276).

In an effort to avoid disputes and strengthen their tenure on a residential plot, some people try to secure land through formal transactions. Although these transactions take a customary form and are between kin, they involve increasing sums of money and written deeds, and appear to fix household allocations of land. One young couple, David and Rita, performed a transaction in 2012 to their clan chief and his sons to pay for a piece of land on which they were building a new house. They had begun to construct their new house on the site in 2010 after David returned from New Zealand for the first time. The site was chosen because it was on higher ground and offered protection from tidal waves and disasters; however, Rita told me that their primary motivation for making the transaction was to help safeguard the future of their two children and to prevent them from being pushed off the land due to a dispute.

The fact that Li-Lamenu are increasingly fixing more permanent stakes in the land in the form of durable houses may be part of wider processes of household nucleation and individualisation of land tenure and emphasis on intergenerational transfers (cf. Ward & Kingdon, 1995, pp. 1–2). Rita said that, in the past, 'the ancestors were good' and would give land to friends or family that needed it. She suggested that, perhaps due to the influence of *waetman* (white people), Li-Lamenu people now expect cash payment. She said that she worried about her children's future, especially if they had no land, although perhaps if they were well educated and managed to obtain good jobs in town they would be alright. These are common concerns among Li-Lamenu parents who worry about land scarcity and disputes, and increasingly look to education as a means of securing a place for the next generation in a changing economy.

Stronger Foundations for the Future? Investing in Schooling

The construction of a good house is not the only foundation for a future good life that migrants seek; educating one's children is seen as an investment in the good life of future generations. Seasonal work opportunities are valued for allowing parents to discharge school fees, and many parents are able to fund their children's education through to secondary and even tertiary education. Payment of school fees was the second most common stated expenditure of remittances in my survey, and is often considered the main driver for workers to keep returning to work, even after a house is completed.

Like the house, expenditure on school fees was morally valued over short-term consumption and imports deemed to undermine aspirations for a good life. A primary school teacher at Lamen Bay indicated that some of the blame for a perceived decline in children's behaviour fell on seasonal-worker parents buying them unnecessary material items:

> Many times, when the parents come back from New Zealand, they bring things like stereos, videos, mobile phones, and DVD players for the children. It really distracts children's interest from their studies at home … It's really a big issue … The parents should only carry things that are good for the child, but the child says, 'I want this, I want that', and they don't realise they are creating a big problem.

Unlike the good house and school fees, other kinds of consumption and expenditure were often negatively valued as a waste of money or for undermining moral behaviour. One returned seasonal worker and mother of three said:

> When I came back the two children said, 'oh mummy, when we visit other children whose fathers have come back from New Zealand, they have this and they have that. They have just about everything'. But my reply was that 'you must get a good education, that's my plan' … In my experience, those children whose fathers go to New Zealand: their lives are different. But in my home, I don't want my children to have all these things. I want my children to live a 'local life', so their thoughts remain good all the time. So, when I came back, they asked me, 'what did you bring for us?' And I replied, 'the things I brought are clothes, and money just for paying school fees, so I bought things to help your future'.

The primary school headmaster saw the concrete house as a less than permanent solution to a future good life. In his view, it was school fees that truly would provide a firm foundation. He told me that parents must prioritise a child's education, as it may be the only means to enable them to achieve and maintain the improved standards of living that the parents were striving for in the long term:

> If this [RSE] scheme in New Zealand stops, where is your investment, the money for which you worked hard? If the scheme closes tomorrow, everyone will see that you worked to invest in your children, and too, the child will be able to support himself because he has a strong foundation. But if it is all for a house and solar, the child will not be able to achieve that if the scheme stops. It is better if you support the child in their schooling.

The class teacher reiterated to her pupils that the standards of living brought about through seasonal work could not be maintained forever:

> I keep telling the pupils in the classroom, 'don't you think this scheme will last forever. It will stop. And if you don't have an aim for your education, if you think that when you finish school you will go to New Zealand, then one day you will find it really, really hard, because one day this scheme will stop. It's not like your land, which will always be there to make gardens on. This scheme belongs to different people'.

However, while many Li-Lamenu realise that the scheme may be short-lived, and are using the money to invest in their children's education, they do not feel they can rely on the fact that the land will 'always be there' for gardens either. Li-Lamenu parents' anxieties about securing a place for their children in the wage economy is often framed in terms of land scarcity or insecure tenure, which makes them fear that there may not always be enough land for the rapidly growing population to provision themselves. Anxieties over land shortages and disputes, exacerbated by high population growth and fears about climate change, are causing parents to pin their hopes for their children's security on their education and employment in the wage sector.

Changing material standards of living creates pressure to maintain or better those standards. The headmaster suggested that if the next generation are unable to maintain or further those standards attained by their parents, they may find themselves in a precarious situation, neither able to make a living like their forebears, nor succeed in the wage economy:

> I keep telling the Year 8s: 'You must get a good education, because it's not good if you stay here, while your parents have flat screens and solar lights and everything, but when you grow up and you get married, you are using kerosene lamps. It will look bad, because you won't be able to use the same lights as the others, because you are used to a "good house"'. When they get married, if they don't get a good education, and the [seasonal migration] 'scheme' is closed, then these children won't be able to live the same life that their parents provided for them. And for them, reaching that standard will be hard, because they don't have the same knowledge that their parents had. And when you see the children today, you see they don't work like the older people did in the past.

As the headmaster implied, while schooling is often understood as preparing children for opportunities for wage work, it is seen as coming at the expense of acquiring knowledge and horticultural techniques that would make young people accustomed to working on their land, as their grandparents did.

The emphasis that parents place on education both contributes to, and is motivated by, youths' disinclination or inability to take up subsistence gardening in the future. Youths are increasingly undertaking secondary school, which involves them leaving the island and taking up residence in boarding schools. Living away from home, often at a great distance, they do not learn the gardening skills that were once essential to making a living. A secondary schoolteacher told me that due to the United Nations Millennium Development Goals, the government was keen to progress every child to at least Year 9. He felt that this plan was detrimental because many youths who were struggling in school, or who had little interest in education, were being encouraged to continue even though they were unlikely to find employment. It was his view that such children were better off returning home and learning traditional cultivation techniques; he felt that it was 'too late' to learn such skills past adolescence.

Educating their children allows Li-Lamenu parents to imagine a future with a future: one, they hope, that will not only lend them security in their older age, but also different standards of living for the generations that follow. However, this conception of a secure future is premised on different ways to make a living and types of mobility. This vision of a 'good life' requires reimagining Li-Lamenu social relations and ways of 'living well' that may be increasingly incompatible with possibilities for living together in one place. Rather than work the land, it seems that youths will be more likely to go to town in search of work or opportunities to work overseas. The increasing education of children to final years of secondary schooling and even into tertiary education suggests that the future of Lamen may be one that is economically differentiated and based on urban–rural flows. This is likely to be a process that creates 'winners' and 'losers'; given the limited opportunities for gainful employment, there is little guarantee that one's child will be able to obtain well-paid wage work in the future. While those who are successful may become the urban elites of tomorrow, older generations fear that a youthful population, disinclined towards garden work, but unable to secure a well-paid job, would drift to town, struggle to get by and get involved in trouble. Increasingly, youth are seen to be adopting foreign lifestyles and ignoring *kastom*, thereby threatening a conception of the good life that is seen as living together well with kin.

Losing Respect

> When you ignore the small things, it builds a big weakness. Now the community will always be in a mess. The power of our culture has been declining every year, since 1989. Now all the children act as if everywhere is a 'free zone'. (Father, gardener)

> If you have respect, you will have a good life. The youths are strong headed: they don't know how to make a garden and they always disobey. They don't have respect. When we die, it will be even worse. Lamen won't be like it is today. (Church elder, grandfather)

Most Li-Lamenu agreed that housing and education were self-evident 'goods' associated with community prosperity and development and securing a long-term future in a changing environment. However, most also feared that the indiscriminate pursuit of imported modern goods also threatened to undermine a conception of the good life rooted in an autochthonous past (albeit one re-imagined to be compatible with Christian values). While most people advocated the incorporation of particular types of material goods and practices, many were concerned about a moral decline and a lack of respect associated with the acquisition of foreign items and lifestyles at the expense of social relations based on ideas of respect for others, and for ancestral knowledge and practices, or *kastom*.

Discussions about the 'good life' in terms of living together well with others often revolve around ideas of respect (*rispek, kohoyana*). As in the quotations above, it is common for people to lament a decline in respect and the 'good life' of the past. Despite the increasing value placed on education as a means to securing a good future, many people worry about the effect of exposure to foreign things and knowledge on 'younger generations' regard for the respectful demeanour and customary practices that are understood to maintain good social relations. The common complaint about a decline in respect among young people not only denotes a lack of deference to authority, but also a lack of observance of avoidance behaviours, ignorance about obligations to kin and a loss of knowledge associated with how to perform *kastom*.

At 'Children's Day' in 2012, a Presbyterian Church elder addressed the children, saying:

> The power of darkness in the 'daylight' of today is even worse than the darkness of before … We claim that today we are Christian and we are in the daylight, but the behaviours emerging today, if you compare with before, are much much worse.

The elder talked about how past attempts to revive customary practices had gone amiss, and how everyone must work to 'pull up' *kastom* and the values of respect and honour:

> Those [customary practices] that are bad; we will throw them out, for example, poison and killing people. But we must take hold of those we think will help us bring back respect and honour to our island … You need to pull all these things and you will see our lives grow and rise up … You must try to pull back honour and respect … *Kastom* is our identity. We don't know our future … Identity shows that this is your place.

For the elder, the value of place and time-honoured modes of respect were crucial to navigating an uncertain future. Like the chief, who talked of a selective approach to the incorporation of 'good' foreign items and practices, the elder advocated a selective approach to customary behaviours, seeking to reject 'bad' *kastom* associated with black magic and conflicts, while retaining the respectful relations seen as underpinning the ability to live together well. He then invited a several elderly people to the stage to demonstrate ideal marriage prescriptions and avoidance behaviours to the children.

Similar complaints about being strong headed, selfish, materialistic and ignoring respect and avoidance expectations are also levelled at seasonal workers, particularly in association with extramarital affairs that take place when married couples are separated during seasonal work. The Assemblies of God pastor, who was also a seasonal worker, told me:

> These behaviours have come from money. People overseas are 'out' of respect; they joke and tease with affines. But it started here and spread outward. If you neglect things, then the next day other things will come in as well … Money flows in but many problems follow this change. For instance, problems with marriages: before they didn't happen. Families have been broken. When change comes, a lot of other things flow in too, if you're not careful.

Money has a good side and a bad side. Parry and Bloch (1989) famously critiqued the assumption that money is a kind of social acid, inevitably dissolving relations and corroding communitarian bonds. They noted a common tendency across different cultures to subordinate short-term acquisition to long-term principles of social reproduction in which 'the totality of transactions form a general pattern which is part of the reproduction of social and ideological systems concerned with a time-scale far longer than the individual life'. The durable house and school fees are justified as moral in so far as they are a means of domesticating money to secure a long-term future for the next generation in a changing economy. However, this household-oriented domestication comes into tension with long-term principles of social reproduction associated with *kastom* in which reciprocity and respect between clans are paramount.

Li-Lamenu often situate different standards of the good in contradictory temporal terms or telos, like the elder above. Many, especially seasonal workers, emphasise a trajectory in which standards of living are improving and development is being created, promising a prosperous future. Others, often older people, talk of a golden age of 'light' ushered in by missionaries to banish pre-Christian 'darkness', in which people cooperated well in community projects and kept the place clean and well-ordered—behaviours that are now seen as in decline. In other contexts, people often evoke a revalorised ancestral past in which people lived well according to time-honoured traditions of *kastom* and kin-ordered respect. Rather than being taken at face value as descriptions of a former way of behaving, Li-Lamenu statements about idealised pasts, as well as futures, legitimate present and future-oriented actions as more or less compatible with achieving a good life together.

Conclusion: Concrete Contradictions

Li-Lamenu pursuit of the good life in the twenty-first century is fraught with paradox. Workers leave home for several months each year, citing concern for the household. The quest for a durable house constructed from imported materials is seen as a self-evident moral and material 'good'; however, it has given rise to a number of 'bads', including conflicts over land and a decline in reciprocal and communal work. Likewise, investment in educating children is seen as a means of securing a future, especially when the likelihood of making a living on the land is seen as diminishing; however, it may also make future life more precarious if the next generation fail to attain good jobs.

Reasoning about the good life is no simple matter of separating good from bad; it requires navigating changing and often contradictory value standards. Such dilemmas may be heightened in the twenty-first century, in which people are increasingly confronted with different moral and material goods, each corresponding with different ways of valuing space and time: development and success in a market economy, Christian and community moralities and enduring *kastom* ideals of respect and reciprocity between kin.

The affective value of *ples* remains strong, and the good house may be seen as a way of investing in a long-term future as part of the community. However, the quest for a good house has propelled people towards dispersed residence patterns and more household-based work over reciprocal labour between kin and for the community. Building a house of durable materials entails staking a permanent claim to household occupation of land, thereby exacerbating land disputes and accelerating a process towards more individualised land tenure, which leads to increased worries over scarcity of land for food and commodity production. Further, investment in education points to a future in which Li-Lamenu will become increasingly spatially dispersed and urbanised.

Different valuations of time are often evoked to evaluate things and practices as good or bad. A durable house and school fees, unlike other kinds of expenditure, are valued because they are understood to have lasting benefits in securing the household for future generations. However, particularly for older generations, the quest for the good house and improved standards of living are creating tensions and uncertainties over the possibility of achieving social reproduction and living well together with kin and community. Opportunities for work, and the money that flows in, open up possibilities for both prosperity and disaster. Idealised pasts, as well as a utopian telos of development or modernity, may be evoked to legitimate or critique things and behaviours as more or less conducive to a good life. These different moral and material trajectories are evoked to emphasise particular value standards in an ongoing 'historically extended, socially embodied argument' (MacIntyre, 1984, p. 222) over the good life. Yet, alongside an idealist dialectical inquiry into the nature of the good, a historical and materialist dialectical approach reveals the contested nature of the good, and the concrete contradictions and paradoxes arising in these precarious times.

References

Callon, M. (1998). An essay on framing and overflowing: economic externalities revisited by sociology. *Sociological Review*, *46*, 244–69. doi.org/10.1111/j.1467-954X.1998.tb03477.x

France, N. (1953). *The jungle drums are quiet*. Christchurch, New Zealand: Presbyterian Bookroom.

Gamburd, M. R. (2004). Money that burns like oil: A Sri Lankan cultural logic of morality and agency. *Ethnology*, *43*, 167–84. doi.org/10.2307/3773952

Gregory, C. A. (2013). The value question in India: Ethnographic reflections on an on-going debate. *HAU: Journal of Ethnographic Theory*, *3*, 116–39. doi.org/10.14318/hau3.1.007

Jolly, M. (1989). Sacred spaces: Churches, men's houses and households in South Pentecost. In M. Jolly & M. MacIntyre (Eds), *Family and gender in the Pacific: Domestic contradictions and the colonial impact* (pp. 213–35). Cambridge, England: Cambridge University Press.

Jolly, M. (1991). 'To save the girls for brighter and better lives': Presbyterian missions and women in the south of Vanuatu: 1848–1870. *The Journal of Pacific History*, *26*, 27–48. doi.org/10.1080/00223349108572645

MacIntyre, A. (1984). *After virtue: A study in moral theory*. Notre Dame, IN: University of Notre Dame Press.

Martin, K. (2007). Land, customary and non-customary in East New Britain. In J. F. Weiner & K. Glaskin (Eds), *Customary land tenure and registration in Australia and Papua New Guinea: Anthropological perspectives* (pp. 39–56). Canberra, ACT: ANU E Press.

Martin, K. (2013). *The death of the big men and the rise of the big shots: Custom and conflict in East New Britain*. New York, NY: Berghahn Books.

Mauss, M. (2007). *The manual of ethnography*. Oxford, England: Berghahn Books.

Mitchell, J. (2013). Objects of expert knowledge: On time and the materialities of conversion to Christianity in the southern New Hebrides. *Anthropologica*, *55*, 291–302.

Parry, J. & Bloch, M. (1989). Introduction: Money and the morality of exchange. In J. Parry & M. Bloch (Eds), *Money and the morality of exchange* (pp. 1–32). Cambridge, England: Cambridge University Press. doi.org/10.1017/CBO9780511621659

Radio New Zealand. (2015). Pam teaches lessons about building. Retrieved from www.radionz.co.nz/international/pacific-news/269786/pam-teaches-lessons-about-building

Rodman, M. C. (1985a). Contemporary custom: Redefining domestic space in Longana, Vanuatu. *Ethnology, 24,* 269–79. doi.org/10.1017/CBO9780511582950.020

Rodman, M. C. (1985b). Moving houses: Residential mobility and the mobility of residences in Longana, Vanuatu. *American Anthropologist, 87*, 56–72. doi.org/10.1525/aa.1985.87.1.02a00060

Rodman, M. C. (1997). Conclusion. In M. C. Rodman & J. Rensel (Eds), *Home in the islands: Housing and social change in the Pacific* (pp. 222–33). Honolulu, HI: University of Hawaii Press.

Smith, R. E. (2017). From colonial intrusions to 'intimate exclusions': Contesting legal title and 'chiefly title' to land in Epi, Vanuatu. In S. McDonnell, M. Allen & C. Filer (Eds), *Kastom, Property and ideology: Land transformations in Melanesia* (pp. 327–55). Canberra, ACT: ANU Press. doi.org/10.22459/KPI.03.2017.11

Sykes, K. (2012). Moral Reasoning. In D. Fassin (Ed.), *A companion to moral anthropology* (pp. 169–85). Chichester, England: Wiley-Blackwell. doi.org/10.1002/9781118290620.ch10

Taylor, J. P. (2008). *The other side: Ways of being and place in Vanuatu.* Honolulu, HI: University of Hawaii Press. doi.org/10.21313/hawaii/9780824833022.001.0001

Tonkinson, R. (1982). Vanuatu values: a changing symbiosis. *Pacific Studies, 5*, 44–63.

Vanuatu National Statistics Office. (2009). *National population and housing census.* Port Vila, Vanuatu: Vanuatu National Statistics Office.

Ward, R. G. & Kingdon, E. (1995). *Land, custom and practice in the South Pacific.* Cambridge, England: Cambridge University Press. doi.org/10.1017/CBO9780511597176

4

'According to *Kastom* and According to Law':[1] 'Good Life' and 'Good Death' in Gilbert Camp, Solomon Islands

Rodolfo Maggio

> We can only discuss the death of a man according to the culture of that man. Culture of man, decision of man. (Nathan)

Those who see the world through the experience of precarity are unable to feel secure about the stability of present conditions or the predictability of the immediate future. Precarious is the equilibrium of balancing on a thin rope! Precarious is the truce between opposed parties! It is the life of those who live amid tensions between incompatible values, for they are constantly under the threat that one position will suddenly snap and the other prevail, destroying, or at least altering, whatever it is they are trying to build. If this is what precarity means for real people living in the contemporary world, then the people of Gilbert Camp can be described as journeying through precarious times.

1 In Solomon Islands pidgin—'*lo sait lo kastom en lo sait lo lo*'.

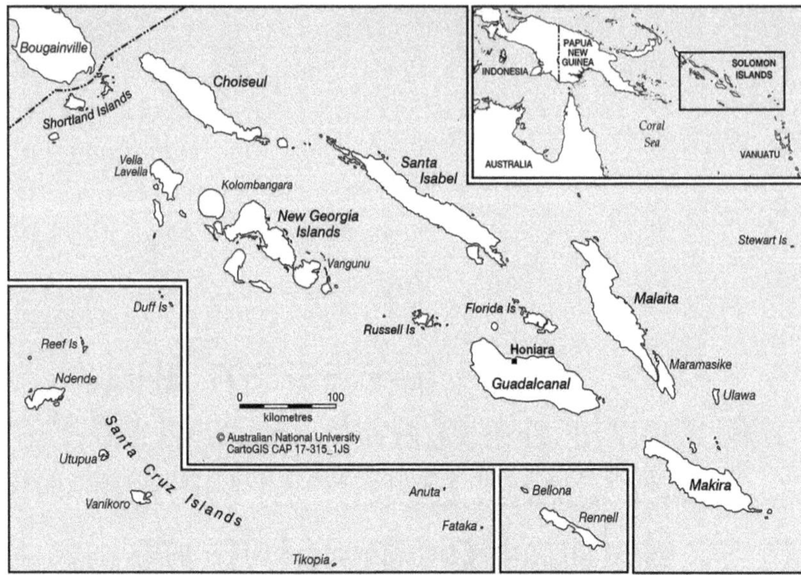

Figure 4.1: Map of the Archipelago of Solomon Islands
Source: CartoGIS, College of Asia and the Pacific, The Australian National University.

Gilbert Camp (see Figures 4.1 and 4.2) is not the original *hom* (home) of those who live there now. They started to migrate to Gilbert Camp from other parts of the Solomon Islands archipelago towards the end of World War II. At the time, Honiara was still a military base in need of builders to make it look more like the capital city. After the labour migrants, others soon followed, having heard about the 'lights of the city' from relatives and friends. Curious about the novelty it represented, they became convinced it offered the prospect of economic growth and the promise of an enriching experience.

However, in the years of Honiara's rapid expansion, migrants struggled to find a place to settle, for the cost of renting in town was prohibitive for the vast majority. The system of subsidised housing put in place by the Solomon Islands Housing Authority benefited only 'the wealthiest members of the urban population' (Nage, 1987, p. 95), so the migrants started to build leaf houses in public places in the town and on its outskirts. This is the case of the land where the Gilbertese contingent camped during the Guadalcanal campaign, which is reflected in its contemporary toponym.

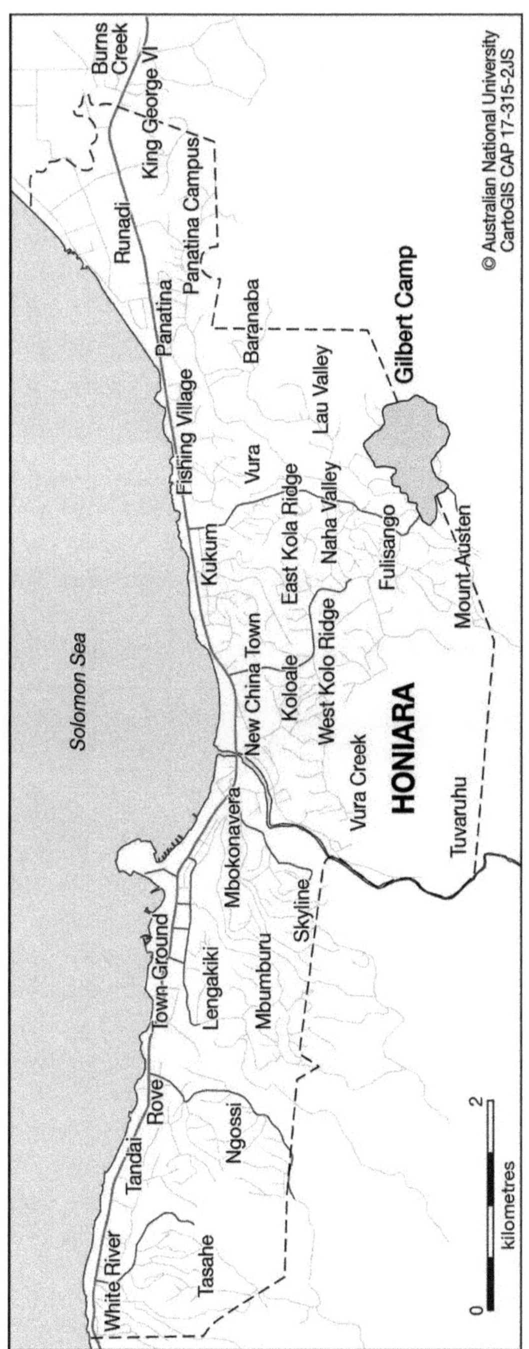

Figure 4.2: Map of Gilbert Camp and the Honiara Town Boundary

Source: CartoGIS, College of Asia and the Pacific, The Australian National University.

In Gilbert Camp today, people habitually declare: 'Honiara is hard' (*Honiara hemi had*)—meaning that living according to their traditional values results in a daily struggle. They face multiple challenges: they must ensure subsistence for their immediate families with the paucity of their financial resources; they must cope with the incompatibility of their market-based social lives and the realisation of the values of relatedness; and they must mediate between the different cultural repertoires of their ethnically diverse population, and even between the different conceptions of Christianity defended by the various denominations. It is indeed hard. Nevertheless, coping with these tensions constitutes the core of their effort to turn Gilbert Camp into the place where they can live according to their values, which is what they indicate as the 'good life' (*gud laif*).

There is no reason to expect that such a condition will be achieved soon. They know that, at any time, they can lose all that they have built, in both material and symbolic terms. It has happened already in the past. As a matter of fact, Gilbert Camp has already been destroyed a few times, and has always risen from its ashes again. Literally. On Tuesday 13 September 1977, a fire left nearly 50 people homeless and only two buildings untouched. Stoically, the settlers immediately began reconstruction. Men travelled to Visale, in West Guadalcanal, cut timber for a week or two, and built new houses.

In the following years, the living standards of the settlers benefited from many improvements. A bridge was built at the bottom of the hill and the road was improved and extended. However, these improvements took place amid problems and difficulties of various kinds, such as the lack of a proper water supply, poor access to electricity, road disruptions, random disposal of rubbish and increasing demographic pressure. In addition, floods occurred on a regular basis, destroying people's food gardens and the newly built houses. Dave Hart (2008), a missionary who lived and worked in Gilbert Camp, wrote a detailed description of a violent rainstorm that hit the settlement on 2 November 1993 and the flood that inundated it as a result. In his diary, he recorded that 'many people lost their gardens and especially the potato crops. They were either washed away completely or so covered with mud that they couldn't be salvaged' (p. 376). Yet, they did not give up; they started everything again.

Next, the indigenous population of Guadalcanal began to voice their concerns about the unregulated occupation of land. They did not receive much attention from the national government, though. As a consequence, their frustration mounted and some migrant households were forced to leave under the threat of violence. Those were the beginnings of what has become known as the 'ethnic tensions'. This is the rather inaccurate tag that is commonly used to indicate the tumultuous events that took place in Solomon Islands between 1998 and 2003. Dissatisfied with the response of the government to the land issue, some Guadalcanese organised themselves as paramilitary groups and evicted about 20,000 settlers (Moore, 2004). While the continuous disputes over previous decades could be explained as resulting from unregulated access to land by different ethno-linguistic groups, the response of colonial institutions and, later, the national and provincial governments, also played an important role. The different descent system (patrilineal for most of the settlers, matrilineal in Guadalcanal) had not been codified in a legal framework sophisticated enough to account for the cultural complexity of this context, and Guadalcanese concerns regarding land boundaries, exploitation of land and overall land policy had not been taken seriously (Fraenkel, 2004). That is why it is inaccurate, at the very least, to label as 'ethnic' a conflict that was arguably caused by ineffective land policy and a superficial understanding of the indigenous point of view about land.

Following the Honiara Peace Accord (2003), the migrants were allowed to return to their settlements. Yet, today, after more than a decade, the land issue is still far from resolved (Maggio, 2017), for the 'real landowners' have not been identified, as the 'right' way of accessing land has not been identified. The people of Gilbert Camp know that, at any time, they may be evicted again and lose everything. That is why they have to use all their cultural competence to cope with the problems emerging from the legacy of the land issue. In this chapter, I illustrate how skilful and sophisticated their response can be.

I take the case of a compensation meeting organised to solve a controversy that originated in an accusation of malevolent magic. The meeting was presided over by independent local headmen and three police officers. They established that no attack had taken place and that the accusation had its origins in a sisterly dispute about residential land. Nevertheless, compensation had to be paid. To establish who was to pay it, how and how much, but especially why and to what effect, the collaboration between the police and the 'local chiefs' was fundamental.

This case is indicative of the processes through which the people of Gilbert Camp are coping with the conflicts that originate from the absence of a sophisticated land policy, the large-scale introduction of foreign capital into Solomon Islands, the monetisation of land, the individualisation of landownership promoted by the state bureaucracy and the inequalities that these processes engender. Sorcery accusations are thrown to make inequality visible. Conversely, hybrid courts are organised to prevent accusations from escalating into potentially deadly conflicts.

The ability to make use of these mechanisms reveals a sharp awareness of the risks connected to the flows of foreign capital, ineffective bureaucracy and the negative incentives that these new possibilities create for the peri-urban population. The memories of the 'ethnic tensions' are a constant reminder of what perceived inequality can cause. It follows that the efforts of the people of Gilbert Camp to make and control accusations is an illustration of their commitment to construct a peri-urban space in which the project of the good life can still be cherished.

In a nutshell, the people of Gilbert Camp are fully aware that the introduction of large quantities of capital and the monetisation of land will encourage predatory behaviours in their fellow citizens who will compromise on their morality to make profits. However, most of the people of Gilbert Camp do not want to live in a community in which immoral behaviours take place with impunity, because that will eventually result in the kind of tensions that caused the eviction and the death of many of their relatives and friends in the past. They migrated because they wanted economic prosperity; however, they do not wish to compromise on the 'art of living together well'. The good life for them is made of both.

The case analysed in this chapter shows that, notwithstanding the general condition of precarity of the people of Gilbert Camp, they are all too aware of the difference they can make in building stability that will reach across the present and the future. In fact, they are making a strong contribution to the identity of Solomon Islands as a nation that ensures the freedom of movement of its people. Rather than 'squatters' trapped in a precarious present, they should be recognised as citizens struggling for a better future.

Such a claim has an important bearing on the ways in which the people of Gilbert Camp are perceived by outsiders. Popular caricatures of peri-urban settlers in Honiara often represent them as criminals (Anti-social behaviour becomes police's concern, 2011), unscrupulous squatters (cf. Fraenkel, 2004) and violent raiders (cf. Sillitoe, 2000, p. 178) who can only be tamed by Christianity and who can only advance with the help of externally imposed development schemes. In contrast, this chapter indicates how they may be considered concerned citizens, inventive creators of practical solutions to potentially dangerous situations and successful mediators between state law and customary law.

This process of mediation is of extreme importance for the people of Gilbert Camp today. Since the end of World War II, they have been leaving their places of origin in large numbers and settling in Honiara, because, generally speaking, they value what is lacking in their former home locations and what can be found in Honiara. However, even in the urban context they would like to live under the aegis of their *kastom*.

The starkest illustration of their commitment to living according to customary values is in their daily efforts to deal with tensions over the meaning and use of these values. Sometimes tensions can escalate into actual disputes, with the explosion of potential violence and consequent blood feuds. To avoid this, some sort of arbitration becomes necessary. In Honiara, though, there is no state-based legal system covering issues related to customary law. That is partly due to the fact that the national legal system withdrew the delivery of local justice services as a consequence of the civil conflict and recent administrative centralisation. Even though the government provides some support for local courts, this is very limited and, in recent budget allocations, has increasingly been diverted to more formalised legal apparatuses (Winter & Schofield, 2007). Most local courts 'exist in name only' (Goddard, Paterson & Evans, 2010, p. 11); those that do have a place to sit, personnel and a budget allocation from government usually deal only with land disputes.

Given the absence of state-based systems of customary dispute resolution and enforcement of customary norms, the people of Gilbert Camp have set up their own ways of dealing with wrongdoing and implementation—that is, 'hybrid courts', like the one I describe in this chapter. The fact that they creatively re-elaborate the principles of *kastom* to concretise them in the non-traditional context of their peri-urban settlement is an illustration of their efforts to change their current conditions.

Before presenting the ethnographic description and analysis necessary to ground these claims, I must delimit the scope of the argument and define three terms fundamental to it. First, the argument presented in this chapter is especially relevant for the segment of the Gilbert Camp population that identifies with the island of Malaita and, most specifically, with the Kwara'ae ethno-linguistic group. Gilbert Camp is largely a Malaitan settlement, the majority of its population being born in Malaita province or having a Malaitan background (82 per cent). People from other provinces, especially Western Province, Central Province and Makira, make up the remaining 18 per cent, along with a few migrants from Papua New Guinea (PNG). Among the people sharing Malaitan origins, most identify with the Kwara'ae ethno-linguistic category (72 per cent), the largest in Solomon Islands.

Second, the three terms that need to be defined are 'hybrid court', 'law' and '*kastom*'. The term 'hybrid court' has been used to refer to forms of dispute resolution in small-scale communities, resting at once on varying degrees of customary practice and state intervention. In the dispute analysed in this chapter, state intervention takes the form of voluntary assistance provided by local police staff. As for the customary part, describing this case as one of customary law would be discursively convenient, but is complicated by the underlying problem of conceptualising both *kastom* and law. The 'concept of "custom", often associated with "tradition" remains notoriously problematic for anthropologists', as Goddard (2010, p. 31) has argued. Further, using the Western term 'law' when referring to the norms involved in processes of dispute resolution might distract from their actual aims and effects (Zorn, 1990). Yet, the importance of local norms cannot be denied, nor should any reflection about tentative terminologies prevent an attempt at understanding the implications of cases of dispute resolution (cf. Goddard, Paterson & Evans, 2010, p. 18).

Concerning the meaning of Malaitan *kastom*, this has been extensively discussed in the past (Akin, 2005; Carrier, 1992; Demian, 2003; Jolly & Thomas, 1992; Keesing, 1982a, 1982b, 1982c, 1993; Turner, 1997). Summing up a great deal of literature, one could say that *kastom* refers both to shared traditions and to contemporary ideas and institutions that people perceive to be grounded in such traditions. Thus, people make use of *kastom* in a rather creative and flexible way, for political purposes as well as within the context of economic mechanisms, such as compensation claims and land dealings (Akin, 2013). However, I think that Kwara'ae people would phrase it more straightforwardly. As the anthropologist,

Benjamin Burt (1982), wrote, '*kastom* represents the values by which they would like to live' (p. 381). For these reasons, they tend to use the terms *kastom*, tradition and *falafala* interchangeably (Gegeo & Watson-Gegeo, 2001, p. 59).

Speaking about the values of Kwara'ae life, the Kwara'ae man, Michael Kwa'ioloa, called 'a community' a place where 'everyone knows each other'. He added:

> We coordinate the chiefs and if there are any problems we deal with them. The chiefs[2] of each place come together and arrange it: 'The meeting will be at our place on Sunday'. That man must come, *as at home*, and the matter is finally settled with a hearing at a police station [emphasis added]. (Burt & Kwa'ioloa 2013, p. 168)

Kwa'ioloa's words aptly summarise the case reported and analysed below, which suggests that what I observed is not an isolated circumstance, but rather an instance of a contemporary tendency.

Background: Two Sisters, One Piece of Land and a Death

Rhoda is an unmarried woman in her 30s who settled in Gilbert Camp when she was a teenager. In January 2000, she gave money and food to Jacob in exchange for a piece of land. Jacob claims to be a landowner; he frequently receives payments from people who seek to regularise their settlement in Gilbert Camp, but he does not issue any written proof of sale. So it was for Rhoda, who was asked to pay SBD10,000. As she only had SBD6,000 at the time, she promised to pay the rest as soon as she had saved it. Jacob accorded her some time, and Rhoda built a house on 'his' land and lived there for six years (see Table 4.1 and Figure 4.3).

In 2006, a maternal relative of Rhoda's died, leaving behind a young daughter and a house in the adjacent settlement of Kobito. Consequently, Rhoda went to live in Kobito with the young girl, and Rhoda's sister, Jane, moved into Rhoda's house with her own husband and children. They built a store in front of the house and lived there for six more years.

---

2 By chief, Kwa'ioloa actually indicates a person who has experience in dealing with cases of dispute resolution and who is not necessarily recognised as a leader in the community. In this essay, I use the word chief with the same meaning.

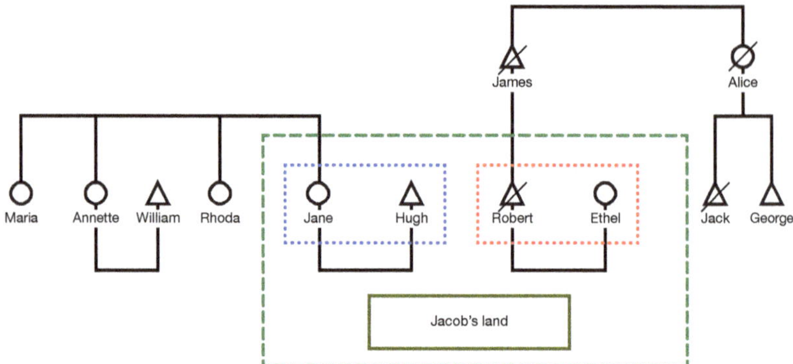

Figure 4.3: Kinship and Spatial Relations Connecting the Opposed Parties

Key: Triangle = male; circle = female; horizontal link below = marriage; horizontal link above = siblings; vertical link = descent; slash = deceased.

Source: Fieldwork data.

One day, a tragic event took place. In the same area, Ethel was living in the house of her late husband Robert. In June 2011, Jack visited her. As one of Robert's cross-cousins, Jack felt he could take advantage of Ethel's hospitality, even though she had been a widow for more than five years by that time. He showed up and demanded to be fed and given a place to sleep. Ethel welcomed Jack and prepared what later became his last supper.

The following day, as the man was not up for breakfast, Ethel sent her niece to wake him. The young girl came back alone; she said that her uncle was not getting up and that he was very cold and looked lifeless. Ethel rushed into her cabin and immediately came out in tears, screaming and shouting that Jack was dead.

George, Jack's brother and second in their patriliny, soon came. From that day, he became the eldest male member of his family. As such, it was his duty to officiate at the funeral. The next day, on her way to the cemetery, Jane met her sister Rhoda and informed her of what had happened in their neighbourhood.

About a year later, Jane and her husband had saved enough money to buy the piece of land where they were living. Even knowing that Rhoda had already 'bought' the area, they knew that they could still 'buy her out' by simply offering Jacob a higher price. So they visited the man and handed him SBD10,000. Rhoda, who initially had given Jacob SBD6,000, never completed the payment. Hence, after more than 10 years, Jacob felt fully entitled to take those SBD10,000 from the couple and forget about the first purchase. It was not his business, after all, if, in this way, Jane was playing a very bad trick on her sister. As a consequence of the double-dealing, Rhoda lost her SBD6,000, 'her' piece of land and her house.

That is why, as soon as she knew about the purchase, Rhoda decided to take revenge. She visited Ethel and told her that Jack had died of sorcery, and that Jane and Hugh were responsible for it. Immediately, Ethel went to George's cabin and informed him. Outraged, the brother of the victim went in search of Nathan, a man he used to call a 'local chief'. Cognisant of the events, Nathan realised the deadly potential of the controversy. He decided to mediate, and called for a meeting in the nearby Naha police station.

Table 4.1: Timeline of Events, 2000–12

2000
• Rhoda gives SBD6,000 and food to Jacob in exchange for land she believes is his. She does not know that her purchase is not protected by state law. • Jacob allows Rhoda to reside on 'his' land and she builds a house.
2006
• Rhoda rents the house to her sister Jane. • Jane builds a small shop in front of the house.
2011
• Jack stays at Ethel's house. Ethel hosts Jack and cooks for him. • Jack dies. Ethel rushes into the cabin when she hears that Jack has died. • George officiates at the funeral in honour of his brother.
2012
• Jane gives Jacob SBD10,000 in exchange for the right to reside on the same land that Rhoda 'purchased'. • Rhoda threatens Jane, requesting money in exchange for not denouncing her. • William threatens Rhoda to prevent her from denouncing Jane. • Rhoda gossips about Jane. • Ethel refers the gossip to George. • George requests compensation for Hugh. • George asks Nathan to set up a meeting. • Hugh asks Luke to hold the meeting in the police station. • Hugh pays compensation to George.

The following Sunday, in the room of the Chief Police Officer (CPO), there were 18 people: the CPO and two policemen sat behind a desk; Nathan and two 'chiefs' were behind a table; on one side of the room sat Jane, her husband and their relatives; on the opposite side sat Rhoda, George, his wife, Ethel, other relatives and me. After a collective prayer, Nathan formally opened the proceedings; he explained that the meeting was held under the authority of the local chiefs, the depository of customary law, and the local police, who were responsible for the enforcement of the national constitution. Then George stood up, explained his reasons for taking offence, and the 'trial' began.

It was a long debate. The chiefs asked many questions, listened to a multiplicity of contradictory claims and crosschecked different versions for more than two hours. At the end of the interrogation, Nathan declared that no evidence of a sorcery attack had been found. Having fruitlessly dissected the sorcery accusation in all its details, the authorities began to interrogate Jane and Rhoda on their dispute over land. After a few clarifications, they seemed to agree about what had happened. Eventually, they asked us to leave the office, as they had to formulate their judgement.

We left the room, sat on the grass and waited, smoking cigarettes and chewing betel nut in haste. I started to look around. Many people were gathering in front of the police station. They were friends and relatives or simply people who could not resist their own curiosity. I could see Helen, George's wife, and their children, plus many of the children who normally stayed with us in Gilbert Camp. Those on 'our side'—Ethel, Jim, Graham and Peter—were sitting with George and me. At the left-hand corner of the building, Jane and Hugh were sitting close to each other. Sometimes they would exchange a few words, but they remained silent for most of the time. On another corner, Annette, William and Maria, who, until then, had been sitting with Jane and Hugh, were talking rather animatedly, although in very low voices

As for Rhoda, she was by herself, walking back and forth on the verge between the grass and the road. At that time, I was not conscious of what was happening. The rearrangement of relationships had already started; Rhoda was not on 'our side' anymore, as she had been at the beginning of the meeting. She was not on her sister's side either. She was alone. It was as if the judgement had already been pronounced.

We re-entered the room when the CPO summoned us. A man who had not been at the meeting in the CPO's office took the stage, introduced himself and gave a brief speech in Kwara'ae, which the knowledgeable Luke translated.

> Luke: 'I have never come across a case of two sisters attacking each other in this way. I am very surprised.'

Nathan also spoke:

> Nathan: 'This case, as we have had the opportunity to ascertain, does not present any evidence concerning the death of our brother Jack. They have made use of his name for their personal problems with the land.'

Finally, Luke pronounced the verdict:

> Luke: 'We chiefs sat down and decided what follows: Rhoda shall pay one *tafuli'ae*[3] to George. Jane shall pay another one to George. Both Jane and Rhoda shall pay another one to Hugh. In case they do not have any *tafuli'ae* readily available, they will give SBD1000 instead.'

Except for a few screams of indignation from Rhoda, the decision was accepted and no appeal was called for. The case, though, left me perplexed. Why was making use of the name of a dead relative, and not the land double-dealing, seen as the main wrongdoing? How should the conflict between the value of land and the value of kinship be interpreted to reflect the point of view of the chiefs? How did they achieve their final decision? Most puzzling—why was Jane considered as responsible as Rhoda, as Jane was a victim of her sister's gossip, not an accomplice?

Analysis: Context, Conflict, Accusation and Outcome

My analysis of the material above is inspired by a conceptual categorisation of cases of witchcraft and sorcery accusations developed by anthropologists Stewart and Strathern (2004). They made an explicit attempt to connect witchcraft and sorcery accusations with gossip and rumours, developing a theoretical framework in which this case seems to fit. The framework consists of four analytical fields: context, conflict, accusation and outcome.

While there are some benefits in undertaking such an analysis, there are also some complications. In particular, the difference between the terminology used by my informants (see Table 4.2) and that used by Stewart and Strathern can be confusing. In the main, I use the term 'malevolent magic' (Goddard, 2010, p. 22) rather than 'sorcery'. If, at times, I switch to 'sorcery' as if these terms were merely interchangeable,

3 Type of shell money.

that is only because undertaking the analysis of my material involves a dialogue between conceptual repertoires produced in different contexts, which nevertheless apply to the same issues.

Table 4.2: Key Terms Used During the Meeting

Term	Example	Meaning
Black magic	Rhoda: '*Hem sei: mifala askem magic man fo mekem wanfala magic wea save kasim Jack sapos Jack traem kilim faestaem*' ['We asked a magic man to make a spell that would turn Jack's black magic against him'].	Black magic indicates a substance used to curse or kill a person.
Man blo taun	William: '*Wanfala man blo taun*' ['a troublesome man who lives in town'].	*Man blo taun* indicates a malicious person who does not belong to any place.
Spoelem	Nathan: '*Kaincross insaet lo toktok mi no laik, hem spoelem toktok*' ['I don't like this type of violent talk, it makes talking bad']. Rhoda: '*O'ta spoelem lo main blo mi, lo erea blo mi, lo lan blo mi*' ['They spoiled my mind, my area and my land'].	*Spoelem* describes an attitude towards someone or something that at once devalues it in the abstract and defiles it concretely.
Kastom	Nathan: '*Rod wea hem stap hem blo kastom en lo, iumi mas settle en sit ya*' ['Our pathway is that of *kastom* and law; we have to act within its limits']. CPO: '*Lo sait lo kastom en lo sait lo lo, death hemi lo top degree*' ['In terms of *kastom* and law, death is the most severe issue']. Phil: '*If argumen blo iutufala, plis, no digimaot ankol blo mifala fo argumen blo iufala, bikos hemi sirius tumas lo kastom*' ['If it is all an argument between you two, then, please, do not pronounce the name of our uncle in vain just for the sake of your argument, because that is really serious in terms of *kastom*'].	*Kastom* refers to shared traditions and contemporary ideas grounded in indigenous concepts and principles. In its political uses, *kastom* is often closely tied to indigenous means of dispute resolution, or '*kastom lo*', set in opposition to 'state' or 'government law'.
Samtin	Ethel: '*Wanfala samtin insaet lo erea blo iufala … Samtin fo kilim*' ['Something inside your area … Something that kills'].	*Samtin* indicates an indefinite substance. In this context, it refers to the mysterious substance that supposedly killed the victim.
Debol	Rhoda: '*Jack go fo paem debol fo kilim Hugh*' ['Jack paid somebody to evoke a spirit that would kill Hugh'].	*Debol* is a supernatural presence that can cause harm to those who encounter it.

Context: The Value of a Dead Man's Name

Understanding the relationship between gossip and accusation requires us to consider the context in which these take place—a fundamental consideration. Stewart and Strathern (2004) wrote:

> For words to be harmful, even lethal … they have to be spoken in contexts of ideology that are congenial to them. It is therefore the ideological and historical context rather than the words themselves that ultimately produces the effects. (p. 30)

Since looking at Kwara'ae history and ideology is beyond the scope of this chapter, I will concentrate on two specific elements of Kwara'ae culture: death and names.

The people of Gilbert Camp at first experienced Jack's death as an inexplicable, perhaps natural, event. Then, when Rhoda's gossip spread, they began to suspect that the death had resulted from an attack of malevolent magic. The difference between these two conceptions of death (*mae*) is very marked in Kwara'ae culture. In general, the death of a relative is something that throws the community into a sense of loss and astonishment, regardless of whether the person died or was killed. However, it is relatively less shocking when an aged person or someone who is known to be sick dies. If it is recognised that the person died as a consequence of aggression, some form of reparation has to take place.

There are two main aspects in Kwara'ae reparation: *to'ato'a* and *fa'aābua*. *To'ato'a* is the compensation given or extorted for an offence. It might take the form of a voluntary payment or the deprivation of life through a retaliatory killing. *Fa'aābua* is the maintenance or restoration of a person's status as *abu*.[4] An offence, such as the killing of a relative, or the desecration of a sacred place, devalues the status of the related person. Such devaluation is called *fa'alia*, a term that is translated as *spoelem* (defilement)[5] in Solomon Islands pidgin. Hence, to put it in Kwara'ae words, following a *fa'alia*, a *to'ato'a* has to be given to *fa'aābua* the victim.

Both voluntary compensation and retaliatory violence are seen as ways to regain the status one has lost as a consequence of taking offence. Traditionally, if it is not possible to identify the perpetrator or to seek

4 Persons towards whom respectful behaviour ought to be shown are referred to as *abu*.

5 See Table 4.2.

reparation from them or their relatives, the victim pursues the restoration of their own status through killing someone randomly (cf. Burt, 1994, p. 47). Nowadays, this institution has been largely, if not completely, abandoned. However, its principle should be kept in mind if we are to understand that the point of reparation is not to punish the perpetrator but, rather, to *fa'aābua* the victim. That a perpetrator is identified is somehow incidental. In contrast, restoring the victim's status is fundamental.

That is valid in both life and the afterlife. Regardless of whether the person died or was killed, he or she will not cease to be a member of the community. He or she will continue to take part in the everyday life of the descent group as an invisible, though sentient, entity. It follows that the relationship between the ghosts and the people is not very different from the relationship that people have with each other. One should make a person *abu* (*fa'aābua ngwae*) as much as one does a ghost (*fa'aābua akalo*). The degree of respect depends on status, not on biological conditions.

There are several ways in which a ghost is made *abu*. One is the prohibition against pronouncing a ghost's name. It follows that *spoelem nem* (defiling a name) is considered a wrongdoing. That is because, as George told me, 'a dead relative must rest in peace'. At this point one must ask: how could Jack rest in peace while somebody was making disrespectful use of his name? It is as if somebody was using the name of a living relative. It follows that the reason why making use of the name of a dead relative was seen as a wrongdoing deserving of compensation was that there could be no 'good life' for the Kwara'ae people as long as there was no 'good death' for their ancestors.

Conflict: The Value of Land and Kinship

Let us now turn to the conflict between Rhoda and Jane and see how it can be interpreted. 'It is always some misfortune that triggers accusations', Stewart and Strathern (2004, p. 27) argued. However, although 'the same human envies and jealousies feed into gossip generally and witchcraft accusations in particular' (p. 28), the causes of envy differ depending on the context. The context of this case study was characterised, among other things, by the problematic issue of land.

Victor Turner (1996) published a study of Ndembu village life in which he interpreted sorcery and witchcraft accusations as forms of 'social drama' that made other underlying conflicts explicit, including conflicts over land. In other words, he explained accusations as the surface indicators of pre-existing tensions. As the local chiefs and the police officers saw it, the accusation that came before them can be seen to fit within the grids of such an interpretation.

Turner (1996) famously identified four sets of events in which the 'processional form' of social drama can be formulated: breach, crisis, redressive action and reintegration or recognition of schism. Although I find that Stewart and Strathern's (2004) analytical model aptly suits the purpose of interpreting the different stages of this case, Turner's processional form better serves the specific purpose of looking at the origin of the conflict. Indeed, while Stewart and Strathern conflate breach and crisis into the single category of 'conflict', Turner distinguishes between these two aspects. This analytical separation allows a more precise examination of the ultimate cause of the conflict.

The origin of the conflict can be conceptualised, in the first phase, as that identified by Turner (1996) (i.e. breach), because a person breached a set of norms that regulated social relations between the members of a community. In this case, the norms regulating the relationship between sisters, as well as between in-laws, were disregarded in favour of personal land interests. In the words of Maria, Rhoda and Jane's elder sister, 'two sisters ought not to fight each other, they are the same blood'. So, although the origin of the conflict was land double-dealing, the chiefs conceptualised this wrongdoing through the idiom of kinship. To look more closely into these two layers of wrongdoing, I must briefly illustrate the controversial issue of land in Gilbert Camp, before looking at the value of sisterhood.

The people in Gilbert Camp see the issue of 'their' land as covered by several layers of confusion. One of the reasons for this is the impossibility of knowing who the 'real landowner' is. The area of land disputed between Rhoda and Jane lies outside the town boundary (see Figure 4.2) under the jurisdiction of the Guadalcanal Provincial Government. That means that it is not easy to verify the claim of landownership by anyone who can prove genealogical connections to the indigenous tribes of the Giana region. People in Gilbert Camp do not know who the 'real landowner' is. So, if someone like Jacob claims ownership over a piece of land to sell or rent it, they could believe him and pay him. A self-appointed 'landowner' can, as happened in this case, accept money in exchange for a piece of land and then, after an unspecified period, decide to sell that same area to someone else. This case of land double-dealing is particularly telling of the many possibilities of twisting the terms of a contract in the absence of written records and a clear-cut land policy.

These and other aspects coexist and come together to create the precondition for land double-dealings to happen and be denounced by means of sorcery accusations. It is happening in other parts of Melanesia too, such as PNG, where witchcraft and sorcery accusations have been interpreted as a reflection of tensions emerging from changing relations between landowners and incomers (Stewart & Strathern, 2004, p. xiii). Since Solomon Islands underwent recent major rapid changes in land tenure (Larmour, 1979, 1984), it is not surprising that land conflicts are found to be at the origin of malevolent magic accusations.

However, even though land double-dealing cannot be prosecuted, it can be proscribed. Here comes the second aspect of this section: kinship values. In Kwara'ae culture, the general principle that relatives ought to help each other is unanimously accepted and generally concretised in acts of mutual care. This principle applies particularly to siblings, who, as Maria effectively reminds us, are 'born in the same basket'. Sisters are especially expected to be kind to each other and to cooperate effectively. They should be mutually helpful, rather than harmful.

It follows that when Kwara'ae sisters have a disagreement, they ought to solve it with each other, or at least try to. Should the matter be so serious that mediation becomes necessary, they should seek the help of their mother or another woman elder in their network. When a conflict between sisters is dealt with in that way, its negative potential can be contained and a resolution found.

Certainly, buying your sister's land is, to use Turner's (1996) terminology, a 'breach of regular norm-governed social relations … between persons or groups within the same system of social relations' (p. 91). An elder woman or a mother could settle the conflict by reminding the two sisters of their reciprocal obligation of care and help. However, if that did not work, the breach could 'extend until it becomes co-extensive with some dominant cleavage in the widest set of relevant social relations to which the conflicting parties belong' (p. 91.). This corresponds to the shift from the first to the second phase in Turner's processual form—namely, 'crisis'.

Since Rhoda and Jane were unable to solve the initial breach, the tension mounted until it reached crisis point. During this phase, the underlying conflict (land) came to the fore, creating a set of actual and potential fissures within the concerned group or groups (kinship). As Turner himself observed, the recognition of the crisis as originating in the infringement of fundamental norms reveals the importance of these very norms for the people involved.

That is true also for the case under analysis. Based on what the chiefs took as evidence, they identified the land issue as the root cause of the accusation. However, the crucial infringement did not concern the 'correct' way of dealing with land. What the chiefs considered scandalous was the infringement of the norm of 'good' sisterhood. Yet, this was not *what* justified the compensation. Rather, this aspect played a role in the decision regarding *who* had to pay.

Accusation: The Values of a Gossiper and Those of a Messenger

How did the chiefs achieve their final decision? It was necessary to identify a specific form of hostility in the accusation. As Stewart and Strathern (2004) wrote:

> We should note … that … accusations centred on people following a death. They were post-hoc attempts to explain the death and pinpoint blame for it. Rumor and gossip particularly came into play on the occasions of death and sickness, bringing out veiled suspicions and animosities … [G]ossip may be seen as picking on someone to *treat* as an outsider, thereby redrawing the boundaries of the community, but the immediate motive may have to do with local politics in circumstances where group cohesion is fragile. (p. 12)

The authorities eventually realised that such were the circumstances of this case; they switched from the idea of hostility as distance[6] to the idea of hostility as local animosity. The alleged sorcerer ceased to be seen as the perpetrator who did not belong to the place; rather, it was Rhoda, the initial accuser, who began to 'be seen as playing the aggressive role' (Stewart & Strathern, 2004, p. xii).

6 The idea of hostility as distance stems from the late fifteenth century: from Middle French *hostile*, 'of or belonging to an enemy', or directly from the Latin *hostilis*, 'of an enemy' (*hostis*, 'enemy', *hospes*, 'host'); from the Greek *hosti-potis*, 'host, guest', originally 'lord of strangers'; and from the Greek *xenos*, 'guest, host, stranger'.

That was possible because the chiefs were able to distinguish the different functions of gossip and rumour. According to Stewart and Strathern (2004), the difference between gossip and rumour is essentially one of extension. Both gossip and rumour refer to information about someone who is excluded from the conversation; however, while gossip consists of information reported or shared among people who are part of a relatively restricted network, rumour consists of the same kind of information when it begins to circulate into wider networks. Such a distinction provides us with a clear terminology to distinguish between the gossip phase—when Rhoda contacted Ethel—and the rumour phase—when Ethel reported to George.

Stewart and Strathern's (2004) distinction between gossip and rumour serves well the purpose of analysing these two phases. One way to elaborate further on this distinction is to connect the two phases with two different theories. Below I interpret the gossip phase according to Gluckman's (1963) theory, before proceeding to interpret the rumour phase according to Paine's (1967) theory.

Gluckman (1963) wrote that 'there is no easier way of putting a stranger in his place than by beginning to gossip: this shows him conclusively that he does not belong' (p. 313). Perhaps this is what Rhoda was trying to do with her sister. According to the interpretation of the chiefs, she was trying to transform her into a stranger, to make her look like someone who deserved to be ostracised by the community so that Rhoda could take her land back. Ethel implicitly initiated ostracism, too, when she reported the gossip to George. However, in doing so, Ethel was not pursuing her own interests. Rather, she was concretising the values of the community. The rumour worked to increase group cohesion, for as soon as the relatives of the victim knew about the attack, they began to 'coagulate' around the area where they were told their blood was spilled.

As Ethel was telling of her reaction to the bad news, she said that she immediately thought, '*brata blo mi mas save*', literally, 'my brother must know'. *Mas*, in Solomon Islands pidgin, can be equally translated as 'ought to'. In this case, it seems that the sentence was intended to express some form of moral obligation. 'Brother' was used to refer to George, who was both related through marriage links and someone with whom the speaker felt a strong bond. In this sense, the two were part of a group. *Mi* indicates the speaker, excluding anyone else. When Ethel used the term *mi*, she intended to stress that it was *her own* duty to report the matter.

An early critic of functional interpretations, Paine (1967) criticised Gluckman because, in focusing on the consequences of gossip for the community rather than on the motivations of the individual, the anthropologist tended to 'attribute to gossipers the "unity" of their community as their paramount value' (p. 280). In contrast, Paine proposed that gossipers defame others to advance, calculatedly, their own status.

Nevertheless, gossipers might present themselves as the denouncers of a wrongdoing—that is, as promoters of the values that are seen as positive by the community from which they seek to extract benefits. This, coincidentally, is the way in which Rhoda, according to the chiefs, tried to mystify her intentions when she denounced Jane and Hugh. Paine (1967) insisted that the analyst should not be misled by the face values under which gossipers seek to conceal their real aims. Indeed, he contended, this kind of reasoning does no better than reaffirm the tautological reasoning that sees every sociocultural trait as an organic contribution to collective equilibrium and unity. In contrast, 'a discussion of the values of gossipers is best related to what we can find out about their self-interests' (p. 280).

Two opposed theories of gossip reflect two opposed interpretive possibilities; one sees the gossiper as motivated by self-interest, the other emphasises the positive repercussions of gossip for the community. Similarly, in his theory of value as the importance of social action, Graeber (2001) considered Nancy Munn's argument that witchcraft and sorcery accusations can be interpreted in two opposing ways. From an egalitarian point of view, witchcraft and sorcery accusations in Gawa are intended to suppress the 'destructive hyperindividualism' of some; from an individualistic point of view, Gawans assert that equality shall be maintained to 'create a situation where everyone is free to enter into exchange relations, engage in *kula*, and thus, spread their own individual names in all directions' (p. 84). The two interpretive pathways are feasible because Gawans are, according to Munn, both egalitarian and individualistic.

In this section, I have been trying to say something similar about Kwara'ae conceptions of gossip and rumour. Indeed, the opposition between two interpretive possibilities of gossip and rumour mirrors that between Gluckman's (1963) and Paine's (1967) theories. While the gossip phase (when Rhoda told Ethel) fits with Paine's theory of gossip as motivated by self-interest, the rumour phase (when Ethel told George) fits with Gluckman's theory of gossip as the assertion of group values. It follows that one single model cannot account for the accusation. Indeed, the case illustrates that gossip can change function depending on the intentions of the gossipers.

These intentions became evident towards the end of the meeting. In the first part of the chapter, I presented the disposition of people in the office where the hearing took place. I contrasted this with their distribution during the break, when we were all waiting in front of the police station. I hinted at the fact that, at that point, the 'rearrangement of relationships had already started'. In particular, I was referring to the position of Rhoda, who moved from being perceived as part of the accuser's group, to being perceived as against it. In formulating their judgement, the chiefs moved from the perspective of Gluckman's theory to the perspective of Paine's theory.

This shift was at the very crux of the compensation meeting. When the meeting began, we were all persuaded that George would receive compensation for the death of his brother. After hours of questioning, it became clear that this was not going to happen, and that compensation was being claimed against the misuse of the victim's name. As the reason for the compensation claim changed, Rhoda's position changed. As a messenger, Rhoda was sitting in the same area as the accuser's group. However, when the chiefs and the police established that the accusation was unfounded, and suspected that Rhoda had used it to attack her sister, she stopped being part of that group. Not being part of the other group either, she found herself isolated. That was the point at which compensation started to be realised in its essential meaning and function—that of a rearrangement of relationships.

Outcome: Rearranged Relationships and the Value of Community

> In all societies there are everyday ways of evaluating evidence, and not all stories are accepted as simply true. A great deal depends on who is telling the stories and what their perceived motive for spreading gossip actually is, that is, their own self-advancement, revenge, hatred, jealousy, and so on. (Stewart & Strathern, 2004, p. 30)

The motives the chiefs identified behind Rhoda's gossip were akin to those identified by Stewart and Strathern (2004): 'self-advancement, revenge, hatred, jealousy and so on' (p. 30). So, why did the chiefs request that her sister compensate too?

Let us begin with the concrete form of the compensation that was requested in this particular case: one *tafuli'ae*. One *tafuli'ae* is considered by Kwara'ae people to be the appropriate compensation for a moderately severe wrongdoing. This is for reasons that do not relate strictly to its economic value.[7] Rather, what matters is its symbolic value. A *tafuli'ae* symbolises the value of unity in diversity. A brief analysis of its materials and the way they are arranged clearly illustrates this point.

A *tafuli'ae* is made up of four types of shell (*kakadu,*[8] *kurila,*[9] *ke*[10] and *romu*[11]) reworked into round chips, and two types of seed (*fulu*[12] and *kekete*[13]) all tied together with strings obtained from the bark of either of two types of trees, *fa'alo* or *lili*. The mid-section of a *tafuli'ae* is made of chips of *romu*, the most rare and valuable type of shell. This mid-section terminates at both ends with a spacer made of wood or turtle shell, which divides it from a series of other segments of shell chips. The shell pattern of these segments varies depending on the type of *tafuli'ae*. It might be an alternation of discs of *kurila* and *kakadu* or a segment made of *ke* only. In any case, it is symbolically relevant that these segments are always in even numbers, whereas the central part is always unique.

Another symbolically relevant feature is that each end of a *tafuli'ae* culminates in a set of red cloth stripes. These, according to my Kwara'ae informants, represent the blood of two people who, for whatever reason, look at each other as separate. Like the cloth stripes, *romu* chips are red, thus, representing blood in their own turn. The reproduction of the metaphor of blood at both ends and the centre symbolises the unification of two groups in one. Kwara'ae people understand this aesthetic arrangement to be indicative of the particular function of *tafuli'ae*, namely, to turn duality and difference into unity and sameness. Therefore, when Kwara'ae people give a *tafuli'ae*, they are making a statement about their relationship.

---

7 As for the economic value of *tafuli'ae*, Kwara'ae people do not especially emphasise it, as opposed to Langalanga people, who produce them and have a more standardised categorisation (Burt, Akin & Kwa'ioloa, 2009, p. 59).

8 Kwara'ae name: *gwarigwari*; scientific name: *arca granosa*.

9 Kwara'ae name: *kurila*; scientific name: *pinna*.

10 Kwara'ae name: *tutu*.

11 Kwara'ae name: *romu*; scientific name: *chama pacifica*.

12 Kwara'ae name: *fulu*; scientific name: *gesneriaceae*.

13 Kwara'ae name: *mumu*; scientific name: *ciperaceae*.

A passage by Strathern (1999) elucidates how compensatory transactions have this effect:

> Collectivities differentiate, identify, and, in short, describe themselves by their role in compensation, a kind of functional heterogeneity. Compensation is part of the wider field of transactions by which social units are defined through exchange. (p. 191)

This appositely describes one of the outcomes of the case, namely, the negotiation of Jane's position. To get back to her normal life, Jane had to pay her compensation to George immediately and in front of everyone; she had to make a statement about herself and her family as people of Gilbert Camp, rather than as outsiders seeking to extract a benefit from the community. With an act of giving, she was required to counter Rhoda's attempt to make a 'stranger' of her through gossip. This process of self-description, identification with members of the community and differentiation from hostile strangers (cf. Strathern, 1999, p. 191) is what makes the reorganisation of social relations possible and is what the chiefs were after when they formulated their judgement.

Still, the question remains: why Jane? As mentioned above, the chiefs considered Rhoda and Jane to be equally responsible. They said it explicitly and concretised this opinion in a demand for equal compensations. Were the women equally responsible? Before attempting to answer this question, I would like to highlight a further point. Jane paid her compensation in cash, at the end of the meeting, straightaway. As instructed by the chiefs, she gave SBD1,000 to Hugh who handed the money to George. The reason I find this interesting is that Solomon Islanders do not usually walk around with SBD1,000 in their pockets. The fact that Jane had such a sum on her proves that she expected to be asked to compensate; the fact that she was expecting what eventually happened reveals that she found the outcome, for some reason, reasonable to expect. Why?

Rhoda and Jane were not asked to pay compensation because they had acted as 'bad sisters', for there was nobody to compensate for that but themselves. Instead, they were asked to pay compensation for the disrespectful use of Jack's name, and for putting Hugh and George's lives in danger as a consequence. The authorities established that it was Rhoda, and not Jane, who initially spread the dangerous words. Hence, Rhoda's 'guilt' and Jane's 'innocence' were converted into their joint responsibility: first, for *spoelem nem* and, second, for causing the conflict between George and Hugh's families.

It follows that the outcome of the case cannot simply be explained in terms of wrongdoing and compensation. It is more complex; it is such complexity that I have tried to clarify in this chapter. True, Rhoda was guilty of misusing the name of the victim and of illegitimately gossiping against Hugh and Jane. However, Rhoda's actions were interpreted as resulting from a pre-existing tension that the two sisters should have solved before it affected other people. Therefore, it was their responsibility to give something to re-establish peace.

If we did not assume that the whole point of a compensation meeting was to identify the culprit, then it would not seem so strange that someone who did not directly commit a wrongdoing would be 'condemned'. This brings us closer to understanding the chiefs' request to Jane. Rather than finding a particular person guilty of a particular wrongdoing, the meeting was intended to identify the person(s) who had the responsibility for restitution. The difference between someone who is looked at as guilty and someone who is looked at as responsible is crucial. The object of guilt and that of responsibility are not the same; guilt refers to wrongdoing, whereas responsibility refers to the maintenance or restoration of *abu*. The former looks back at the past and the latter looks forward towards the future.

If we briefly look back at the section on 'context', we might recall that in Kwara'ae *kastom*, a man who suffers an offence only seeks compensation from the perpetrators if they can be identified. In a situation in which that is not possible, he regains his status by killing someone else, randomly. This old-fashioned institution suggests that the priority of compensation in Kwara'ae *kastom* is not to identify and punish the perpetrator but, rather, to re-establish the value of the victim—that is, the victim's condition as *abu*.

To make this possible, it is necessary to identify the party who is 'responsible for giving' rather than 'guilty of taking'. To clarify this point, another quotation from the work of Strathern (1999) is useful:

> First, compensation enrols a rhetoric of body expenditure, covering both physical and mental exertion, based on an image of body process as the giving out and taking in of resources. What is embedded as substance in artefacts and bodies is the energy with which persons have acted. (p. 189)

The 'energy with which people have acted' is entrenched in the object of compensatory transactions, because this is the substance of what has been subtracted in the first place: the values of the community as a whole. The imbalance created by such subtraction has to be reconverted into balance through the reinsertion of an appropriate and proportionate amount of substance. The main problem for this compensation meeting, then, was to determine who had to put his or her hand on his or her resources to re-create the pre-wrongdoing equilibrium. Once such equilibrium is re-established, the basic conditions for prosperity are back in place. The fact that the Kwara'ae people of Gilbert Camp, in collaboration with the police officers, were able to put this compensation mechanism into effect is an illustration of their efforts to establish these conditions, and to create a 'good life' in the urban context, according to their values.

Conclusion

The social anthropologist Marwick (1965), in his study of 'the link between sorcery … and the social process', argued that sorcery accusations tend to emerge in response to socially stressful situations in which people 'belonging to a close-knit group … are unable to settle their disputes by the judicial procedures available' (p. 3). In their later study, Stewart and Strathern (2004) showed how such circumstances might create the preconditions for gossip and rumour to become powerful weapons in the hands of disputants. In this chapter, I took up Marwick's position, and the subsequent move by Stewart and Strathern, to explore how a group of Kwara'ae people living in Gilbert Camp managed to turn accusations of malevolent magic into means for enforcing customary law to protect their values in the absence, or given the inadequacy, of a state-based legal response to local disputes arising from the legacy of a land issue. Land, kinship, death and names are values that the series of events analysed above brought to the fore; they were concretised in actions such as Jacob's double-dealing, Jane's purchase, Rhoda's gossip, Ethel's rumour, George's demand for compensation and the chiefs' final decision.

The chiefs concluded the compensation meeting as they did because they believed that such an outcome was beneficial for the community. However, some issues were left unresolved. In particular, the two sisters were still divided by their conflict over a piece of land. Arguably, the land conflict was not resolved because that was not the intention of the chiefs in the first place. The way they directed their judgement was a statement: the value of a dead relative has priority over the value of land. The issue of land 'has to wait', as Nathan said towards the end of the meeting.

For the chiefs, establishing Rhoda and Jane's responsibility for compensation was an accomplishment, because that was the primary aim of the meeting—neutralising the ill-effects of the unresolved issue of land that had created the structural conditions for such wrongdoing to happen. As wrongdoers, Rhoda and Jane concretised values that Kwara'ae people recognise as foreign and wrong, and the compensation meeting was the instrument to counter such acts through concretising another set of values. These are the values by which the Kwara'ae people want to live. By concretising them into actions, such as compensatory transactions, they were trying to make Gilbert Camp a better place, a place where they can live the good life, whatever that means for them.

This chapter provides a clear counterargument to the widespread tendency 'to scapegoat and even demonise the residents of urban settlements' (Barber, 2003, p. 288; cf. Goddard, 2001) as blameable for the decay of Melanesian capitals. Rather than seeing these 'squatters' as responsible for a stagnant present, this story demonstrates that the people of Gilbert Camp are doing their best to minimise the negative consequences of historical processes largely beyond their control. They do this without the slightest certainty about their future.

References

Akin, D. (2005). Kastom as hegemony? A response to Babadzan. *Anthropological Theory*, *5*(1), 75–83. doi.org/10.1177/1463499605050871

Akin, D. (2013). *Colonialism, Maasina rule, and the origins of Malaitan kastom*. Honolulu, HI: University of Hawaii Press. doi.org/10.21313/hawaii/9780824838140.001.0001

Anti-social behaviour becomes police's concern. (2011, 13 May). *Solomon Star*. p. 4.

Barber, K. (2003) The Bugiau community at Eight-Mile: An urban settlement in Port Moresby, Papua New Guinea. *Oceania 73*(4), 287–97.

Burt, B. (1982). Kastom, Christianity and the first ancestor of the Kwara'ae of Malaita. *Mankind, 1*(4), 374–99. doi.org/10.1111/j.1835-9310.1982.tb01001.x

Burt, B. (1994). *Tradition and Christianity: The colonial transformation of a Solomon Islands society.* Newark, NJ: Harwood Academic Publishers.

Burt, B., Akin, D. & Kwa'ioloa, M. (2009). *Body ornaments of Malaita, Solomon Islands.* Honolulu, HI: University of Hawaii Press.

Burt, B. & Kwa'ioloa, M. (2013). *The chiefs' country: Leadership and politics in Honiara, Solomon Islands.* Brisbane, QLD: University of Queensland Press.

Carrier, J. (1992). *History and tradition in Melanesian anthropology.* Berkeley, CA: University of California Press.

Demian, M. (2003). Custom in the courtroom, law in the village: Legal transformations in Papua New Guinea. *Journal of the Royal Anthropological Institute 9*(1): 97–115.

Fraenkel, J. (2004). *The manipulation of custom: From uprising to intervention in the Solomon Islands.* Wellington, New Zealand: Victoria University Press.

Gegeo, D. W. & Watson-Gegeo, K. A. (2001). 'How we know': Kwara'ae rural villagers doing indigenous epistemology. *The Contemporary Pacific, 13*(1), 55–88. doi.org/10.1353/cp.2001.0004

Gluckman, M. (1963). Papers in honor of Melville J. Herskovits: Gossip and scandal. *Current Anthropology, 4*(3), 307–16. doi.org/10.1086/200378

Goddard, M. (2001). From rolling thunder to reggae: Imagining squatter settlements in Papua New Guinea. *The Contemporary Pacific 1*(13): 1–32.

Goddard, M. (2010). *Villagers and the city: Melanesian experiences of Port Moresby, Papua New Guinea.* Wantage, England: Sean Kingston Publishing.

Goddard, M., Paterson, D. & Evans, D. (2010). *The hybrid courts of Melanesia: A comparative analysis of village courts of Papua New Guinea, island courts of Vanuatu, and local courts of Solomon Islands.* Washington, DC: The World Bank.

Graeber, D. (2001). *Toward an anthropological theory of value: The false coin of our own dreams.* New York, NY: Palgrave Macmillan. doi.org/10.1086/200378

Hart, D. (2008). *Solomon boy: An island journal: Adventures among the people of the Solomon Islands.* CreateSpace Independent Publishing Platform.

Jolly, M. & Thomas, N. (1992). The politics of tradition in the Pacific. *Oceania, 62*(4), 241–48. doi.org/10.1002/j.1834-4461.1992.tb00355.x

Keesing, R. M. (1982a). *Kastom* in Melanesia: An overview. *Mankind, 13*(4), 297–301. doi.org/10.1111/j.1835-9310.1982.tb00994.x

Keesing, R. M. (1982b). *Reinventing traditional culture: The politics of kastom in island Melanesia.* Sydney, NSW: Anthropological Society of New South Wales.

Keesing, R. M. (1982c). *Kastom* and anticolonialism on Malaita: 'Culture' as political pymbol. *Mankind, 13*(4), 357–73. doi.org/10.1111/j.1835-9310.1982.tb01000.x

Keesing, R. M. (1993). *Kastom* re-examined. *Anthropological Forum, 6*(4), 587–96. doi.org/10.1080/00664677.1993.9967434

Larmour, P. (1979). *Land in Solomon Islands.* Suva, Fiji: Institute of Pacific Studies, University of the South Pacific and the Ministry of Agriculture and Lands, Solomon Islands.

Larmour, P. (1984). Alienated land and independence in Melanesia. *Pacific Studies, 8*(1), 1–47.

Maggio, R. (2017). 'Big confusion': The land question in Honiara and the history of land policy in Solomon Islands. *People and Culture of Oceania, 32*, 1–28.

Marwick, M. (1965). *Sorcery in its social setting: A study of the northern Rhodesia cewa.* Manchester, England: Manchester University Press.

Moore, C. (2004). *Happy isles in crisis: The historical causes for a failing state in Solomon Islands, 1998–2004*. Canberra, ACT: Asia Pacific Press.

Nage, J. (1987). Immigrant settlement in Honiara, Solomon Islands. In L. Mason & P. Hereniko (Eds), *In search of a home* (pp. 93–102). Suva, Fiji: Institute of Pacific Studies, University of the South Pacific.

Paine, R. (1967). What is gossip about? An alternative hypothesis. *Man, 2*(2), 278. doi.org/10.2307/2799493

Sillitoe, P. (2000). *Social change in Melanesia: Development and history*. Cambridge, England: Cambridge University Press.

Stewart, P. & Strathern, A. (2004). *Witchcraft, sorcery, rumors and gossip*. Cambridge, England: Cambridge University Press.

Strathern, M. (1999). *Property, substance, and effect: Anthropological essays on persons and things*. London, England: Athlone Press.

Turner, J. W. (1997). Continuity and constraint: Reconstructing the concept of tradition from a Pacific perspective. *The Contemporary Pacific, 2*(9), 345–81.

Turner, V. (1996). *Schism and continuity in African society*. Oxford, England: Berg.

Winter, J. & Schofield, K. (2007). *Annual performance report 2006/2007—a report on the performance of the regional assistance mission to Solomon Islands*. Honiara, Solomon Islands: Regional Assistance Mission to Solomon Islands.

Zorn, J. G. (1990). Customary law in the Papua New Guinea village courts. *The Contemporary Pacific, 2*(2), 279–311.

5

'This Custom from the Past Is No Good': Grassroots, 'Big Shots' and a Contested Moral Economy in East New Britain

Keir Martin

In the aftermath of the volcanic eruption of 1994, the people of Matupit village in Papua New Guinea's (PNG) East New Britain Province were offered a resettlement scheme at Sikut—a rainforest location a long distance from Rabaul—where many of them were given agricultural blocks. Many Matupit families have settled at Sikut. More have returned to Matupit, with many families spending time keeping up houses and interests in both locations. The reallocation of land to the Matupi was partly a response to the disaster; however, it was also an opportunity for the provincial government to address the existing problem of overpopulation and land pressure at villages near Rabaul, such as Matupit.

The eruption was clearly a disaster for the population of Matupit, but it was by no means an unqualified disaster. For many of those who had had trouble gaining access to land or finding paid employment in Matupit, if they were willing and able to commit to the move from the peri-urban coast to the virgin rainforest, the 3 hectare blocks at Sikut held out the prospect of an income from cash crops that would have been unimaginable at home. I was struck by the number of occasions on which Matupi described the eruption to me as a 'blessing from God'; this was because, by relieving the land pressure at Matupit, it had also taken the sting out of a growing number of increasingly ferocious land disputes that threatened to tear the village apart. It was not only the villagers who tended to see the destruction of their village as an opportunity. Klein (2007) has described how the forced displacement of populations, whether as a result of war or natural disaster, can act as a kind of shock that gives those with the power and desire to restructure local political economies a chance to put their plans into action. The eruption of 1994 acted as just such an opportunity. However, unlike some of the sudden changes imposed in the aftermath of other disasters—for example, the expropriation of Sri Lankan fishing villages to make way for tourist resorts after the South Asian tsunami of 2004 (Klein, 2007)—it is too early to judge the extent to which the changes in East New Britain will have the effect their authors desire.

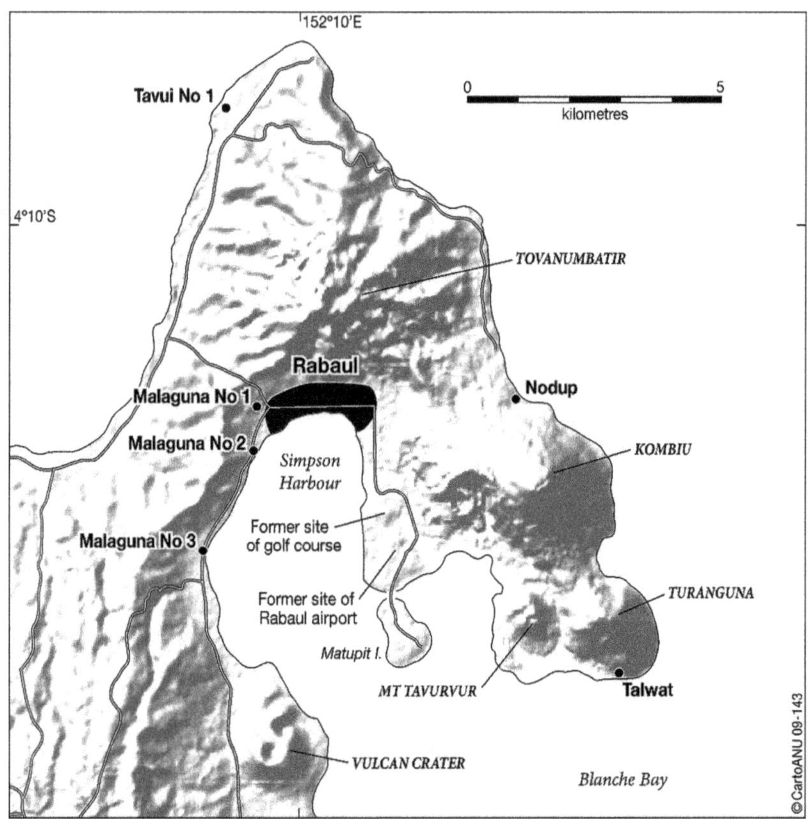

Figure 5.1: Map of the Gazelle Peninsula

Source: The Australian National University Cartography Department.

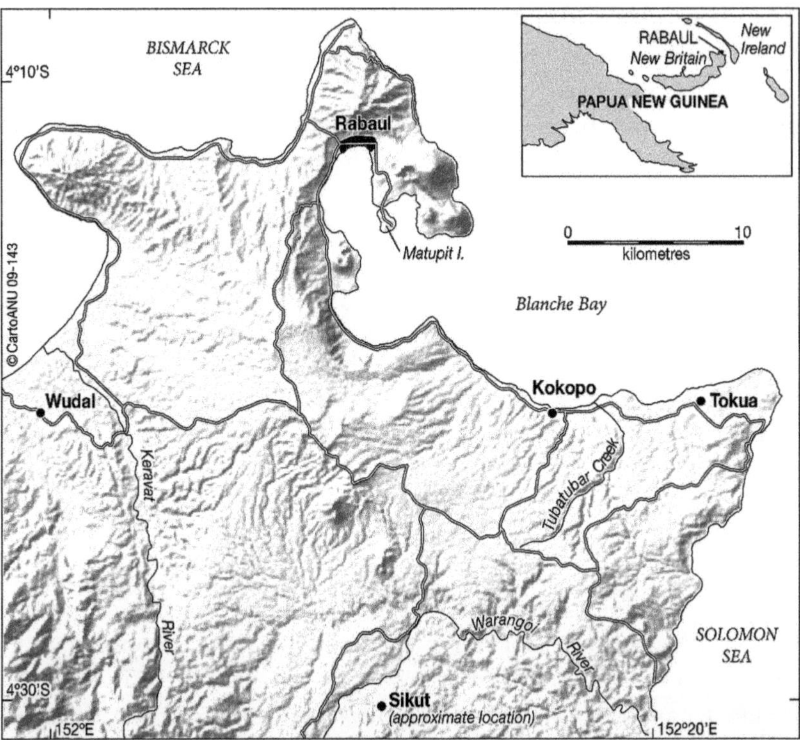

Figure 5.2: Map of the Rabaul Area

Source: The Australian National University Cartography Department.

The most obvious way in which the volcano became the pretext for a restructuring of the local political economy was the decision to relocate the provincial capital from Rabaul town to nearby Kokopo. This was justified on safety grounds. Kokopo was said to be less at risk from future volcanic activity than Rabaul. It was also claimed that major donors to the reconstruction process, such as the World Bank, had made the move a precondition of releasing funds, although those who suspected that corruption and political manoeuvring lay behind the decision believed this to be a story made up by some of those with an interest in blocking the reconstruction of Rabaul. Whatever the reason, the move negatively affected villages like Matupit, close to Rabaul, which had already suffered in the eruption. It had effectively wiped out the major local source of jobs and services, and shifted the balance of political and economic influence in the region to Tolai villages in the Kokopo area.

However, in terms of the local political economy, this headline-grabbing dispute was, perhaps, of less fundamental importance than a more silent revolution encouraged by the East New Britain Provincial Government in the eruption's aftermath. Resettlement was used as an opportunity to try to kickstart a revolution in land tenure in the Gazelle Peninsula. There is nothing new in the desire of politicians and administrators to effect the kind of changes pioneered by the East New Britain Provincial Government after the eruption. At both the national and provincial level, customary land-tenure regimes, which involve a large number of overlapping, inalienable rights and obligations, are commonly seen as an impediment to economic development. They are said to act as a disincentive to invest time and money in the land, as an individual's investments can never be secure.

Resettlement and Reconstruction

The eruption and resettlement of Matupit and other Rabaul-area villages provided the provincial government with the perfect opportunity to attempt to develop new land under a new regime in the hope that this would act as a catalyst for a more general shift in land-tenure practices. This was made clear to me in a number of conversations with politicians and senior government officials during my period in East New Britain (February 2002 – February 2004). I will recount one such conversation as an example. This was with Horim Ladi, a Tolai, who was head of the East New Britain Lands Division. I met him one morning in May 2003 at his office in Kokopo. As I sat down, he asked me how much I knew about the government's latest planned land-registration scheme. He described it to me as 'beautiful', and told me that the registration of customary land was essential to the future of East New Britain. When I asked him why registration was so important, his answer was clear and simple: 'What is important is the establishment of ownership, whether it be the individual, the clan, or the incorporated land group'. Customary tenure, as it currently stood, with its tendency to disperse rights across a wide variety of persons and groups, did not establish such ownership. In many respects the ideal might be ownership by an individual person or family; however, if ownership by a clan or land group constituted as a 'collective individual' (e.g. similar to the constitution of a corporation under US commercial law) could be established, with the overlapping claims that complicated ownership or called it into doubt increasingly expunged, the land could be seen as a productive resource that its owners might have an interest in developing. Ladi accepted the possibility that the PNG national government might be forced to pull out from implementing the land-registration scheme, as they had been on previous occasions, but he insisted that East New Britain would be able to go it alone if that were the case. East New Britain, Ladi asserted, was always at the 'vanguard'.

This was true in respect of both externally imposed changes to land practices and Tolai adaptations of their own customary practice. Whereas 97 per cent of land in PNG is commonly reckoned to still be under customary tenure, around 40 per cent of land in the Tolai Gazelle Peninsula had been alienated by the start of World War I, primarily by foreign plantation managers. The process by which this alienation occurred remains controversial on the Gazelle to this day, and was perhaps the major contributing factor to both the intense land pressure experienced by the Tolai over many decades, and to the rise of the anti-colonial Mataugnan Association in the 1970s.

Local villagers themselves have introduced new practices that have, to use Ladi's words, put East New Britain in the vanguard. In the 1970s, Tolai villagers were among the first to start registering customary transfers of land with legally binding statutory declarations. These customary transfers, known as *kulia,* did not act as a purchase, at least as it would be recognised in a Western legal context. Full ownership rights were never unambiguously alienated, and there was always the possibility for the original landholders to find a way to claim the land back if the other party did not maintain a cordial relationship and exchange of gifts (see Epstein, 1969, p. 132). Such a situation came to be seen as increasingly problematic by many Tolai in the 1960s and 1970s when land was frequently being used for permanent financial investments, such as cash crop trees like coconuts, which might live for 80 years, or for the permanent 'European'-style houses that were increasingly replacing bush-material residences at Matupit and other villages near Rabaul (Epstein, 1969, pp. 147–48). In such circumstances, land transfers that could be terminated at any point, and that were reliant on a relationship of ongoing reciprocal interdependence and exchange—relationships that might break down in acrimony at any point—were more problematic than they might have been at a time when transferred land was used for the production of short-term food gardens or bush-material houses that would need replacing only every four or five years. The practice of registering *kulia* was not a government-driven process. Instead, it was Tolai villagers themselves who increasingly began to use the statutory declaration as a means of attempting to confirm that rights in land had been unambiguously and finally transferred (Fingleton, 1985, pp. 178, 181–82; Fitzpatrick, 1983, p. 19; Jessep, 1980, pp. 123–24). However, the local government did recognise and encourage the process, keeping records of the statutory declarations and commonly referring to them in the course of land-dispute hearings.

Although the registration of *kulia* had not turned land exchange unambiguously into a completely uncomplicated commodity transaction entailing the total alienation of property rights, it nevertheless made transfers more secure than in previous generations; it also became significantly more difficult for vendor clans to reclaim land if they felt vendees had been remiss in observing their customary obligations. To this extent, Ladi's claim that East New Britain was in the vanguard of change made sense. The province's long history of deep entanglement with global trade and commerce relative to other provinces seemed not only to have left the province's administrators with a pressing desire to reform land tenure, it had also bequeathed them a population that was itself moving in that direction.

It Is Better Because It Is Not Customary

From the perspective of the region's administrators and planners, *kulia* was not the only potentially problematic form of customary land transfer in East New Britain. Of even more pressing concern was the matter of the transfer of land rights between generations on the occasion of the death of the previous resident. Tolai land tenure is commonly described as matrilineal, with prime landholding rights being vested in named matrilineal clans (or *vunatarai*). This means, ideally, that upon a father's death, his widow and children will 'return' to the land of their clan (i.e. the widow's clan, as the children are part of her clan); often the children will be 'returning' to land with which they are unfamiliar. Although tensions between the father's clan and his children regarding the transfer of certain kinds of valuables (in particular, secret ritual or magical knowledge) have a long history (e.g, Martin, 2013, p. 107), the development of these kinds of tensions with regard to land seems to have intensified greatly in the years following World War II, when a combination of the effects of the previous massive land alienation, population explosion and, most crucially, the previously mentioned introduction of permanent investments in land, led to a rash of the most common variety of land dispute—that is, between a man's children and his nephews and nieces on his mother's side (i.e. his clan 'descendants'), often centred on the children's right to remain on land upon which the father had made permanent investments.

During my fieldwork in East New Britain, I divided my time between the village of Matupit and the resettlement camp at Sikut. The provincial government had made sure that the land at Sikut would not be held by matrilineal extended clans but by named individuals, normally the male head of a nuclear family unit, whose children were expected to be the main inheritors of the block of land. When I arrived at Sikut, one of the phrases I heard repeatedly from those who had committed to make the move was that 'the land at Sikut is better because it is not customary land'. The expectation that their children would be able to hold onto their land and receive the benefit of any investments made on it was the commonly given explanation for this view. Most Sikut residents seemed to be fully in favour of this move by the provincial government; they seemed to think that the perceived reintroduction of 'custom', as had occurred at places like Wudal, would not occur today at Sikut. Indeed, only a small minority believed that this experience would be repeated at Sikut. As one Sikut resident angrily exclaimed to me during the course of one conversation:

> Now custom is fading away. What happened at Wudal won't happen here. Sometimes the nephews do just take over. But that can't happen now. You've got no right to come and just grab the land from my family. Why do I have to grow my kids? Why do I have to settle someplace? This custom from the past is no good. Our ground is clan ground, but my ground is my ground automatically. I will never give it to the clan—no way. This kind of thinking is just for the old or the ancestors. Now we've been to school we've got better ideas. If I develop this ground with my children? With my sweat? I'm just going to come and let the nephews kick them off?! No way. Not now! Why should I bother getting married? This kind of thinking is bloody rubbish and bullshit from before … The nephews won't be able to put demands on the kids just because the father was the same clan. It's different now. The kids will be able to get a bush knife and chase them away! My kids haven't seen a cousin come and help, and if they come and ask, I'll tell them no way. If the nephews take over, the people today see it's no good. You're making the man's family suffer. If I behaved like this on clan land, of course there would be talk, and yes at Wudal it happened, but this generation we've seen it's not good. Because the father raised the children. The father planted the cocoa. It's not the nephews'. It's not the clan's.

Or, as Horim Ladi put it to me during my conversation with him:

> The attitude that you see now at Sikut—'this land is better land because it's not customary'—is a new development over the past 30 years. It's a result of all the pressures and problems with land. And the government today would be very strong with any attempts to bring custom back in at Sikut.

Horim Ladi, in common with other senior administrators in East New Britain, saw the establishment of individual property rights in land at resettlement camps such as Sikut both as a good thing in its own right and also as a potential spearhead that, if successful, might make the process of registering customary land easier across the rest of the province. One crucial problem with investing on customary land, whether that land had been transferred by *kulia*, and whether any such transfer had been registered with a statutory declaration, was the lack of clarity as to who the 'original' landholder truly was. Even the best registered and least acrimonious *kulia* transaction was potentially liable to a claim 20 years hence from a third party arguing that the vendors had no right to sell the land; that they were not the true landholders; or, perhaps, that their ancestors were children of the clan who had been allowed to stay on the land after a paternal ancestor's death out of this third party's generosity, but now they wanted to claim the land back after discovering it had been sold without their knowledge or consent.

The main purpose of land registration (as it was described to me by key players such as Ladi) was to draw a line under this kind of confusion. At the registration process, anyone who disputed the rights of *ownership* of a clan currently *resident* on a piece of land would have to make that objection clear at that point so that it could be legally assessed. After that, so the argument went, they would not be able to make a claim years or decades later, after others had made investments on the land. It was hoped that such a scheme would, at one stroke, remove one of the key disincentives to investment on land. Even if it could be said that such a development would not solve the problem of potential disputes between a man's children and his nephews after his death, it is easy to see how it could be viewed as a step in that direction. For if registered land strengthened the property claims of a clan over a piece of land, then, perhaps paradoxically, this could be seen as creating the grounds for stronger individual land ownership in the future. That is, if a man could negotiate to purchase land from his own or another clan, then as long as such a 'purchase' was strengthened by a statutory declaration, it would ideally amount to an even stronger property claim, as it was now free of potential third parties disputing ownership in the future. Hence, although land registration did not establish individual ownership, in strengthening group (i.e. the clan as 'collective individual') ownership, it created the preconditions for more successful individual alienation and was seen by many administrators as a desirable step in that direction.

One noticeable aspect of these discussions was the way in which they focused on the quest for a good life, and often seemingly dismissed custom as a barrier to that quest. Thus, the man quoted above argued that custom from the past was 'no good'; he returned to this theme on two more occasions in the course of his exposition. For the likes of Ladi, the way in which traditional matrilineal patterns of land transmission worked against a man's children was not only unfair, it was one of the biggest barriers to economic development in the province. To this extent, regional planners and administrators had a perspective that could be seen as fitting into a wider discourse on the economic disadvantages of customary land-tenure regimes, as seen in both the Pacific literature (e.g. Hughes, 2003) and globally (e.g. De Soto, 2001). It is not my intention to go into the pros and cons of this policy position here beyond the observation that, regardless of its desirability or otherwise, the exponents of a radical, sudden introduction of individual property rights in land in PNG are far greater idealists (in the technical philosophical sense of the term) than any of their opponents. The maintenance of individual property rights in countries such as Australia relies upon the existence of a state with the power to enforce legal norms. However, no such state exists in PNG at present; nor is likely to in the foreseeable future. One can produce as many individual land-title deeds as one likes, but without a state to enforce them they will not have the effect that the decrees of enclosure had in seventeenth- and eighteenth-century England, despite what some advocates of land-tenure reform imagine. A more apposite historical comparison might be the promises of land and title deeds made by the Marquis de Ray as the basis upon which he convinced Italian subscribers to join his ill-fated expedition to settle New Ireland in the 1880s.

Problems with Custom and Problems with Customary Land

In the remainder of this chapter, I want to focus on how this perspective on the desirability of restructuring customary land tenure ties into a wider discourse of the backward and anti-development nature of customary relations and practices (known locally in Tok Pisin as *kastom*) in East New Britain, and how that discourse of the need to remove custom from governance is simultaneously subverted, at certain points, often by the people who are normally its strongest proponents. *Kastom* is a term that is used to refer to a wide range of activities and things, from land (*graun bilong kastom*) to the rituals (usually centred around ceremonial gift exchange) and day-to-day practices of small-scale sharing. Given its various manifestations, it is often portrayed as a barrier to political and economic development. Why do we elect bad leaders? Because most of us don't choose the best party or person to vote for, voting instead for someone according to whether they are part of our clan or a clan that our clan is related to, as that's our *kastom*. Why do village-based enterprises such as trade stores nearly always collapse? Because people don't respect the business and cripple it with demands for credit that the entrepreneur is forced to accede to, as that's our *kastom*. Why can't people afford to pay their kids' school fees or fix the roof on their house? Because they had to spend what little money they had on *kastom*, such as contributing towards the cost of clan ceremonial gift exchange. Why did I not buy a new water tank when I had the money and knew that I would need more water storage in preparation for the dry season? Because I knew my lazy neighbours and relatives, who have no money, would come and insist on taking all the water and, because of *kastom,* I would not be able to refuse them, so what's the point making the investment?

This kind of discourse is commonly produced by all kinds of people across the Gazelle Peninsula, from impoverished grassroots villagers to successful entrepreneurs and foreign expatriates. As one grassroots villager put it to me on his way out of the polling booth on election day in 2002: 'none of it makes much difference, it's *kastom* that holds us back'. It is worth stressing at this point that all such criticisms of *kastom*, including criticisms of customary land arrangements, share a common basis, namely, criticism of the ways in which overlapping claims and obligations, often based on a shared but disputed history of reciprocal exchange, can be seen as a drain on both resources and individual initiative. Indeed, the case of land is best seen as an example of this general trend. What is at stake in the attempt to restructure land tenure is ultimately an attempt to restructure the nature of the social relations of those who are linked by the land. This is the case in all attempts to restructure property rights, which, given that property is ultimately the expression of a particular kind of social relationship, are, in the final analysis, always attempts to restructure particular types of social relations. When Horim Ladi and his peers try to restructure customary land tenure, they are simultaneously attempting to restructure the kind of problematic social relations that are often glossed under the term *kastom*: relations of interdependence and mutual obligation that create a particular kind of person who cannot escape those claims. They wish to replace that person with a different kind of person, one who is able to invest and accumulate free from the demands of *kastom*.

As I have detailed elsewhere, this denigration of *kastom* is only half of the story. Most Tolai, from impoverished grassroots villagers to the emerging indigenous elite—often contemptuously referred to as 'big shots'—have an ambivalent attitude towards *kastom*, denigrating it in the terms mentioned above in some contexts, and praising it in others as the heart of Tolai culture. Indeed, it sits at the base of what many believe makes Papua New Guineans morally superior to whites who can be denigrated for their individual acquisitiveness, for which, in other contexts, they may also be admired.

Unsurprisingly, this negative discourse surrounding *kastom* is particularly common among administrators and planners with an interest in promoting development. Although land is the most common context in which this perspective is advanced, it is also advanced in others, such as by those wishing to promote local entrepreneurship. The example of the trade store that is bankrupted by greedy relatives is often given. Yet, even among this group, who often seem to occupy a social position that might lead them to be the most unambiguously suspicious of *kastom*, their position is often ambiguous, or even contradictory. Rather than a blanket denunciation of *kastom*, their position is more one of wishing to delimit it: to keep it in its place so that it will not infect the sphere of development in which an ethic of individual economic rationality should be paramount. *Kastom* is viewed as being important in promoting cultural identity and a kind of civic consciousness. This desire to wipe out *kastom* and the ethic of reciprocal interdependence that underpins it in some contexts, while preserving and promoting it in others, is, of course, a desire beyond the power of regional governmental officials to realise. In the final part of this chapter, I aim to briefly outline an example of the wish to delimit *kastom* in the context of resettlement, and suggest why this might be an unrealisable desire.

As we have seen, *kastom* is often presented by Tolai and other residents of East New Britain as the thing that holds PNG back from development. The attempt to re-engineer customary land as individual property should be seen as part of a wider attempt to engineer a new kind of modern 'possessive individual' who would be free from the demands and obligations of *kastom* that hold him or her back. However, at other points, it seems as if there is not enough *kastom* to ensure progress; the same planners and administrators who berate villagers for their backwardness suddenly discover that the Tolai are, in fact, too modern to develop successfully. I will provide an example from a conversation that I had during my fieldwork. As with the conversation with Horim Ladi at the Lands Division, I could have chosen a number of other conversations with other representatives of this segment of East New Britain society who would have made a similar point. This conversation was with two senior officials of the Gazelle Restoration Authority (GRA), the body set up by the PNG national parliament to deal with the reconstruction of the Gazelle after the 1994 eruption. The GRA was controversial in some quarters (e.g. its officials were blamed by Rabaul loyalists for pushing the move to Kokopo) and, on many occasions, its position diverged from that of senior officials in the provincial government who were resentful of its influence. However, the broad policy objectives of restructuring East New Britain's political economy to promote economic development by encouraging individual landholding were shared across the board.

The first official involved in this conversation, James, was from England, but had been married to a Tolai woman for over 20 years and lived in a Tolai village near Kokopo. The second, Timothy, was a Tolai who also lived in the Kokopo area. I had not intended the conversation to be about *kastom*; instead, it was a quite technical and dull interview about the mechanisms by which the PNG Government secured counterpart funding from the World Bank for restoration projects and the competitive tendering process by which contracts for those projects were allocated. It became apparent in the course of the conversation that there was supposed to be a division of labour between the GRA and the provincial government, whereby the GRA would construct the infrastructure in resettled communities such as Sikut, and the provincial government would take over the maintenance. Both men were adamant that it was not the GRA's responsibility to make sure that the new community buildings, water tanks or so forth were maintained. This explained why the list of completed projects on the report sheet that the GRA had produced to show funders, such as the World Bank, bore no resemblance to my experience of having lived at Sikut for over a year. The completed projects seemed either not to exist or to have fallen into a state of complete disrepair. When I asked what the point was of spending the money to build these projects when the provincial government was either unwilling or incapable of maintaining them, James shrugged his shoulders and repeated that that was not his job. Eventually, after I repeated the question a couple of times, he became slightly exasperated and asked, 'why can't the community look after their own assets? Communities have to learn to look after these assets. No one's going to repair constantly vandalised assets'.

I had heard this kind of complaint from members of the provincial government as well. Local communities were being provided with infrastructure projects; however, they refused to maintain them and, worse, allowed their disaffected youth to vandalise and destroy them. I asked my two informants why they thought that the community was incapable of looking after the assets. Thomas replied that, whereas 15 years previously there had been 'a lot of respect for community assets', since then there had been 'a lot of change within the community'. Some of the problems were the result of large-scale political restructuring, such as the decision by the PNG national government to centralise the collection of VAT revenue, which had left the East New Britain Provincial Government with much less money for maintenance. However, the main problem was vandalism and that, according to my informants, 'begins in the family'. When I asked if the communities' inability to maintain and protect infrastructure assets had come as a surprise to them, they both nodded vigorously. It was clear that they had expected the community to be able to police itself. Timothy explained what he thought had gone wrong:

> When the Big Men were there, there would have been respect, and you would be sanctioned if you stepped out of line. What we have now is totally different from 20 to 30 years ago. Now it's a Westernised life. People are struggling for themselves and their families; we don't have the kind of relations that we had before, working together as a community. Today we don't give things freely; we sell … today it's an individualistic approach. My brothers and my sisters—they don't support me. I have to struggle for my wife and kids.

Later, Timothy went on to describe how the problem was the decline of 'customary authority' in the villages, meaning that there was no way of stopping the destruction of community assets. This was a narrative with which I was very familiar from grassroots Tolai villagers at places like Matupit and Sikut. There were no more 'big men'—of the kind described by ethnographers of the Tolai in the 1960s, such as A. L. Epstein—who lived in the village and had influence over young men by virtue of their position of power in relations of gift-exchange obligation (crucially, a young man in the past would nearly always be reliant on a 'big man' to provide the shell wealth or *tabu*) necessary for him to marry and establish his own household. I have detailed these perceptions elsewhere (Martin, 2010); at this point, it is crucial to note that, despite the difference of opinion as to the nature of social changes over the past 40 years, which are common among many Tolai, it is impossible to find anyone who believes that 'old-style' village-based 'big man' leadership still exists.

Custom as Barrier and Precondition for Development

The point here is that very often *kastom* is portrayed as a barrier to development and modernisation by elites in PNG, yet, on closer examination, their attitude is often far more nuanced and context dependent. In fact, the same grassroots villagers who are condemned for being the slaves of wasteful and de-incentivising *kastom* are simultaneously condemned for not preserving it and for becoming too individualistic. Perhaps it is often forgotten that the kind of Western possessive individualism that so many planners wish to encourage relies on a social context of strong states and civic institutions to flourish. As Polanyi (2001, p. 3) observed many decades ago, free markets are conditional upon certain kinds of state and civic institutions being established if they are to function. In the absence of such social institutions in East New Britain, planners often take the very *kastom* that they denigrate for impeding individualism for granted, as a kind of social framework that will enable that individualism to flourish and be safely regulated. Paradoxically, the perceived abandonment of *kastom* by the grassroots is now seen to stop proper development, as it leads to a kind of antisocial individualism that pulls the whole community down. Rather than making a blanket denunciation of *kastom*, planners and managers want a delimited *kastom*, one that provides the social framework that would allow what they see as a progressive individualism in some contexts, but that simultaneously does not hinder its development in others. In this hope they are, of course, likely to be frustrated, as these processes are largely beyond their control. This is not just an issue in PNG; it is increasingly an issue for governments and policymakers around the world.

Take the career of Michael Young, who, as well as being probably the most important British sociologist of the twentieth century, can lay claim to being one of the main figures in both the construction, and dismantling, of the post-war British welfare state. In 1945, Young was one of the two co-authors of Labour's manifesto that established the welfare state following Labour's surprise landslide election victory of that year. In 1957, along with Peter Wilmott, he authored one of the most important books in the history of British sociology, *Family and Kinship in East London*. The book applied ethnographic methods of in-depth interviewing and participant observation to demonstrate how extended kinship networks, based on matrifocal extended households several generations deep, were the basis of community cohesion in the working-class East End, contrary to theories that suggested such kinship networks had died out with the industrial revolution. Here we might note (in response to some recent discussions) that there is nothing necessarily geographically Melanesian about the 'Melanesian city', at least not if the kind of sociality Young and Wilmott revealed is taken as one of its defining characteristics. By the time their book was published, Young was already beginning to have doubts about some of the effects of the revolution that he had played such a central role in establishing. At the time, many across the political spectrum had some hope that the new welfare state would enable the brightest and best in these working-class communities to escape their bonds and take up positions in the managerial middle class that was expanding under conditions of the post-war boom. For these leaders, the welfare state and individualised payments were meant to enable the talented to escape and transcend the confines of their communities, which were widely seen as holding them back. However, Young was concerned that this would weaken the fabric of these communities; he coined the now commonplace term 'meritocracy' as a satirical attack upon the idea of a society based upon merit (Young, 1958). If talent was inherited, then 'meritocracy' was as unjust as 'aristocracy'; not only this, it robbed working-class communities of those whose talents and drive held those communities together.

A similar argument is made at Matupit regarding those talented members of the post-independence generation who had to leave the village to take up national roles in politics and business. It is one of the main reasons advanced for the 'death of the big men'. By the end of his life, in the early 2000s, Young had become a strident critic of what the welfare state had become. In the final book to bear his name, *The New East End,* he argued that:

> From the mid-1960s onwards the administration of supports and benefits became increasingly freed from community reciprocity and oriented instead towards the needs of individuals. This shift of principles has … weakened the fabric of working-class communities. (Dench, Gavron & Young, 2006, p. 5)

In the current climate, in which the state wishes to withdraw as far as possible from a duty of care to the poorest and weakest, whether in PNG or the UK, 'community' is all the rage. As Dench, Gavron and Young argue in another part of their book, there will always be winners and losers, and community is a vital safety net for those who fall into the latter category (p. 228). No wonder that senior politicians from both major parties lined up to praise Young's final book, which chimed with this zeitgeist almost perfectly.

The reason I end with this discussion of the nature of welfare payments in East London is because I want to conclude with the following point. From the perspective of government and business elites around the world, the problem with the poor is not, as is often assumed, their backward custom; rather, it is that they simultaneously have too much and too little custom at the wrong points of social life for their betters' liking. For all of its different manifestations, this aspect of the problem of managing the poor's necessary, yet limiting, attachment to networks of reciprocal obligation is neither uniquely a Western nor a Melanesian phenomenon.

Governments may not control these processes but they have a part to play in shaping them. Although moves towards a perceived lessening of customary authority and partial individualisation of land tenure have been ongoing on the Gazelle Peninsula for decades, the eruption provided an opportunity for these planners to accelerate and intensify these processes via the resettlement program—an opportunity that they grasped with both hands. One of the key factors in the decline of customary authority reported by many Tolai is the loss of the control over land once held by 'big men'. Today, young men reportedly just settle on clan land without getting the permission of clan elders in a manner that is perceived by many as a deliberate provocation. Yet, it is a problem to which there appears to be few answers. The reasons for this are complex and beyond the scope of this essay; however, like the tendency for young men today to buy their own bride wealth, or to not bother paying it at all, it is clear that this is another trend that lessens the potential sanctions and control over young people's behaviour. This is a process that has reportedly been going on for years. Yet, the move to individual land tenure (if *kastom* does not reappear at Sikut as a small number of people predict) intensifies that process, further reducing the impact of the ties of obligation of which customary authority was an expression. Although it would be naive to imagine that, if the land at Sikut had been parcelled out on the basis of traditional Tolai matrilineal clan tenure, customary authority would rule at Sikut (the perceived decline of customary authority is a Gazelle-wide phenomenon), the introduction of individual tenure does mark another example of the kinds of changing social relations and obligations that have led to its perceived weakening. In attacking *kastom* in the interests of development in one area of social life, the planners have contributed to wider processes that weaken it more generally, providing an example of the kind of 'unintended consequences' that so often bedevil bureaucratic attempts to remake the people in the planners' image.

References

De Soto, H. (2001). *The mystery of capital: Why capitalism triumphs in the West and fails elsewhere.* London, England: Black Swan.

Dench, G., Gavron, K. & Young, M. (2006). *The new East End.* London, England: Profile.

Epstein, A. L. (1969). *Matupit: Land, politics and change among the Tolai of New Britain.* Canberra, ACT: Australian National University Press.

Fingleton, J. (1985). *Changing land tenure in Melanesia: The Tolai experience* (Unpublished doctoral thesis). The Australian National University, Canberra.

Fitzpatrick, P. (1983). The knowledge and politics of land law. *Melanesian Law Journal, 11*, 14–34.

Hughes, H. (2003). Aid has failed the Pacific. *Issues Analysis, 33*. Sydney, NSW: Centre for Independent Studies.

Jessep, O. (1980). Land demarcation in New Ireland. *Melanesian Law Journal, 8*(1 & 2), 112–33.

Klein, N. (2007). *The shock doctrine: The rise of disaster capitalism.* New York, NY: Henry Holt.

Martin, K. (2010). The death of the big men: Depreciation of elites in New Guinea. *Ethnos, 75*(1), 1–22. doi.org/10.1080/00141840903581576

Martin, K. (2013). *The death of the big men and the rise of the big shots: Custom and conflict in East New Britain*. New York, NY: Berghahn Books.

Polanyi, K. (2001). *The great transformation: The political and economic origins of our times.* Boston, MA. Beacon Press. (Original work published 1944).

Young, M. (1958). *The rise of the meritocracy, 1870–2033*. London, England: Thames and Hudson.

Young, M. & Wilmott, P. (1957). *Family and kinship in East London.* London, England: Routledge and Kegan Paul. doi.org/10.4324/9780203802342

6

A Moral Economy of the Transnational Papua New Guinean Household: Solidarity and Estrangement While 'Working Other Gardens'

Karen Sykes

Introduction

Transnational Papua New Guinean (PNG) household members provide for each other while making new forms of traditional marriage, often resulting in changes to their access to land in their homelands in PNG. They capture the sense of that experience of migration away from clan lands with the idiom 'working other gardens', by which they mean they have migrated from PNG to 'other gardens'. Although they sustain their household's livelihood as employees of firms and as parents of students, public speculation about Papua New Guineans' reasons for taking up residence in Australia focuses wrongly on their geopolitical demographics rather than this moral economy of the transnational PNG household. Neither the state and its agencies nor the independent service providers, who assume the political economy of PNG-born residents in Australia is precarious given the transience and landlessness of the members of this community, grasp the moral economy of the transnational household. Contrary to the precarious political economy imagined by representatives of the state, ethnographic research reveals a moral economy of resilient solidarity within the transnational household. PNG women live at its centre, often having multiple residences in PNG and Australia. Nevertheless, it is one within which disaffected household members might find they are estranged from traditional land.

'Working Other Gardens'

I learned to turn my attention to the experiences of PNG women in Australia, and away from census data and the moral judgements made about their households, during a short fieldwork trip in 2011. I had made a journey with several PNG women from Cairns, in Queensland, to Darwin, in the Northern Territory. Among other plans, we hoped to view the 10,000-year-old petroglyphs in Kakadu National Park and to visit some old friends settled there. We were guests for an evening in the household of a PNG woman whose husband worked in the uranium mine several hours out of the city. Our host had once hailed from Western Province, PNG, as had another family (from the mouth of the Fly River) who had travelled with us from Queensland. Another guest in the house that evening had come to Darwin from PNG to attend a technical education college for a three-month course. He arrived with two other Papua New Guineans from Enga who had been recovering in a Darwin hospital, receiving treatment for injuries sustained on a mining site at their employer's expense. That night, I joined the gathering with my three friends who had been born on the New Guinea islands.

I asked the PNG women and men present that evening how such a disparate group of Papua New Guineans had come to be living in Australia, how they sustained their lives there and what they made of their experience of doing so. I posed my questions to the group over a late-afternoon meal, which was served in traditional style: generous amounts of root vegetables—sweet potatoes, taro, cassava and sago—with portions of roast chicken. They were bemused by their realisation that they were eating many of the same foods enjoyed for centuries, and I asked them to clarify their thoughts. My companions answered, but talked more about the deep past than the present. They spoke of their ancestors, the Pacific navigators who had accomplished one of the greatest triumphs over space and time of any migration in global history, moving westward out of South-East Asia to Madagascar and eastwards to Rapanui (Easter Island) over 10,000 years ago. They spoke of seagoing canoes peopled by their ancestors and loaded with bundles of taro and yams, models of which stood in the Northern Territory museum nearby. They spoke of the deep history of their ancestors, who, they believed, had had the ability to make a life wherever they landed—not by marine crafts but by expert horticulture. They also remembered the modern migrations of workers to plantations in Queensland, and recounted stories of meeting the descendants of these men and women. Perhaps the authenticity of these ancient and modern stories rested more on my friends' view of their own peripatetic lives in the present than on the archaeological record? Taking new jobs, moving to a new house and even visiting relatives across many Pacific islands had remained a common habit throughout their history.

In this introductory section, I have described my understanding of a gathering of Papua New Guineans in Australia. How that fieldwork experience reconfigured my research questions follows in the rest of this chapter. I learned that the twenty-first century form of association, the modern PNG household, emerged out of the migration of household members from PNG to Australia, Europe, South-East Asia and the Americas. However, the principal destination for the last four or five decades has been Australia, where increasing numbers of PNG women have settled with their husbands and children. I also learned that many migrant PNG households in Australia are composed of the descendants of two or more generations of marriages across the language or cross-ethnic groups of multicultural PNG. At best, they had complex means of access to their clansperson's land in PNG; at worst, no rights to use it. How they came to migrate to Australia and find other work there arises from their generational histories, rather than only from contemporary, individual motives. Their ancestors' intention to work 'other gardens' wherever they landed to make a good life together in the future appealed to my friends' sense of their current moral reality of making a livelihood in a widely dispersed network of household members; they used the idiom to capture the character of their new livelihoods in Australia, where they now 'work other gardens' because they must do so.

The Limits of Geopolitical Accounts of the PNG Transnational Household

The moral economy of the transnational PNG household was unknown to local government and businesses. When local councils and their business partners in Queensland began to investigate these further it was because they most often relied on the census data, which was too thin to provide a picture of how the transnational PNG household lived. Most often, business and government officials mistook the particularities of the PNG householder's moral economy for their response to the loss of more general economic rights. The government officials raised the ethical principle that communities must not only survive, but also thrive and flourish. They raised concerns with the PNG householders rights to thrive within the optical economy of the region, which were based on the assumption that members had a right to make a livelihood based on access to residence, work, and social care. I was encouraged by the agents of local government and business to enrich their demographic picture of the transnational PNG household so that they might assist the PNG community to make a good life together.

Ethnographic fieldwork yields knowledge that is different from the information that methods like census data collection and analysis allow. My research among transnational PNG families had begun simply enough with my inquiry into the PNG community in Australia and how they constituted their relationship with each other there. I began in their households in Far North Queensland, a region of more than 225,000 residents in the Australian state of Queensland. The total number of Papua New Guineans there is unrecorded in the census because their residency is so fluid and their identity unfixed. Many people I knew kept one home in the political jurisdiction of Far North Queensland because of its proximity to PNG's national capital, Port Moresby, a mere one-hour flight away. Often, they also had a home in Port Moresby, where some household members lived; perhaps a third had another home in either a more distant part of Australia or in a PNG province. However, the PNG families I worked with in greater Cairns showed me that the household was transnational because it was defined by how its members related to each other. I came to see that the strength of kinship and friendship connections across distances mattered more to their identity as Papua New Guineans than the location of their residences.

My first acquaintance with the transnational household had been in the 1990s when I broke my travels to PNG in Cairns to visit people I had first met in their PNG village. Often the Australian-residing arm of the household asked me to carry messages to relatives in towns or villages in PNG, but I did not realise that fluidity is deeply characteristic of the PNG household until I settled in Far North Queensland myself in 2012. Beginning in the greater Cairns area, which had a population of about 50,000 people, I mapped those PNG households geographically to other Queensland towns and cities and to Australian cities in different states, as well as to the PNG towns and cities where household members owned or rented other houses. This was daunting at first but became less so as I followed the connections they had already made, thereby coming to see the transnational household in distinctly PNG terms, rather than geopolitical ones.

I found that PNG households typically settled in Cairns for several months, after which their members made longer visits to other homes in PNG and Australia. It can be said that, rather than the physical residence itself constituting the household, it is the PNG women who form the centre point of these large extended households of relatives and 'friends' for whom they choose to care, and who might be called, in Tok Pisin, *wantoks*. I met with the members of approximately 60 households of this character between 2011 and 2014. All the households in my survey centred upon relationships between a PNG woman, her clanspersons and her in-laws, or affines. Her husband might have been white Australian or European, or identified as Chinese or Malaysian. Comparatively few PNG women were married to men from other Pacific island nations, but many had married a PNG man, often from a different language group, or an entirely different PNG region. The PNG woman's point of view of the domestic moral economy of the transnational household often encompassed concerns with household and financial debt, as well as 'marriage debt', as I describe in two cases of mortgages held by transnational PNG families (Sykes, 2013). Certainly, a PNG woman might feel challenged to sustain the members of such a household and, in coming to define the ground rules for inclusion in it, she might exclude certain *wantoks* and relatives from care by the household, thereby limiting the demands made on her and the household.

Just as PNG women were concerned about the resilience of their transnational households, so too was regional government. However, by contrast with the point of view of PNG women, which centred on relations between households (i.e. the domestic moral economy), the perspective of local service providers and regional government was something like 'geopolitical-centric', following the assumption that simple residence in the region is the most significant factor in understanding PNG households. This assumption confounded service providers' ability to acknowledge and report on the transnational quality of these households. They were often heard to say that the PNG population of greater Cairns was 'a very roughly estimated number in the neighbourhood of something between five- and eight-thousand people'. Their geopolitical-centric perspective focused on Cairns being home to the highest concentration of PNG households in Australia, with it being commonly rumoured in business and government that the Cairns-area population represented 'between a quarter or a half of the total number of Papua New Guinean people resident in Australia as of 2011', but there were not official data to show it. The more that officials tried to clarify the census data, the less convincing was their hold on any significant knowledge of Papua New Guineans in Australia. As I learned to be sympathetic to the trials of interpreting the lifestyle and residence patterns of a somewhat mobile form of household, I also realised that census data are not a good guide to how Papua New Guineans thrive in Australia; the data are not even a measure of how many people live in such households. That requires an account of the moral economy of the PNG transnational household, which I describe below.

Closer analysis of census data shows how little value it brings to the clarification of even the geopolitical profiles of people of different ancestries. Despite not providing the solid evidence needed for developing shared political visions or social planning, a powerful moralising discourse emerged around census data. Regional politicians mapped a trend across Australian census years that showed an increase in the absolute number of people declaring themselves to be PNG-born residents of Australia, with the two largest increases coinciding with particular events in immigration policy. Table 6.1 shows that the largest increase in numbers occurred in 1976, the year after PNG independence. This was when Australian families returned to Australia after decades of working in PNG, started new businesses and took up jobs in various Australian states, often in Queensland. The increase in 2006 coincided with shifts in Australian immigration policy regarding the issuing of education visas for PNG children. Whereas in past decades, students had come to Australia on scholarships offered by the Australian Government, in the twenty-first century, PNG children were given visas for study, with one PNG adult offered a guardianship visa to accompany them. The significance of official moralisations about these historical developments is clearer when examined at the level of the household.

Table 6.1: PNG-Born Migration to Australia, 1954–2011

Census Year	Number
1954	1,723
1976	15,562
2006	24,024
2011	26,787

Source: Department of Immigration and Citizenship, Australia (n.d.).

Despite official trust in these figures, they overstate the number of PNG migrants, as many of those PNG-born migrants in Australia are the children of Australians who were working in the former territories of PNG. In addition, many hundreds of people who are recorded in the 2011 census as PNG-born residents were those temporarily visiting (six to 12 weeks) as adult students at Australia's many technical and further education colleges. In short, the numbers do not record merely residents of PNG descent; nor do they distinguish longer term or permanent residents.

To better grasp the aggregate size and significance of PNG-born migration, census data on 'ancestry' was also gathered. Notably, this data were volunteered: it was not *required*. In the Australian census, a total of 15,460 responses indicated PNG ancestry. However, it must be remembered that this is not the same as saying that 15,460 persons identified as having PNG ancestors. There are several reasons for this. First, by 'ancestry' the census question meant the birthplace of the respondent's parents or grandparents, and not their nationality or 'race'. For example, as I learned during my ethnographic inquiries, a respondent with a parent born in PNG would list PNG ancestry even if that parent were the child or even grandchild of (white) German residents in PNG. Second, the voluntary nature of responses necessarily skewed the results, making them non-representative; many people simply did not respond to the question (i.e. they listed none of their ancestries). Third, those who did respond to this question could identify either two ancestries or one, as they wished. For all these reasons, the Department of Citizenship and Immigration could not clarify just how many people chose to respond with information about both, one or none of their parents and grandparents.[1] Hence, those analysing the data were warned not to divide the number of respondents into the aggregate number of responses because it would not determine how many PNG-born people also identify as having PNG ancestry.

Of all the responses to the question about respondents' ancestry, the responses given by people who also identified as PNG-born can be expressed in tabular form. Table 6.2 shows that of the major ancestries named by those who were born in PNG, only 23 per cent indicated PNG ancestry, a raw number of 8,752 out of 37,625 responses. Notably, 'other ancestral responses' has the largest percentage of all responses, being the total number of responses that do not name the top four named ancestries of the PNG-born: Papua New Guinean, Australian, English and Chinese. Table 6.2 shows the aggregate number of responses to this question.

Table 6.2: Ancestry Responses of PNG-Born Migrants, 2011 Census

Ancestry responses	Number of responses	% all responses
Papua New Guinean	8,752	23
Australian	7,313	19
English	6,736	18
Chinese	2,972	8
Other	11,852	32
Total Responses	**37,625**	**100**

Source: Department of Immigration and Citizenship, Australia (n.d.).

Quite wisely, the compilers of the data warn against translating aggregate responses into percentages of people, and percentages into absolute numbers of people of PNG descent. Hence, the number 8,750 is neither an absolute nor approximate number of people of PNG descent in Australia. Instead, it represents the aggregation of responses to the category 'PNG ancestry'.

1 There is no analysis that can reveal how many people surveyed actually listed PNG ancestry, let alone were actually of it. Given that the census counted 26,787 people who identified as PNG-born, their total possible numbers of ancestry responses, at the limit of two per respondent, would have been 53,574. However, the total ancestry responses of the PNG-born were 37,625. Not surprisingly, perhaps, this figure is the aggregate of responses that listed one or two ancestral birthplaces of parents and grandparents.

'PNG-born and resident in Australia' is a fuzzy category, one that offers little clarity about those whose lives it describes, except that Queensland is their favoured destination, as Table 6.3 shows.

Table 6.3: Geographical Distribution of PNG-Born, 2011 Census

State	Number of PNG-born	% total PNG-born
Queensland	14,500	54
New South Wales	5,428	20
Victoria	2,534	10
Western Australia	1,763	6
Other	2,562	10
Total	**26,787**	**100**

Source: Department of Immigration and Citizenship, Australia (n.d.).

However, it remains as difficult in this as in other tables to understand to whom the figures refer. In the course of my fieldwork, I met many white Australians who invested in Queensland farms and small businesses after the sale of plantations in PNG. By their own account, they preferred to resettle in Queensland because they could more readily gain access to their remaining business investments and personal commitments in PNG.

In the course of my fieldwork, I heard how the Far North Queensland regional government and service providers were increasingly perplexed by the disjuncture between reports of an extensive PNG presence in their region and their actual experience; they simply did not meet as many Papua New Guineans as the census figures suggested they might. At first, they set out to find more PNG people. When they were unable to do that they came to doubt the census figures. Some government officers admitted that they had misread the figure of 26,787 as the measure of PNG migrants in the country, not realising that it was an aggregate that included many more people who were born in PNG but of Australian ancestry and citizenship. Others misread the number of responses identifying PNG ancestry for the number of individuals of PNG descent. The next section shows that the Australian Government Department of Citizenship and Immigration correctly warned users of their data to take care when extrapolating from it to comment about the PNG community.

Moral Economy Versus Political Economy in the PNG Transnational Household

It is common to use census data to describe the political economy of a population. However, the case of the PNG transnational family is better grasped via an account of their moral, rather than political, economy, which requires ethnographic methods. In this section, I show how geopolitically informed census data misshaped knowledge of the political economy of the PNG transnational family and led service providers, business managers, financial institutions and government officers to err through speculations about the meaning of the numbers, a form of insight called 'quantitative gossip' by E. P. Thompson (1993, p. 413). Searches were made by officials of the registration records of the Queensland Department of Education and those of the state's health services for better evidence of the needs of the community, and they contacted representatives for the Pacific Islanders in the region to elaborate on these needs. However, searches of the property register, in particular, generated morally charged debate about the make up and political economy of the PNG household. Following an overview of some of the first responses to the census by health and education offices, as well as to the Queensland property register, I focus on the moral economy of the PNG household as the lived reality within which PNG livelihoods are made.

The Queensland Department of Education records the arrival of new students from PNG every school year, but it does not have a distinct record of PNG households that have settled permanently in Australia. In 2011, 30 PNG students began studies in Far North Queensland for the first time; in 2014, that number more than doubled, with the arrival of over 30 students on an Ok Tedi company scheme, accompanied by family members. The department's figures represent new migrations in the hundreds each year from 2011 to the present, as parents and their non–school age children have taken up residence.

The Queensland Department of Health wanted better information about those who called a parent or a grandparent PNG-born because the census data was 'too soft' to provide them with good evidence for decision-making. They commissioned an independent study of the PNG community's health needs and held focus group meetings in Townsville and Cairns, where it believed the greatest number of PNG-born people lived. A survey of stated needs, based on 15 respondents from each city, showed that diabetes and heart disease were the most commonly occurring non-communicable diseases suffered by members of the community, just the same as for non-PNG, white Australians. Citing the importance of meeting Pacific Islanders' health needs, the department hired a health officer from PNG to work with Papua New Guineans in Queensland. They made special attempts to develop links with PNG women, who were thought to be vulnerable in Australia, and who were also considered the key to the wellbeing of PNG networks in the region. On the latter point, they were right.

Individual public officials, service providers and business people reflected on how the figures did not fit with their experience; they did not see as many PNG-born residents on the street as census data suggested they would. PNG neighbourhoods do not exist in the greater Cairns region, nor can any distinctive pockets or enclaves be found in the wider political region of Far North Queensland. Despite acknowledgement of the vagueness of the census data, Cairns residents were still surprised by the extent of PNG involvement in local home ownership. In 2010, the *Cairns Post* reported that research into the Queensland property register showed Papua New Guineans investing more money in Far North Queensland property than any other foreign buyer, except those from Singapore who led in land purchases with AUD11.5 million covering 11.1 hectares. However, PNG purchases totalled 181 properties covering 10.3 hectares by comparison to Chinese purchases of 19 properties covering 108 hectares (Dalton, 2014, p. 13). The most common purchase was a three-bedroom family home, even if the common wisdom was that an office building would provide a better return on a comparable investment.

In the first analyses by journalists, most PNG activity on the property market was seen to be driven by the purchase of personal residences valued under AUD500,000, rather than for the purchase of housing as an asset or financial investment. Notably, Queensland house prices are similar to those of comparable houses in the neighbourhoods of Port Moresby, where many professionals and civil servants live. When families have a house in PNG and another in Queensland, often the Queensland house is of a lower price and in better repair than the Port Moresby one. Some families had simply sold a high-priced house in the old suburb of Boroko and purchased one in Cairns.

Rumours of 'corruption' and speculation about the morality of PNG purchases in Cairns spread among white Australians, as some property purchases appeared to be way beyond the means of buyers. Some white Australians made suspicious comments about property investments by PNG political leaders or businesspeople simply because they handled contracts for the royalties from mining-industry operations on traditional land. However, these claims were hard to substantiate. Papua New Guineans shared their suspicions and doubts with me, but also questioned the verity of the stories in circulation. For example, Papua New Guineans in Cairns protested that the price tags on their Australian homes were much lower than those on good-sized lots in Port Moresby, where old colonial housing (c. 1950–70s) built on quarter-acre lots sold for hundreds of thousands of PNG kina, often triple the value of the same period-style house on the same size lot in Cairns. They admitted that the allegations of corruption could not be proven or disproven without a full inquiry. Some civil servants faced the possibility of a tribunal in their workplace that would investigate those personal financial arrangements that were not usually publicly known. Rumours of their misuse of funds led to few full investigations, but they made the PNG household in Cairns far more visible in both Australia and PNG than previously. While PNG-born residents were nearly invisible in the greater Cairns region, they became the focus of public speculations about their integrity.

Speculation and gossip by white Australians connected even Papua New Guineans who sought to live quietly, out of the public eye, to prominent Papua New Guineans and Australians. Most Papua New Guineans in the region make ordinary livelihoods and sustain quiet lifestyles so as not to draw attention to themselves in the mostly white Australian neighbourhoods in which they reside. However, their hope of a quiet life does not mean they wish to hide from their Australian neighbours. Indeed, they do not wish to live close to other Papua New Guineans. Rather than establishing homes close to their *wantoks* from the same village, province or workplace, new buyers aim to find property at some distance from them. They said they wished to escape other Papua New Guineans because they would make uninvited demands on their households, in the manner and style of *wantokism*. In Cairns, they hoped to escape the avarice they perceived as having come to permeate contemporary PNG-village, settlement, suburb and town life.

My own records show that keeping multiple residences was not specifically tied to an upper-income or upper–middle income group, and did not require large salaries. Many of the transnational PNG households in Cairns lack money; they keep very modestly priced houses in both Australia and PNG, counting among these even bush-material and rough-cut timber houses in villages where they or their parents were born. While some houses in PNG might be rented to family members, whose payments might help support mortgage payments in Australia, it is more common for relatives to live 'rent-free'. In such cases, a house is not an asset first and foremost but, rather, a means to provide for relatives whose own residence on clan grounds might offer a PNG-born migrant to Australia some hope of access to it in the future.

In the absence of better knowledge of PNG-born residents in Australia, most attempts to explain the census data generated moralising claims about the PNG community. In greater Cairns, councillors earnestly voiced support for the needs and interests of 'Papua New Guineans' residing in Far North Queensland; however, when counting them proved daunting, they soon gave up. Instead, they sought out individuals to represent Papua New Guineans on the multi-regional committee of local government. They accessed state funds for this, and invited several prominent PNG women to speak about the concerns of the PNG community in Cairns. Although the details of that work fall beyond the scope of this chapter, it proved to be a good plan of political action for accessing larger networks of PNG people.

I have reviewed the information derived from the census, and shown how that scant and speculative knowledge, assembled from what Thompson (1993) once referred to more generally as 'the gossip of quantitative data' (p. 413), is first comprised and then comes to effect PNG households. Therefore, an entirely different approach to understanding the transnational PNG household is called for. The idiom 'working other gardens', as used by some Papua New Guineans, shapes a wider ethnographic understanding of the transnational household by escaping the political and economic framework that girds the Australian census data and the many decisions about its use. For moral economy to provide the better bones to support the fully fleshed out sense that people make of their lives, I turn to marital and generational relationships in the household over several generations. As women and men remake traditional marriage arrangements for transnational lives, they must struggle to define the reach of affinal obligations and the change these bring to their access to traditional land.

My fieldwork in Cairns showed me how difficult it was to locate or even see Papua New Guineans in the geopolitical region, and revealed the complicated nature of the claim that they were part of a precarious political economy. Most Papua New Guineans do not have secure, ongoing access to traditional land in PNG; in any case, they worry that they might not enjoy the benefits of any livelihood that could be made from it. In addition, few PNG-born families own homes outright so the economic security of their household relies on a steady flow of money to repay mortgages. Many PNG-born women are unemployed, some by reason of their visa requirements as parents or guardians of children enrolled in Queensland schools, others because of lapsed qualifications and breaks in their employment as a result of their move to Australia. The security of the PNG transnational household relies on the wages of the husband, whether he is Australian or PNG-born, or on the businesses developed by PNG-born women with assistance from their relatives and access to traditional land at home. The latter provides only an irregular flow of money, as it requires long-term, ongoing negotiation with relatives. However, I argue that these are not signs that the moral economy is underdetermined by a new and precarious political economy. Instead, the moral economy is the very form and structure of the political economy of the PNG transnational household.

The moral economy of the PNG transnational household in Australia secures the moral, political and economic livelihoods of its members. It should not be contrasted abstractly to stability or instability in political–economic terms, as scholars of industrial capitalism have done. This particular moral economy produces social life, and thereby encompasses political–economic factors. It is a moral, political and economic reality, and it is within this that the transnational household is defined by the practices of its members. They keep households in Cairns, at some distance from the jobs household members may hold in PNG cities and towns, and far from their PNG-based relatives, who make a living by horticulture and live in rural villages. They make long-term visits to relatives in PNG and to friends living in North Queensland and faraway in other parts of Australia. They say they feel more deeply and regularly connected to relatives in other Australian cities and in PNG than they do to their neighbours in their streets. 'Working other gardens' outside PNG, the paradoxes of their daily lives unfold as a moral reality of estranged relationships with some relatives, rather than a moral economy at odds with a political economy.

Therefore, the rest of this chapter examines the idea of a moral economy as a social reality, outlining the social norms of everyday living that inform the PNG household's search for the good life with relatives. The uses of the idiom 'working other gardens' highlight that the lives and livelihoods of transnational PNG households can be judged as moral realities rather than value-neutral statistical ones. In Durkheim's sense, it calls forth the sociological meanings of the division of labour in the traditional family and its extended kin, rather than an identification with the people of the deep history of Austronesian migrations across the Pacific, which was hinted at in the late-night storytelling that I described earlier as people contemplated what they had lost in their migrations south. Different from the census data, my ethnographic research shows that it is not the historical 'waves' of migration as such (from those of the colonial period to independence to the present) that shape the transnational PNG household. Rather, in the late twentieth century, the PNG transnational household is shaped by patterns of marriage, both by relationships with marriage partners who think of themselves as *wantoks*, 'speakers of the same language', and with those who do not come to the marriage as *wantoks*.

'Working Other Gardens': Creating Solidarity in Transnational Households

Details of households founded on marriages between PNG women and non-PNG men, and PNG women and men from different regions of PNG, show how most people struggle to keep alive traditional forms of access to land, even as they are 'working other gardens' outside PNG. Traditionally, women access garden lands through marriage, usually following their husbands to work on the land he can claim to access from his clan. Some women retain access to the gardens of the clan into which they are born. Generally, it happens that a woman loses access to much-wanted gardens by making a marriage to a partner who has none, and even risks losing access to gardens of her clan when clansmen distrust her use of the gardens after making a non-traditional marriage to either a non-PNG man, or a man from another region or language group in PNG. The loss is made more profound when, as happens to some families, a woman's son and daughter are denied access to gardens by clansmen of their mother, who would otherwise assist them with accessing the land and cultivating it. 'Working other gardens' is an idiom deeply rooted in the traditional relationships between systems of kinship and land tenure, and the sense of the idiom is strengthened by knowledge of the matrices of marital and generational relationships that I set out in this section of the chapter.

Marriages Between PNG and Non-PNG Spouses

The older generation of PNG-born women who migrated to Australia in the 1970s came predominantly as the wives of men of non-PNG descent (usually white Australian or white European, but often Chinese). Their marriages were celebrated in vastly different ways: either according to the traditions of the wife's clan, by legal register or in church ceremonies. Even today, there are lively discussions in PNG transnational households about the making of marital unions, and these can help clarify the different investments people have made in the process. Many tales are told of trucks and household appliances being given as one-off payments of bride wealth. There are many stories too of situations where an individual white Australian man, on the advice of his PNG wife, made a traditional offer of a gift of bride wealth to her clansmen, but with a non-traditional sensibility. Often the aim was to give generously so that the wider network of relatives could enjoy, and even share the bride wealth with the entire clan, and even the entire village. Such was the case of one husband who, after his children were born, sent a shipping container of school equipment (desks, boards and books) to his wife's village in Milne Bay to thank it for his family, which he called 'the best gift they could have given him'. However, many Australian men married to PNG women who made one-off gifts of money at the time of the marriage never sent anything more, as they had 'completed the bride price payment'. Others, in choosing a 'church wedding', refused to enter into customary marriage exchanges from the outset.

Most Australian husbands who did not originally make bride wealth gifts have not maintained ongoing relations with their wife's relatives, although the wife will often do so. It is her choice whether to support her clansmen. Some women with businesses in PNG use their profits to support clansmen in their village. One woman I knew operated an arts and craft business selling her relatives handwork, in particular, *bilums* (net bags), to international customers. Her business also moderated the loss to her husband's salary from contributions to her clan sisters' households, gardens and children's school fees. Several women with personal wealth supported natal kin without their husband's knowledge, but the majority of PNG women married to Australians do not have the personal means to do so.

These Australian–PNG households form a loose social network. They meet annually to celebrate PNG Independence Day and milestone events in the life of the household. Those who have lived in Australia for a full generation come together to join in retirement parties and birthdays, or to attend the funerals of old friends, who always seem to have died 'too young'. Conversations are peppered with memories of past decades when people lived in the towns of what were then the Territories of Papua and New Guinea. It is not clear that they will reproduce their community by these measures, but they are creating a bank of memories for use in the future.

Marriages Between Spouses from Different PNG Regions

A younger generation of PNG women and men are moving south in the twenty-first century to educate their children in Australian schools. They form households founded predominantly on marriages between PNG men and women from geographically and culturally distant parts of PNG. Some of these marriages are recognised in PNG law as traditional marriages, where bride wealth is arranged by the husband's family and received by the wife's kin, but others are not. In most cases of traditional marriage, people debate the social norms and come to an agreement about what 'feels right', with the husband agreeing on an arrangement for a gift to his wife's parents, which they accept as his bride wealth payment. Many choose to have a religious ceremony in a PNG church; alternatively, some ask a magistrate to perform the marriage in his office. Sometimes, couples ask for a church blessing by a priest or pastor, who will perform a ceremony for couples who have lived for many years as husband and wife with their children in a 'traditional marriage'. Some couples insist that church weddings still meet all the obligations, given that traditional practices are diverse and unclear, especially when the two parties hail from places as distant as Manus and Milne Bay. In both cases—traditional and non-traditional—a man will seek to have his marriage registered by a magistrate, who provides the legal record to accompany a couple's migration to Australia.

For these younger migrants to Australia in the twenty-first century, the choice to work in Australia is not simply about salary. They have few opportunities in PNG to advance their livelihoods, largely because it is unusual for members of this educated younger generation to have easy access to clan lands for gardening or businesses. Some are involved with their clanspersons in larger financial enterprises, but they are frequently subordinate partners to relatives who hold elite jobs in Port Moresby and who keep close relations nearer to the villages and land of their birth. The transnational family member with a firmer foothold in PNG generally claims clan land for business ventures and the economic development of their village. Most of this generation of PNG migrants to Australia have much more fragile connections to clan land.

Working in Australia provides this generation with the only real way of advancing their lives and those of other members of their greatly dispersed households, as waged professional employment is the only way they can make a living. They say it became clear to them in their school days that educational success would be the product of their own hard work, and that schools and workplaces would be their 'gardens', as they lacked access to land. They rely extensively on non-PNG workmates, often because their marriages were not made in keeping with the traditions that would solidify their affinal relations. Usually the spouses come to Australia together, each having had an independent career in business or the professions. However, in finalising their migration to Australia, one, usually the wife, foregoes their career to relocate.

This generation of PNG-born migrants to Australia is not as closely tied to affines by traditional marriage as their grandparents or great-grandparents' generation, but they do maintain commitments to sustaining their siblings and parents in PNG. Thus, the habit of sending remittances to their village-residing kin is common. They remit money, automobile parts, used clothing and traditional arts and crafts, including a small number of cowrie shells, but they do this when and for whom they choose. Their generosity towards some of their clanspersons is recognised and welcomed, and their record of giving is only a bit less unreliable than that of the older independence-generation women. Most maintain an attenuated correspondence with relatives by telephone and email, largely because they have discovered that they can control how they use and give their free time. I have been with PNG women many times when their mobile phone has lit up with a PNG number. Usually, the caller, short of credit, asks 'auntie' for a call back. The women have the choice of not picking up, and they often let the phone ring out. I learned that it is common to receive answering machine and text messages, but the PNG-born woman usually chooses to return them later, not immediately.

A comparison of the two different generations of migration shows common patterns. As noted, the first migration of PNG women occurred with the repatriation of their husbands who were colonial agents at the time of independence. The second occurred with the movement of PNG families redeployed to an Australian subsidiary of a company employing them in PNG. These later migrations, which allow the continuation of work and education in Australia, are made under employment policies agreed by multinational mining companies and the Australian Government. Notwithstanding the political and historical differences between the two waves of migration, the transnational PNG household in both eras has rested on common ways of reorganising relationships to accommodate PNG traditions in a different land and, in that sense, both sets of PNG migrants have 'worked other gardens' than the households into which they were born.

It has been the practice of members of both waves of migration to send material goods to relatives in PNG; this in a common pattern of giving to clanspersons. Typically, individuals in both waves of migration have sent monetary and non-monetary gifts to their clanspersons. In the first wave, it was the women who did this; their Australian husbands did not send remittances. In the most recent wave of migration, I have found that both PNG women and men send remittances to clanspersons. Like Australian spouses of PNG women, they do not send gifts to the clanspersons of their spouse, their affines; instead, like the PNG women of the previous generation, they send money and goods to their clanspersons. With only a few exceptions, neither PNG nor Australian men choose to send gifts of ceremonial shell wealth and money onwards to their wives' brothers to complete bride wealth payments, as they would have done in past years.

The tradition of arranging for the gift of bride wealth from the husband's to the wife's clanspersons has not been present in either migration. However, there has been innovation of that custom to assert the legality of marriages. In most cases, the bride wealth is given once, in the very early years of the marriage, to the wife's parents only. Few gifts of bride wealth are made to them after that ceremonial gift. Where affinal relations are honoured or recognised by exchanging traditional forms of bride wealth at the time of the marriage, no one believes these imply an ongoing interdependency in making a livelihood, as would be the case in a village sustained by horticulture. While these innovations in giving bride wealth symbolically solemnises, and legally secures, traditional marriage, it does not become a basis for either Australian or PNG men to continue to give gifts to their wives' relatives, either to complete traditional bride wealth payments, or to contribute to the livelihoods of affinal relations.

'Working Other Gardens': Estrangement from Traditional Land

Estrangement is a relationship, one that does not require that the partners to it believe in their absolute alienation from shared resources. 'Working other gardens' captures the sense in which the transnational PNG household exists even in the absence of some marriage partners' access to clan lands. In this section, I investigate the nature of estrangement from clan lands and gardens typical of the transnational PNG household. My ethnography shows the moral paradox that grounds it; the PNG household rests on the solidarity created through international remittances and on the estrangement that is felt by people who no longer work together in gardens made on their clan lands. Here, I am concerned to show how that moral paradox shapes the household's history and its present.

There are three ways in which the transnational PNG household emerges as a social unit for 'working other gardens': first, through the loss of access to traditional lands used to support non-traditional economies and means of creating wealth; second, through long-term, multi-generational neglect of payment of bride wealth; and, third, through marriages made across cultural and linguistic groups with very different patterns of inheritance. Case Set 1 shows households constituted by traditional and non-traditional marriages under conditions where land has been used for non-traditional purposes. Case Set 2 shows what I interpret as symbolically constructed *wantok* households constituted by marriages made without strong commitments to meeting clan-wide obligations to bride wealth gifts, and often in the absence of shared traditional practices for these. Bride wealth in these cases is used to legalise a marriage for the Australian immigration office, or to solemnise it with the symbols of tradition. Case Set 3 shows non-*wantok* households constituted over several generations by marriages made between men and women who are not of the same language group and, thus, have come to have no access to clan lands through their marriages, as well as a fragile relationship to clan lands through their descent from parents from different regions and language groups.

Case Set 1: Traditional and Non-Traditional Marriages, Estrangement from Land

The first set of case studies shows marriages between *wantoks* that have been made according to tradition. Nevertheless, some of their kin have agreed to pass clan lands into non-traditional use, and have thereby excluded other kin from access to it. Clanspersons are excluded when the land is harnessed for use in primary resource extraction, preventing horticulturalists from enjoying its use for gardening. They are also excluded when land is degraded by timber extraction or following over cropping for corporate or industrial agriculture. In these cases, clanspersons' access to garden lands remains secure, but the means of gaining a livelihood from the gardens does not.

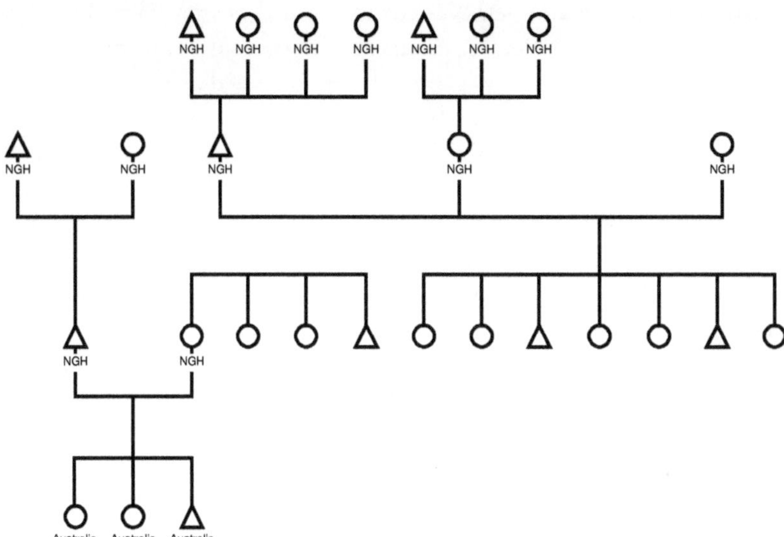

Figure 6.1: Traditional Marriage, While Land is Under Development

Key: Triangle = male; circle = female; horizontal link below = marriage; horizontal link above = siblings; vertical link = descent.

Source: Fieldwork data.

In Figure 6.1, which shows three generations of a household in a coffee-growing region of the PNG Highlands, the residence of different members shifts over the years. The eldest generation, all of whom were born and lived a lifetime in the New Guinea Highlands, planted the coffee and benefited from the crops. The second generation were educated on the profits from the coffee plantations and found work in provincial capitals, as well as Port Moresby, after training to become health and education professionals in PNG during the time of independence. The household genealogy shows that they were born and married in different places across the country. The third generation attended tertiary education institutions and hold degrees. They arrived in Australia in the same decade that the coffee plantation failed to bear profits to support their lives in their home region. Citing violence between household and clans as a reason for leaving, and prepared to make their livelihoods while employed on company contracts with a mining company, these families say that their careers in Australia are 'their only remaining gardens'. In short, they are saying that they are environmental and economic refugees seeking a substitute for making a living from horticulture.

Figure 6.2 shows marriages that, over several generations, have alienated relatives from one another. Not surprisingly, these marriages have been made between Papua New Guineans and 'Europeans'—for the most part, white Australian. Of the two cases from this set that I have chosen to discuss, one stands out for its depth of knowledge about the generational history of a family. It links the household history of a marriage in the early colonial era, between a German man and a New Guinean woman and, a decade later, between an Englishman and a Papuan woman. After World War I, the German father was repatriated and the wife remarried a man of 'mixed ancestry' from the south coast of the Territory of Papua. Subsequently, the children of the family were split between the Territory of New Guinea, Germany and Australia. In the second generation, each of the children experienced difficulties just making their marriages and in finding land to settle on. In the period between the wars, social norms dictated that people of 'mixed race' would be treated as undesirable marriage partners unless they were in regular employment. Relatives often refused bride wealth from 'mixed-race' men, sometimes even if the man had the means to make a bride wealth payment. They did not marry according to tradition; rather, most marriages of this kind took place in the church.

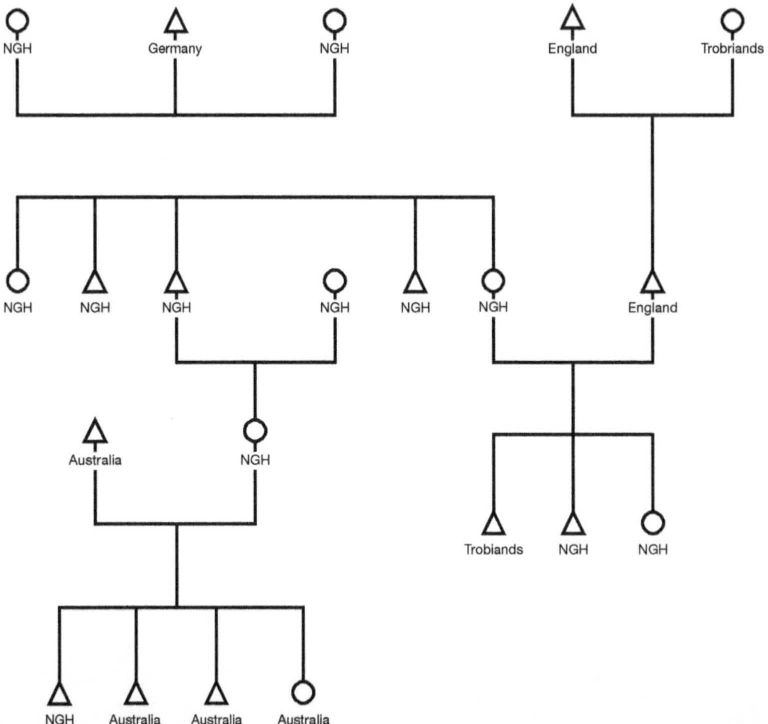

Figure 6.2: Non-Traditional Marriage, Changing Residence

Key: Triangle = male; circle = female; horizontal link below = marriage; horizontal link above = siblings; vertical link = descent.

Source: Fieldwork data.

Over the next two generations, siblings and cousins sent letters to each other and sought to reconnect. The household established in Cairns today provides a point of connection for some of the members. Some of the large, loosely related household members identify with the clans from which they might descend, but this is voiced as a memento of their history, not as evidence of a relationship to that clan or as claims over ownership of clan ground. No members of this household have claims to land in PNG, as so few of their marriages were made according to the traditions that normally would secure access to it.

Case Set 2: Innovative Bride Wealth, Uncertain Access to Traditional Land

The second case set concerns innovative marriages that are not recorded as customary. Figure 6.3 records the history of two generations descending from the marriage of a PNG woman to a New Zealand man. A member of the wife's birth mother's clan adopted her at the age of five. Her adoptive parents educated her, and she acquired a certificate to teach in secondary schools. She did not remit money or gifts to her mother's clanspersons in the village in the years during which she drew a salary for her work as a teacher in PNG. However, she did send money to her father, who was of a different clan than she was, as he had paid her school fees. Now she sends money to her brother and her mother's clanspersons in her village of birth. Her husband reports that he never knew her birth parents, and that her adoptive father did not want to receive bride wealth. He believes sincerely that a gift should be given as if giving a part of himself; he does not wish to give to people he has never met and who did not raise his wife as their daughter. The children of the marriage are young adults who have no claim on land in PNG because the family says that the father did not marry the woman according to custom.

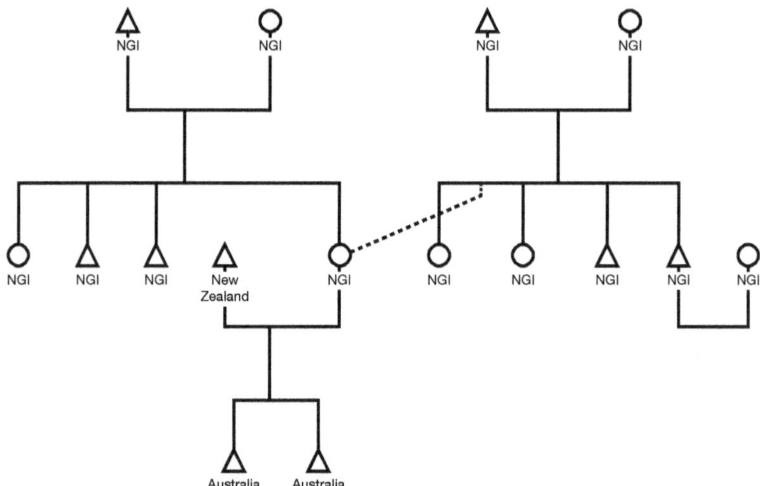

Figure 6.3: Non-Traditional Marriage, Including Traditional Adoption

Key: Triangle = male; circle = female; horizontal link below = marriage; horizontal link above = siblings; vertical link = descent; dotted line = adoption.

Source: Fieldwork data.

What is interesting in Figure 6.3 is how misunderstandings about the history of the wife's parentage and failure to make gifts to key relations attenuated her claims on clan ground while also solidifying her potential claim on it for her sons. Over the 30 years of their marriage, her husband paid to have a house built for her adoptive brother. She had urged him to do this after her parents died, and he had agreed because he liked the idea that a modern house would be more comfortable for him on the annual visits that he and his wife made to her birth village. However, despite her gifts, the woman still struggled to assert any claim on her clan's ground. Her husband had acted without understanding the gift part of a traditional ceremonial exchange, and had thereby unwittingly married his wife by traditional rituals of the exchange of labour. When an accident occurred and his adoptive brother-in-law died suddenly, he assumed he had lost his advocate for access to clan grounds, but he had not. His wife continued to make a case for him.

There is an irony here; it lies in the fact that because a woman from her own clan had raised her, and because, by PNG law and by her local custom, her mother's sister is also her mother, the woman was a member of both her mothers and her brother's clan by matter of her birth to her mother and her adoption into her mother's sister's clan (the same), which are both conventional ways of affiliating members to a matrilineal clan. A deeper irony lies in the fact that bride wealth normally is given from the husband to the brothers of the wife, rather than to her father or mother, and this woman's husband did exactly that by building a house for his brother-in-law. In short, her relatives did not recognise the house as a form of bride wealth, largely because her husband had made it in accordance with his intention to give them a gift, and not in accordance with their requirements that ceremonial exchange of traditional bride wealth meet their expectations.

Case Set 3: Bride Wealth Household Solidarity and Estrangement from Land

The third set of case studies shows marriages between PNG men and women from different parts of PNG, for whom regional differences in place of birth means they were not *wantoks* before marriage. The example is that of a household founded on a marriage between a man from Port Moresby and a woman from Lae. They are the children of parents who lived and worked in different regional capitals. He was the son of man from Rabaul, where (matrilineal) tradition rules that individuals gain access to ground by way of their mother's claims on it, and of a mother from the Highlands who had been working as a nurse in the provincial capital and whose clan's (patrilineal) tradition rules that individuals gain access to gardens by way of their father's claims on it.

In the case of the husband, neither of his parents had secured traditional access to clan lands in the regions of their birth. They were children of marriages in those regions that did not give them simple access to clan lands by way of clan membership. In addition, the careers of his parents and grandparents' generation took them to different regional centres and away from the opportunities they needed to establish access to clan grounds by working alongside their cousins and winning respect for their efforts to meet traditional obligations. The wife of the household was the daughter of a woman from Bougainville, where civil war had prevented her return to develop clan grounds, and of a man from the Trobriands who could not easily pass on land to his children without disrupting his relationship with his younger clanspersons, who were his nephews and nieces. In the past, her grandfathers had married spouses whose offspring would not have ease of access to the clan land of their mother. She had no claims on land through either her grandfathers or grandmothers.

Members of households founded in marriages made across such great social and traditional differences say they do not even begin to consider how they might access each other's gardens. Neither do they believe they have claims to the clan grounds of their respective parents; custom prevents transfers of access to gardens for the children of men or women who are not clanspersons or *wantoks* of the traditional owners. Working gardens in PNG is impossible for the couple I knew, although their PNG-resident kin recognised them as members of their large and complex transnational household by accepting the bride wealth gifts that the man offered. In such cases, bride wealth is 'only symbolic' and is inadequate for the work of winning access to garden lands. Poignantly, the husband commissioned a portrait of his wife adorned in traditional bride wealth, but she had never worn such wealth, neither for her marriage nor for her sittings with the artist.

The children of marriages similar to the example given in Figure 6.4 cannot make direct claims on clan grounds, and will not do so in later years. Instead of trying to access garden lands, or trying to form businesses with clanspersons in PNG, they imagine that a better future for themselves and the next generation of their wholly PNG family exists overseas. One such family chose to resettle in Australia from Port Moresby. They hope, over the course of the next 10 years, to finish their obligations to living relatives, thereafter ceasing to make any ceremonial gifts to kin. Summing up their perspective on the value of meeting their obligations through ceremonial exchange, or through remittances, the couple asserted that it is 'just a waste of money that we need for the household'.

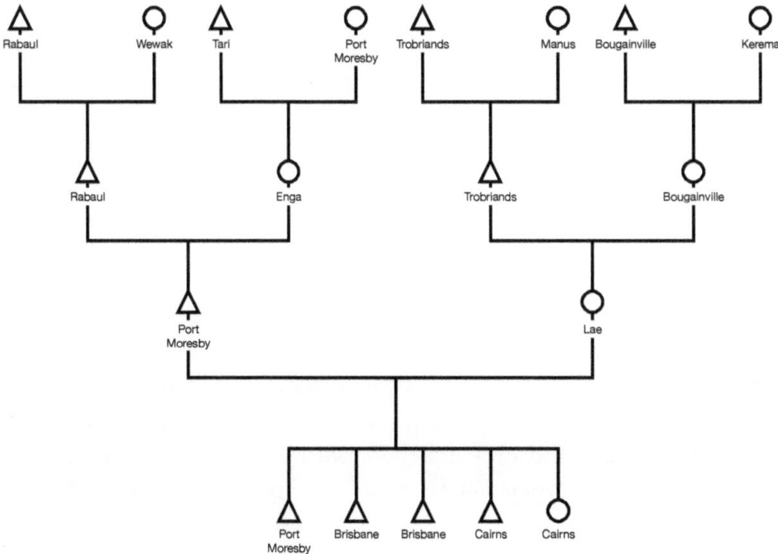

Figure 6.4: Marriage Across Regions Occurring over Four Generations

Key: Triangle = male; circle = female; horizontal link below = marriage; horizontal link above = siblings; vertical link = descent.

Source: Fieldwork data.

All three case sets show that meeting obligations to give ceremonial wealth for marriages, or sending remittances as gifts to clanspersons, is a means for creating a sense of solidarity through the work of making exchanges happen. However, all cases show as well that the same ceremonial wealth and remittances give no assurance that the givers of either form of wealth will not be estranged from the clan lands in which they might have hoped to share, should the receivers of the gifts choose not to recognise it as fitting. Access to land is not ensured; however, members of the diaspora do not live in alienation from their lands, even when estranged from relatives who live on clan grounds. As this moral reality unfolds, the transnational PNG household might turn elsewhere than PNG to satisfy its search for ways to create a good life with its members. At the same time, such households might well keep their link to their country of birth and to kin who do make livelihoods on clan ground.

Papua New Guineans in Australia say that while they are living outside PNG they are 'working other gardens'. Although migration raises opportunities to reflect deeply upon what has been left behind, the idiom does not simply refer to the loss of gardens and their replacement with skilled and professional work in jobs overseas. It is certainly the case that there are many reasons that transnational Papua New Guineans cannot access land, including regional conflict, long-term leasing to resource extraction companies, environmental degradation after years of misuse of soils and obstruction of people's use rights to traditionally owned land. However, none of these experiences of loss of gardens fully embrace why or how they come think of work-life in Australia as 'working other gardens'.

The Papua New Guineans who taught me about their way of making a livelihood said that 'working other gardens' is a new form of 'powerful speech', a complex idiom that carries the sense of the quality of social life created by work. Beyond the obvious meaning of 'working abroad' or 'working overseas', their work is often directed towards the goal of creating a good livelihood, and provides them with a rationale for attending to social norms even as they seek to realise their individual hopes. 'Working other gardens' is a metaphor. The phrase grasps both the moral economy of working *other* gardens, and evinces the sensibility of a political economy in which they must work *others'* gardens. There is ruefulness in their tone; as they shared their bitter humour about the conditions of living transnationally in that evening's gathering in northern Australia, the idiom 'working other gardens' took on new meanings. Replacing 'other' as an adjective meaning 'different' with a plural possessive pronoun connoting 'dispossession' creates a revolution in their understanding of social life, one in which solidarity with others becomes uncertain, and accompanies estrangement from others as a mobile, or uneven, moral reality unfolds in the transnational PNG household.

The Moral Economy of 'Working Other Gardens' as Moral Reality

My conclusions, drawn from interviews with 60 PNG households with residences in Australia, have been analysed as four distinct claims. First, the PNG household is distributed across several nations, and is, therefore, transnational. Second, the PNG household comprises relationships by marriage with those who are not Papua New Guinean by descent as well as those who are, and relationships by friendship with those who are committed to household solidarity. Third, marriages in the PNG household constitute the moral reality of the household by enhancing its solidarity. Fourth, that solidarity is won with the household member's recognition of their deepening estrangement from traditional access to land in the homeland. Finally, having analysed the ethnography of the transnational PNG household, it is possible to interpret the conversation I introduced at the beginning of this chapter to comment on the insights won with an ethnographic approach to moral reality.

In introducing the transnational PNG household, I conveyed the sense that contemporary movement across the Coral Sea to 'work other gardens' is difficult for reasons quite different from the ancient fear of rough crossings. In the twenty-first century, the narrowest crossing of the Torres Strait between PNG and Australia is a shallow passage that can be traversed easily by boat. Flights between Cairns and Port Moresby leave every two hours, and those between Brisbane, Sydney, Melbourne and PNG's national capital are nearly as frequent. However, travellers must give good explanations for their coming and going to immigration officers in Australia. Papua New Guineans who are now Australian citizens hold hard-won PNG work visas in their hands. Immigration officers inspect carefully secured temporary residency permits and permanent residency papers; the Papua New Guineans I spoke with were increasingly finding that work movements and bureaucratic difficulties in securing documents in PNG were taking a toll.

Papua New Guineans in Australia feel a growing frustration and anxiety about the restrictions on their movement. Over the course of an evening with a half-dozen PNG men and women in Far North Queensland, I heard them complain about the various contemporary visas, which they described as impediments to ease of movement and as detrimental to the quality of living for members of the transnational PNG household.

They also spoke about how the many Australian investments in PNG terribly affected the PNG environment. Industrial effluent had damaged some PNG coastal waters. Only in the previous week, some of those newly arrived in Australia by boat from PNG had seen silt from mining operations emptied into a harbour, making its shallows difficult to navigate. They considered this a tragedy.

After a brief pause, followed by a heavy sigh, one man made a loudly spoken observation that it looked like 'the land bridge will rise from the sea again to link PNG and Australia' as a result of damage from Australian mining in PNG. He smiled. Although this was certainly a bitter sense of humour—seeing a long-term positive in an environmental disaster—the group erupted with laughter. They surmised that soon they would be able simply to walk across the narrowest parts of the Torres Strait and arrive in Queensland. 'Forget airplanes, boats and visas. The countries of PNG and Australia will be one whole place again', and Australians and Papua New Guineans will live on the wretched earth together. For some time after, people wiped tears of laughter from their eyes while they repeated to the room that the land bridge once present between New Guinea and Australia would rise again, and 'everyone can walk on that bridge to find our pre-history'. Their joking played with the ordinary historical account. Instead of looking to the past, they gave a tragicomical account of how they had come to be where they were now 'working other gardens' in Australia, distant from the clan-owned lands and gardens they had left behind.

How people recount the ways in which they come to live with each other reveals much about their identity and also provides a record of the moral reality of their present and future social actions. The anthropologist, like the historian, finds many ways of telling and writing other people's shared experience. One example is the work of anthropologist turned novelist Drusilla Modjeska. In *The Mountain*, Modjeska (2012) uses literary devices to create a novel peopled with compelling characters imagined through the details of the lives of the complex personalities who led PNG to independence in the mid-1970s. Another example is that of journalist Sean Dorney (2016) who has called for better contemporary history of the deep association between PNG and Australia, including Australian involvement in PNG's recent political and social tragedies and triumphs. The retired parliamentarian Carol Kidu (2014) has called half a century of international relations between Australia and PNG a 'gentle history' of individual people in families, schools and shared work. Here, I am concerned with the moral reality expressed as 'working other gardens' by which people share in each other's interests in a good life together.

In this chapter, I have described idiomatic usages of the notion of 'working other gardens' to capture its centrality in the many levels of the contemporary moral economy. I have shown how the ethnographic idiom 'working other gardens' captures the reality of the twenty–first century division of labour that defines the PNG transnational family's solidarity and estrangement today, yet ties this family to abiding moral qualities of PNG-village life thriving on garden work. I used their insight into the power to make sense of their contemporary experience in ancient ways by describing it as 'working other gardens' in contrast to how their residence in Australia is accounted for in the analysis of 2011 Australian census data. The sense of the idiom shaping household solidarity is found in the social and moral core of the political history of migration, which I show is shaped by the legacy of marriages of PNG women to non–Papua New Guineans, or to Papua New Guineans from different regions of their country. The third sense of the idiom, found in their estrangement from traditional land, is revealed in close analysis of bride wealth payments made by men who were not members of the same language group, or *wantoks*, before marriage. For them, the consequence of paying bride wealth inappropriately has meant that both they and their children have been estranged from clanspersons and clan lands.

The different uses of the idiom show that 'working other gardens' is a 'moral fact' (Karsenti, 2012) in Durkheim's sense; that is, it reproduces the material social conditions that sustain the idea of a good life as they work to realise it. In classical anthropological terms, moral facts, like those expressed by the idiom 'working other gardens' and working as a form of practical reason, exist as the very ground of people's livelihoods, displacing any notion of the primacy of utilitarian or ends-based reasoning. Durkheim, and those working in his legacy (Evans-Pritchard, 1937; Mary Douglas, 1973) have been much criticised for failing to distinguish the social from the moral life (see Howell, 1996). However, others believe that an upending of this criticism is overdue because it has obscured the strongest points of Durkheim's (1984/1933) early book, *The Division of Labour in Society* (see Fassin, 2012). After Durkheim, anthropologists could claim profound understanding of the grounds for speaking of society, and for reflecting on how a good life is shared. To grasp the importance of Durkheim's early studies of morality, one must contemplate the more provocative question of what people intend when they up stakes and move to unknown places. This chapter works critically within that tradition, revealing the moral reality of the transnational PNG family by describing how its members are 'working other gardens' as the ground of both their solidarity and their estrangement.

Thinking of 'garden work' as an ethical and aesthetic claim to relations that span seas and land is not new in the region. When Malinowski (1936) wrote in *Coral Gardens and their Magic* (his most significant volume on the Trobriand Islands, to the south-east of mainland PNG) that the aim of gardening was to make good yams to give to others, he was asserting the nature of moral reality. In later years, Alfred Gell (1999) reminded us that good yam gardens are also beautiful because they make food available to others to eat. Working a good garden means creating a good life together; thus, seeing a good yam could come to be attractive to anyone. However, the transnational PNG household is also estranged from those kin who are landowners. This too is a moral fact.

By working other gardens, the transnational PNG household emerges as a fact—a moral reality. Karsenti (2012) called on a theory of moral reality in his insightful Kantian reading of Durkheim's (1984/1933) work, exploring the revolution in moral philosophy as an event with the power of a bomb dropped on the ground of economic reason. For Karsenti, Durkheim revolutionised scholarly knowledge about the grounds of society by showing how they exist in human moral judgements, as well as in the prescriptive social norms that such judgements make and challenge. Morality is not to be studied as philosophy, but rather as a reality people make. For Durkheim, and for those who have worked critically within the legacy of his work, morality is a living, unfolding moral fact, and not just a social norm instituted by the ideal of a distributive morality in liberal democracy (for a different interpretation see Giddens, 1971). Accordingly, the living moral fact is constituted by crossing the gap between the sanctions raised against moral and legal infractions and the individual desire to 'do good' (Karsenti, 2012, p. 23) because neither the rule nor the collective desire for the good is a satisfactory definition of morality in itself.

A moral economy of the transnational PNG household exists at the level at which 'reality unfolds as actions and judgments of actions' (Karsenti, 2012, p. 35)—as the ethnography of moral reasoning (Sykes, 2009)—where words become deeds and social actions become important for their capacity to capture contradictory processes. With a sustained description of the idiom 'working other gardens' as a point of critical reflection and political action, this chapter captures the transnational PNG household's understanding of the division of labour in society. It explains PNG households' sense of estrangement, as much as solidarity, at the very least in the sense that 'other gardens' are others' gardens, and not fully possessed by the gardener working them.

References

Dalton, N. (2014, October 25). 'Island states' buyers love Cairns. *Cairns Post*, p. 13.

Department of Immigration and Citizenship. (n.d.). *The PNG-Born*. Canberra, ACT: Government of the Commonwealth of Australia. Retrieved from www.dss.gov.au/sites/default/files/documents/02_2014/papua_new_guinea.pdf

Dorney, S. (2016). *The embarrassed colonialist: A Lowy Institute paper*. Canberra, ACT: The Lowy Institute, Penguin Specials.

Douglas, M. (1973). The logical basis of constructed reality. In M. Douglas (Ed.), *Rules and meanings: Essays in the knowledge of everyday knowledge* (pp. 23–70). Oxford, England: Routledge.

Durkheim, E. (1984). *The division of labour in society* (E. Halls, Trans.). New York, NY: The Free Press. (Original work published 1933).

Evans-Pritchard, E. E. (1937). *Witchcraft, oracles, and magic among the Azande*. Clarendon, England: Oxford.

Fassin, D. (Ed.). (2012). *Moral anthropology*. Oxford, England: Blackwells.

Gell, A. (1999). *The art of anthropology: Essays and diagrams*. New Brunswick, NJ: Athlone Press.

Giddens, A. (1971). *Capitalism and modern social theory: An analysis of the writings of Marx, Durkheim and Max Weber*. Cambridge, England: Cambridge University Press. doi.org/10.1017/CBO9780511803109

Howell, S. (1996). *The ethnography of moralities*. London, England: Taylor and Francis.

Karsenti, B. (2012). Durkheim and the moral fact. In D. Fassin (Ed.), *A companion to moral anthropology* (pp. 19–36). Oxford, England: Blackwells.

Kidu, C. (2014, 3 November). The importance of people to people relationships between PNG & Australia. *Australia-PNG Network*. Retrieved from auspng.lowyinstitute.org/publications/importance-people-people-relationships-between-papua-new-guinea-australia

Malinowski, B. (1936). *Coral gardens and their magic* (Vols. 1 & 2). London, England: Routledge.

Modjeska, D. (2012). *The mountain.* Sydney, NSW: Vintage Australia.

Sykes, K. (2009). Residence: Moral Reasoning in a Common Place—Paradoxes of a Global Age. In K. Sykes (Ed.), *Ethnographies of moral reasoning: Living paradoxes in a global age* (pp. 3–40). New York, NY: Palgrave. doi.org/10.1057/9780230617957_1

Sykes, K. (2013). Mortgaging the bridewealth: Problems with brothers and problems with value. *HAU: Journal of Ethnographic Theory, 3*(2), 97–117. doi.org/10.14318/hau3.2.007

Thompson, E. P. (1993). *Customs in common.* New York, NY: The New Press.

7

Cycles of Integration and Fragmentation: Changing Yolngu–Balanda Sentiments of the 'Good Life' in Northern Australia

Fiona Magowan

Introduction

Almost 20 years ago, on 24 June 1998, the first woman elected to the Northern Territory parliament, Senator Trish Crossan,[1] began her opening speech by defining the 'good life' as living on Yolngu country, learning cultural ways and upholding and acknowledging the rights of the Indigenous citizens of her constituency. In political discourse around Indigenous issues, such 'good' intentions can counter the 'authoritarian moralism' that informs Australian neoliberal ideology, as Wacquant (as cited in Altman, 2010, p. 266) has argued, but they

1 Crossin taught at Yirrkala in the 1980s and is Chair of the Senate Legal and Constitutional Affairs Legislation Committee. She made an apology to the Stolen Generations in this speech. She is also a speaker of Yolngu matha (language) and addressed members as follows: *Nhamirr bukmak? Manymak walnga nganapurr nhinan ngarra ga gurrutumirr ngarrak, ngunhal Yirrkala wangangur. Yolngu walal ngarrak djaka, ga gurrutu gathar ngarrak ga marnggikungal ngarran Yolngu Romgu. Buku—wekan mhuma, wanga—watangun Yolngun, nhe ngarrak, djaka.* 'Those words translated mean thank you for welcoming my family and I, for allowing us to live on your land and for the opportunity to understand your culture. I give a public undertaking to work hard to represent them and to continue to respect and acknowledge their rights' (Lawrence, 2013).

may also unconsciously mute competing perspectives by highlighting sameness over *différance* (Derrida, 1968).[2] Therefore, the intersubjective complexities and politically motivated agendas surrounding terms like the 'good life' in cross-cultural settings require close attention to how *différance* is 'announced' or 'recalled' through language, in turn inviting new forms of temporality, 'play' and the emergence of 'a middle voice' (Derrida, 1968, pp. 261, 284).[3] Forty years after Derrida coined the term *différance,* Hart's (2013, 2015) theory of the 'human economy' placed the plurality of human perspectives at the core of achieving 'economic democracy' working from the grassroots to the global. He argued that 'the human economy was everywhere, including in the cracks of modern societies. This goes with treating markets and money in a variety of forms as human universals' (Hart, 2013, p. 18). Hart (2015, p. 6) specifically argued for an approach that views the global as an extension and outworking of local values and practices. Thus, the imagined futures that local people aspire to should be recognised and encouraged by the larger economic system and those in power (Hart, 2013, p. 18). Since the terms of recognition require agreement, it is in this nexus that Hart (2013) perceived 'the scope for revolution' (p. 22) and the recombination of different kinds of economic institutions and frameworks. By giving credence to the 'body of customs, laws and history' that have been concealed or indeed 'repressed' by dominant forces, he argued that their value was potentially to 'humanize' economic processes (pp. 24–25).

In this chapter, I suggest that the tools needed to engage effectively with economic struggles in Aboriginal contexts are those of language and culture. By bringing out how linguistically mediated practices shape socioeconomic change, some scholars have shown how the language of relationships may be used to manage intercultural ventures and handle

2 Derrida's (1968) term '*différance*' combines Freud's definition of 'differing' as 'discernibility, distinction, deviation' with 'deferring' as 'detour, delay, relay, reserve' (pp. 292–93). In a complex treatise on *différance*, Derrida, following Bataille, argued for 'the economic character of difference' and its delayed effects or 'trace' that 'dislocates, displaces and refers beyond itself' (pp. 294, 297). The application of *différance* in this chapter is intended to draw the reader's attention to a play of positions, concepts and linguistic disruptions that shape crisis, precarity and hope in aspirations for and imagination of the 'good life'.

3 Some aspects of this essay were first presented at the final Economic and Social Research Council (ESRC) Domestic Moral Economy conference, 'The Quest for the Good Life in Precarious Times: Grassroots Perspectives on the Value Question in the 21st Century', 24–26 March 2015, University of Manchester. I am most grateful to Jon Altman for insights and discussions on these issues, and to Chris Gregory and Karen Sykes for broader perspectives on the domestic moral economy in the Asia–Pacific. The project was supported by the ESRC (2011–15).

conflicts (Adler & Elmhorst, 2008).[4] Yet, while some reviews of Australian employment statistics claim that the situation is improving in certain areas (e.g. around Closing the Gap targets for Indigenous employment), the language of what constitutes advantage and disadvantage continues to be variously misunderstood cross culturally.[5] This situation presents challenges for achieving a sense of parity between Yolngu and Balanda (non-Aboriginal people of European descent). It manifests where Balanda governments use the language of 'target setting', a notion that is typically at odds with Yolngu ways of asserting their 'self-perception of presence' (Derrida, 1968, p. 291) in a range of economic contexts.

The spaces in which the presencing of a 'middle voice' occurs receive less attention than policies that propound economic gain and productivity, resulting in play becoming enfolded in, and constrained by, competing political positions. As Altman (2009) noted, the self-regulation required for neoliberal productivity can entangle citizens in complex relations with the state, in which it 'at once acknowledges difference while simultaneously disciplining, constraining and regulating otherness' (p. 10). Moreover, as Peterson (2005) observed, 'there is always the threat of politicization of inequality by any one of a number of external interests' (p. 13). While recognising such constraints, I follow Hart's (2013) approach to human economy, which is:

> Informed by an economic vision capable of bridging the gap between everyday life (what people know) and humanity's common predicament, which is inevitably impersonal and lies beyond the actor's point of view (what they don't know). (p. 3)

In the Australian context, Altman (2010) outlined how this tension is embedded across four key tropes influencing culture and policy discourses around the 'crisis of [Aboriginal] culture' (pp. 266–270). First, the crisis

4 Adler and Elmhorst (2008) have shown that misunderstandings do not only arise from material demands or their lack, but from the kinds of conflict-management styles and concepts that workers experience as either confrontational or non-confrontational. S.-Y. Kim, J. Kim and Lim (2013, p. 58) also discussed how Westerners engage with confrontation, which involves competition and collaboration, while Easterners adopt non-confrontational practices of avoidance and compromise (Morris et al., 1998; Tang & Kirkbride, 1986; Ting-Toomey, 1988).

5 The Prime Minister's *Closing the Gap* report (Australian Government, 2015, p. 5) asserted that decreasing gap targets in areas of mortality rates for children under five, and Year 12 attainment rates, are both on track. Meanwhile, the language of the good life in the new Forrest review (Altman, 2014) has been criticised for failing 'to demonstrate an appreciation of the significance of local cultural and social realities in shaping the existing forms of economic activity in which Aboriginal and Torres Strait Islander people already engage' (Lahn, 2014, p. 2).

is represented in a tension between economic impoverishment and rates of violence in the media; second, scholars and politicians (e.g. Noel Pearson, Peter Sutton and others) highlight negative influences in particular regions where they consider cultural practices to have contributed to 'passive welfare'; third, the idea of a crisis is promoted by 'neoconservative thinkers' who champion entrepreneurial independence for Aboriginal people; and, fourth, the goal of such independence is evidenced in an overemphasis on education as a panacea for welfare ills, regardless of lived differences (Altman, 2010, p. 267). In this framework, the reason why 'closing the gap' has been difficult to advance is because issues are 'intergenerational', changing trends are hard to estimate and disadvantages need to be considered in terms of 'reducing disparities' (Altman, Biddle & Hunter, 2008, pp. 17–18). By comparing competing interpretations of crisis, we can see how the incommensurable aspects of intercultural *différance* are evoked in the spaces in between, although they often are too diffuse or difficult to account for or to enter political agendas. For example, the 2008 Closing the Gap reforms[6] unproblematically assumed a shared language related to proposed outcomes across Yolngu and non-Yolngu domains, which ultimately rendered differences in Yolngu culture, language and life, as well as *différance*, invisible.

Some anthropologists have shown how commodification has created new kinds of conflict. In Central Australia, Austin-Broos (2003, as cited in Peterson, 2005) has demonstrated how relations around commodities compete with relationships that are long established through connections to place, land and religious law, and which once provided the basis of economic engagement. Peterson (2005) asserted that understanding the interpersonal dynamics of cultural issues is critical to achieving successful development processes for Indigenous livelihood, but that it has been extremely difficult to bring these cultural issues to the fore in development projects because the premises they raise present a complexity not readily able to be taken into account. However, as we shall see from the cases presented below, optimal modes of engagement take seriously the implications of *différance*, since achieving goals and targets involves 'allocative power', which MacDonald (2000, pp. 96–99) defined as the 'relative ability to respond to demands'. Allocative power entails

6 The Minister for Indigenous Affairs, Jenny Macklin, delivered the 2008 annual lecture commemorating the Mabo judgment on native title and questioned the poverty experienced by many Aboriginal Australians living on great wealth in terms of land ownership, a paradox a former federal minister, Amanda Vanstone, had identified (Altman, 2009, p. 1).

understanding how Yolngu wellbeing is dependent, in part, on the extent to which Yolngu linguistic and cultural interpretations of the good life diverge from neoliberal agendas, and how their effects create imbalance.

For Yolngu, the good life is more accurately translated as the 'right path', the 'right way' or as 'having power'. Understanding the good life for Yolngu entails recognising the emotional, practical and cultural dimensions of 'aspiration and agency' and implementing 'structural opportunities' that lead to 'dignity and fairness', as well as 'commitments to meaningful (moral) projects' (Fischer, 2014, pp. 207–12).

This chapter examines how Yolngu concepts of the good life work through cycles of integration that stem from periods when a broader sense of 'allocative power' is admitted in relation to all aspects of livelihood. It considers how these perspectives alternate with experiences of alienation or competition, which can lead to unhealthy individualism and fragmentation, dispersing energies in conflict negotiation rather than allowing them to be managed effectively or capitalising on them for other kinds of outcomes. As we shall see, some Balanda recognise the paradoxes (and presencing) of *différance* that new targets for employment or development create, and have devised means of exploring such issues with Yolngu themselves, rather than simply aiming to introduce change to achieve targets. However, understanding a 'middle voice' of shared practice requires movements and mediations from both providers and workers to enable healthy interdependence and to develop immunity from policy that detracts from wellbeing.

The Good Life on Galiwin'ku

The town of Galiwin'ku is 550 kilometres north-east of Darwin, located in the southern corner of Elcho Island in north-east Arnhem Land.[7] The island is 55 kilometres long and 6 kilometres wide at its broadest point. In the 2011 census, 1,890 Aboriginal and Torres Strait residents were accounted for in a total population of 2,124. Established in 1942 by the Methodist Overseas Mission and run by the mission superintendent, Reverend Harold Shepherdson, Yolngu were benevolently disciplined

7 Galiwin'ku is the name of the town on the island and also of the island itself. In English it is known as Elcho Island. The regional population of north-east Arnhem Land is 9,098, of which Aboriginal and Torres Strait Islanders make up 91.2 per cent (Australian Bureau of Statistics [ABS], 2011).

into a Protestant work ethic. The mission sought to provide a Christian education as well as to skill the population for work. Men were trained in carpentry and agriculture and women in domestic-related tasks. Following the Whitlam Government's introduction of self-determination policies in 1972, the mission administration was handed over to Galiwin'ku Community Incorporated to empower local decision-making. The Galiwin'ku Community Council, comprising 12 clan elders, was created under the *Aboriginal Councils and Associations Act 1976* (see also Schwarz, 2006, p. 74). In 2008, the East Arnhem Regional Council was established under the *Local Government Act (NT)* to provide services to nine remote communities, including Galiwin'ku, which belongs to one of six wards, the Gumurr Marthakal Ward. In 2014, nine local authorities replaced the former community advisory boards of the remote communities. Elected representatives from the regional council meet with representatives from the Galiwin'ku local authority to agree on the administration of services on the island. Residents in town also have access to 29 homelands across the region, whose infrastructure is delivered by the Marthakal Homelands Resource Centre.[8]

Visions of the good life often refer to the early mission periods when there were key individuals to whom one related. Today, the good life is consistently referred to by Yolngu men and women aged 30 and above as living on their homelands with the potential to hunt, gather, spend time in the bush looking for yams, collect shellfish and being on country, whether simply being there, or painting, or organising or participating in ritual activities. Homelands offer year-round access to a wide range of bush foods, marine life, shellfish and mammals, which supplement a Western-based town diet.[9] These activities bring a sense of dignity, interconnectedness and relationship with land and family, shared toil, commensality, generosity and camaraderie. The reasons why the emotional and dietary benefits of homeland life are felt to outweigh the practical challenges of living away from town for this age group is not just because they provide a release from the pressures of semi-urban living, and a change from Western food—the latter most commonly comprising meat, some vegetables, bread, rice, damper, syrup, biscuits and tea, alongside popular

8 The 2011 ABS census notes that there were 184 private dwellings occupied across these homelands and 264 homes occupied in Galiwin'ku town. In total, in 2011, there were 393 families in the town and 2,124 residents (ABS, 2011).

9 Homelands in the Northern Territory will continue to receive basic levels of funding until 2022 as part of the Stronger Futures policies. (Altman, 2015).

daily use of three takeaways in the town—but because homeland living fosters empowerment and affinity with the right paths (*dhukarr*) of moral and physical sustenance for a healthy lifestyle. In addition, there are also serious jural reasons for living on homelands or outstations—to ensure the proper maintenance of the country both ritually and environmentally and to tend graves and transmit the crucial knowledge of law and order that persists within environmental relations.

The positive effects of living on homelands include distance from problems in towns, opportunities to enhance culture and language for the next generation, inspiration for art and ritual, having a sense of being at home with the authority and power to decide for oneself and the time and space to teach the stories that hold the power of the Law. Yingiya Guyula (as cited in Christie, 2010) spoke about how his ancestors:

> Told stories through looking at the first thunderstorm of the year, standing tall and straight when it calls out, and I feel strong, stand up strong and the tears run out from my eyes remembering the land, where I am, and it gives me a new knowledge. (p. 72)

Support for homeland living is provided by chartered flights, visits from health professionals, access to solar power and care for the environment in ranger activities and government bushfire management programs.[10]

The Language of 'Allocative Power' in the Good Life

In an effort 'to engage more concretely with the world that lies beyond the familiar institutions immediately securing people's rights and interest' (Hart, 2013, p. 6) and to generate dialogue around how the good life is constituted from different perspectives, a small group of Balanda service providers and Yolngu were invited to share their aspirations for, and experiences of, the good life during a half-day focus group in Darwin in 2015. The event brought together seven stakeholders (two Yolngu and five Balanda)[11] from financial services, the Anglican and Uniting churches, linguistic services and community development to consider the language

10 Further information is available at apo.org.au/system/files/14480/apo-nid14480-35086.pdf

11 The Balanda comprised three women and two men; one Yolngu man and one Yolngu woman also attended.

of the good life and intercultural difference. These participants emphasised that the good life was underpinned by wants and needs (*djäl)*, noting that the Yolngu term goes beyond self-centred or selfish expressions to mandated desires relating to Yolngu law that should be complied with, alongside transcendent desires such as serving God and making a positive contribution to society.

However, given the competing referents of *djäl*, one Balanda participant noted that 'you don't really know what the good life is until it is tested'. In response, a Yolngu contributor explained what the good life meant to him: 'Everything would be good within the family and between families as well. Our homeland too … *mägaya wänga* (a peaceful place)'. He went on to consider how, when the balance between clans, land and law is disturbed—perhaps when some people win greater access to resources than others—it can affect the emotional energy or power of those involved in decision-making, leaving them feeling disempowered (*märrmiriw)*. This sense of societal imbalance generates a state without peace (*mägayamirriw*) that can only be rectified by a return to right relations through customary law (*rom*). He emphasised the moral process involved in understanding the right way of taking responsibility for managing and distributing resources by kin rather than having or acquiring products or material items as status symbols of the good life.

One participant noted how different expectations around practices of measuring can emerge between the two-value systems due to the different emphases given to qualitative and quantitative mechanisms of apportioning and distribution. A community development worker put it this way:

> When you're into distributions you look around and you give and make some sort of assessment, some sort of calculation how it will work: that looks about right, enough, yes, that's the right amount *(gana, yo, dhunupa)*. But when you apportion, then there is this cutting and dividing (*mittmitthun ga djalthan-ngupan*): all measured, all calculated, all estimated. But no-one is doing that. People are allocating not apportioning.

Among Yolngu, there is trust among their own leaders and those with authority that they will make the right allocations and distributions, aligned with the relative power that they have to make those decisions. Yet, in contrast, the Balanda banking system requires that trust is also placed in those who have knowledge of national and international strategic investments and income-management processes that rely upon techniques of apportioning. These distinct processes can, at times, lead to misconstrual by some Balanda who deal with Yolngu finance as mismanaging monetary affairs instead of recognising that they are prioritising culturally distinct modes of 'allocative power' through their knowledge of monetary and relational practice. Such differing values, and the embodied practices they infer, are further underlined by the ways in which banks have generated 'borrowed' terms to explain their services. For example, to translate the concept of a bank, it was noted in this focus group that the equivalent would be a 'money house' (*rrupiyang dhu wänga*), but more often people would talk of going to the 'TCU' (Traditional Credit Union), a term that they say is taken for granted and, as such, does not necessarily facilitate a full understanding of the banking processes involved.

In exploring this issue, Balanda and Yolngu participants discussed how they might educate Yolngu families about bank loans. In the Yolngu context, it was explained that a bank loan is like a *garul*, a place where you can collect and eat yams. The concept of the loan was aligned with asking someone from another clan whether they could take their *garul,* which would otherwise be forbidden. Just as the bank decides whether to approve a loan, so, in the Yolngu context, it was explained how a traditional owner might debate whether to allow the *garul* to be harvested. Such translations of economic practice can offer conceptual and linguistic conduits for the negotiation of values to assist in realising intercultural business models.

In situ service providers have, for some time, identified the need for an 'economic literacy program' in Yolngu language to convey contemporary economic terms (Trudgen, 2014, p. 35). Much careful, detailed work on the cross-cultural competencies needed to facilitate enterprise development, as well as culturally nuanced analyses of human resource management, has been undertaken by the Arnhem Human Enterprise Development Project (AHED) since 2012. This project runs in conjunction with the Why Warriors organisation, established on Galiwin'ku in 2001 by Richard and Tim Trudgen. It is recognised that one of the key elements in facilitating sustainable development projects is the need to educate families about business requirements. To this end, a series of programs on Yolngu economy have been broadcast on Yolngu Radio, and an e-learning program has been established for facility in Yolngu matha (language). Working with 15 leaders on Galiwin'ku, the AHED project has identified more than 40 possible industries and potentially hundreds of businesses that could be established if full support were available (Trudgen, 2014, p. 2).

These Yolngu aspirations are not new. Over 30 years ago, Yolngu visions of business development were evident in their decisions about how they should run their affairs on homelands. In 1987, there was one Balanda builder on Galiwin'ku working for the outstations along with a Yolngu (Watt, 1988). At this time, there was recognition by those on the Resource Centre committee that clans ought to have more say from the start in the development of their homeland priorities. The following year, at Yirrkala, the Laynhapuy Homelands Association outlined their goals as needing 'to determine [our] own future; to manage our own affairs; and to develop towards gaining self-sufficiency' (Watt, 1988, p. 26).[12] Yet, as Hart (2013) explained, 'the real task is to work out how states, cities, big money and the rest might be selectively combined with citizens' initiatives to promote a more democratic world society' (p. 4). Thus, when considering the mechanisms needed to effect culturally appropriate business development, it is important to know both what constitutes the good life—the 'right way' (*dhunupa dhukarr*) to 'empowerment' (*mārrmirr*)[13]—and, also, how hardship or disempowerment is conceived and from whose perspective. By privileging a self-sustaining economy *and* the infrastructure costs needed to deliver it, the concerns of the financial system often override cultural and relational dynamics. A senior Yolngu woman explained to me how she viewed the ongoing effects of neoliberal government agendas[14] that have tried to reshape Yolngu society, and which have affected the 'right blood' and feeling of respect that people have for their culture and their law:

12 High on the list of priorities at that time were housing developments that would include baths, laundries, toilets and kitchens at Baniyala. Work was required on a windmill, water supply and solar pump at Yangunbi. Yolngu envisaged home management education around cooking, sewing, keeping clean yards, tropical gardens and healthy communities that would flourish with arts and crafts activities (Watt, 1988). These goals covered 11 homeland centres ruled by the Laynhapuy Executive and Homeland Council. Rather than comprising separate units of development, the committee included representatives from Yirrkala, the Fijian resource centre. coordinator, also resident at Yirrkala, a Dhalwangu outstation pastor and the vice-chairperson of the Laynhapuy Homeland Resource Centre.

13 Trudgen (2014) has noted that '*märr* is like a spiritual energy force that all humans have and when a person works at something, that force or spiritual power is transmitted to the article produced or the service provided. The more effort used to produce the product or the service the more *märr* the article or the service contains. This happens whenever food is produced and harvested, things are made from raw products, or when an article is obtained and then value is added to it, or whenever a service is carried out. Whoever then receives that product or service also receives the person's *märr* or spiritual power, which builds up in them. As the spiritual power builds up in the receiving person their own *märr* or spiritual power is decreased. They become *märr-miriw*—without spiritual power … As other people's *märr* builds up in you, your *märr* is depressed and a person can feel sick and even die' (p. 62).

14 The Northern Territory Emergency Response, known as the 'Intervention', was announced on 21 June 2007 and introduced a raft of draconian measures to discipline and monitor Aboriginal communities.

> Like, some know, some don't know what Intervention does to our body and to our system, our blood. It's a foreign system that's going into Yolngu's blood. For example, if I have a wrong blood line going into my blood, it makes me sick, see, and that's a new law, government law whatever the policy is. That's a new law, it's like that. I think they [government] should have made it differently, firstly telling that story around the camp, what is going to be happening, but it just came like water, coming rushing and just going in to all our laws and all our culture and everything there. Why are they ruining that? Within our body system—inside, in our blood—where the culture [is], [it] helps to communicate life, helps the environment, work together, good leadership, everything. But, if you try to put your power and your system into ours, it's hard. We wouldn't go to you and force you to do that, you wouldn't like it.

Her critique shows how Yolngu are deeply affected by the places where they feel at home, and how changing policies and practices not only take away control, but also affect people's trust in working through negotiated settlements. The 'foreign system' that is referred to is not confined to the Northern Territory Emergency Response, known as the 'Intervention', but is indicative of other kinds of cultural shifts as well. Indeed, as the many excellent and carefully detailed Centre for Aboriginal Economic Policy Research (CAEPR) reports on homelands, housing, welfare, basic cards, employment and income-support mechanisms show (e.g. Bray et al., 2012; Hunter, 2014; Yap & Biddle, 2012), there can be no single approach to addressing the economic demands of what are essentially very different modes of living opportunities and lifestyles. Instead, each context requires careful support to affect a conjoined system of 'moral optimism' (Trouillot, 2003) as people move between locales and the different economies of wellbeing that they afford.

'Moral Optimism' in Yolngu Enterprise

In the next half of this chapter, I draw upon Muehlebach's (2013, p. 298) analysis of Trouillot's (2003) concept of 'moral optimism' to consider how Yolngu have always used 'self-guiding principles' as a means of extending generosity to others while remaining resilient against systems that may misconstrue or misunderstand the relational and customary norms of the economy. 'Moral optimism' relates not simply to improved conditions of materiality through capital works or better infrastructure but, more fully, to the changing emotional, cultural and spiritual dynamics of human relationship. In two examples, I show how moral optimism was promoted on Galiwin'ku by the entangled nature of work, mutual appreciation, reciprocity and finance in the development of an agricultural work scheme devised during mission times from the perspective of the missionary who ran it. I then compare the relational aspects of this productive mission-run enterprise with housing and infrastructure projects in the town to consider how they operate on principles of '"waiting, following and carrying", all notions inherently expressing the task for relation' (Thiele, 2008, p. 26).

Growing Generosity in Relationships

By examining successful work relations in the past, we can understand how Yolngu view culturally appropriate development in the present. One example of how historical labour relations have informed the present is the way in which homelands have long offered opportunities for gardening, which was encouraged by missionaries and supported by government. As Myers and Peterson (2016) noted, 'the emphasis on "gardens" can be understood as a comprehensible mediation between Indigenous aspirations for autonomy and governmental/mission concerns for learning to labour as a basis for "self-sufficiency"' (p. 5). During the 1970s, a large area of market garden flourished on Galiwin'ku. It was established over many years with the tireless efforts of various mission staff, including the Reverend Wendell Flentje, who worked on Galiwin'ku from 1973–81. Wendell, who had trained in Victoria as an agriculturalist, left the island to study for the Uniting Church ministry. He returned to the Northern Territory Synod as the minister of Casuarina Uniting Church in Darwin in 2004. He was Moderator of the Northern Synod from 2007–10. His time on Galiwin'ku overlapped with Reverend Harold Shepherdson. 'Sheppy', as he was known, had a family background in farming and sawmilling, and was a pilot. Flentje (personal communication) recalled:

> All the Balanda were church staff employed by the mission. There were no government employees. There were about 100 Balanda, not all of them being Christian. The vast majority were Christian and came from all over Australia and from many different backgrounds. Teachers, nurses, tradespeople, [a] mechanic, plumber, electrician, agriculturalist, powerhouse worker, fisherman—all these were mission staff. Some of the houses were pretty old, but the government had supplied some housing for teaching staff and they were those houses down from where the store is now.

Flentje worked half-time in the school at post-primary level and half-time in the garden for two years, until he decided he needed to be full-time in the garden, due to its demands. The produce was prolific—more than the store could manage—so it was sold from the back of a truck driving through the town; the remainder was sent by plane to community stores in other mission communities with the assistance of Missionary Aviation Fellowship, which had been established in 1974. Flentje was successful in negotiating sales of bananas at Katherine and then Milingimbi and Gapuwiyak. The garden was, as he put it:

> Quite an enterprise—bananas and sweet potatoes—up to 1 tonne of bananas a week, watermelons in dry season, pawpaw, limes, sugarcane for sugarcane drinks. With the bananas and sweet potatoes and fish [they had the] basis of a really good diet and they always ate a lot of fish.

These ventures were successful because the emphasis was on the interpersonal, moral and cultural advantage in the interstices of relational engagement rather than market outcomes and financial sustainability or development of the market venture.

Flentje's aim was to provide food for the community, promote relationships, support needs and enhance lives while, at the same time, offering meaningful employment and training to workers. There was also a desire on the part of some garden workers to learn more about the techniques of gardening via the Resource Centre. One garden worker told Flentje how he wanted to pass on his knowledge of gardening, which he had learned over the previous year, to others in homelands right around the islands, and on the mainland, teaching them how to cut the grass, seed and plant, and water and grow banana suckers and other roots. The relational process of 'waiting, following and carrying' was evident in on-the-job training based on a system of kin reciprocity among the workers. Eight Yolngu men were key in the process over the years: a Wangurri man, a son of Battangga, who had worked with Shepherdson; a D̲at̲iwuy man and his son; a group of four brothers from Golumarri homeland on the island; and a young Djambarrpuyngu man who had been involved in the school garden project in 1973 and 1974. A number of women also worked in the garden. The realisation that this was a 'long-term business'—not something that was done overnight—was one of the changes in attitude that took place in the process of educating people through on-the-job training. It was critical to the success of these ventures that the workplace took on its own family dynamic, since the processes needed to complete the ordering of materials, such as fertilisers, irrigation parts and so forth, required investment from everyone working together, waiting on one another and following through with their various roles.

Trudgen (2000, pp. 48–49) has discussed the decline of the garden after this period, arguing that the enterprise was seen as mission owned—as Yolngu working for missionaries in return for pay. With increased welfare being paid to individuals by government, he believed that Yolngu no longer considered it necessary to work for pay in the garden. However, Flentje (personal communication) told me that, from his perspective, it was the holistic system that had been put in place based on relationships and learning through concepts of the land that had determined its success, at least in part, rather than it operating around financial benefit. He highlighted how moral generosity in working for others' wellbeing was key to the success of mission endeavours on Galiwin'ku. Despite this generosity, the difficulties of sustaining a communal enterprise rather than a family run system—in which responsibilities and obligations are clearly defined—was also viewed as the reason for its demise.

Moral generosity is a cultural principle that runs through all Yolngu relationships with Balanda. An early missionary-art curator and, later, anthropologist working on Galiwin'ku, John Rudder (personal communication), put it very clearly when he explained to me that:

> When I started taking in paintings and paying them [Yolngu] for the paintings on the spot, they were doing it for me and were doing it for the mission. They weren't doing it to make money. They were doing it to support the mission. That was a reciprocal relationship thing. It was almost all on relationship and was nothing to do with economics. These [Balanda] craft workers who go out and work to build an industry, the minute they leave, that's the end of the relationship and the person who comes in has to start all over again.

With the departure of former mission staff, employment systems were handed over to the Galiwin'ku council and its workers, but gardening as a community enterprise gradually ceased. Thus, while good intercultural relations are critical to effective enterprise, as some argue, monetary return may play a role in ensuring the flow of productivity. Nevertheless, the same faithful Yolngu worker who started with Wendell and the other mission staff is tending his own garden today, this time with the assistance of AHED and a Balanda community development worker. This garden, located slightly further away from the residential area, is flourishing. Although operating on a smaller scale than the earlier garden, it provides fruit and vegetables for family and extended kin. This engagement not only illustrates the loyalty shown to a missionary who passed on his gardening skills 40 years ago, it also demonstrates a yearning for the past that had 'a stable horizon of expectation' and which had to confront the many dilemmas of precarity over time (Muehlebach, 2013, p. 297). In sum, these examples demonstrate the importance of culture in shaping job choices, which have been recognised in planning processes since 2014 as integral to supporting and informing employee choices around cultural values in the workplace.

From Jobs to Homes: Affordability and Sustainability

By extending intercultural relations in the area of work and gardening to housing issues, we can see how Yolngu on Galiwin'ku also understand their land and homes as sites of relational and ritual practice that face challenges from wider processes of capital-infrastructure planning and development. Housing is not only a concern for Balanda in the quest for the good life, it also constitutes a key focus of Yolngu aspiration. Yolngu have long become accustomed to the fortnightly rents that, even 30 years ago, were recycled back into the maintenance of housing 'to fix any broken pipes, windows, doors, lights etc.' (National Aborigines Week, 1985).[15] Thirty years ago, the majority of communication around the town and to homelands was limited to satellite radio receivers; only 10 telephone lines were available, connected via an antenna located behind the council offices. More than 30 years on, mobile technologies are expertly used by Yolngu and rent not only applies to Yolngu housing but also to housing for Balanda and migrant workers of other ethnicities who come as health workers, teachers and construction workers. Visitors pay a higher fee for short stays at the local 'Galiwin'ku Hilton'—the Visitor Accommodation.[16] Even though 92.9 per cent of housing is rented on the island (ABS, 2011),[17] rent equates in some people's thinking to ownership, due, in part, to longstanding

15 Rent for housing was introduced in 1985 on Galiwin'ku; it was to be paid at the council office at the rate of AUD10 for pensioners, AUD15 for unemployed people and AUD34 for those in work.

16 The construction cost of a duplex was in the region of AUD407,000 in 2004. See www.cordellconnect.com.au/public/project/ProjectDetails.aspx?uid=238887

17 According to ABS 2011 census data, 2.5 per cent of homes are fully owned, but none are currently under mortgage. See galiwinku.localstats.com.au/demographics/nt/northern-territory/darwin/galiwinku

agreements about who has rights over particular houses. A policy of rental needs drives housing requirements and there is no guarantee that Balanda who have lived in a house for many years, developed its gardens and invested in its infrastructure will return to the same house if they go on leave. One Balanda who left for six months was upset when she came home to find that her years of gardening, plant cultivation and care of mature banana plants had been unattended by short-term residents.

Relational and capital investments continue to be worked out as housing developments expand in towns, encouraging people to stay in a single place rather than being dispersed around homelands. For Yolngu, this presents the added dilemma of how to manage the upkeep on housing in homelands when they are absent for part of the year. Mobility costs involved in caring for country, and less individual disposable income due to the system of demand sharing, variously translate into financial burdens in trying to meet the needs of families living between homelands and the town; financial burdens are also incurred where homeland living presents challenges to employers' Community Development Programme ('work for the dole') and Newstart benefit requirements. The fact that homelands are expensive to maintain and that the delivery of remote education and 'monitoring' of homelands is difficult led, in 2008, to government recommending their closure if they were not 'viable': 'only those passing a viability test should get access to services such as schools and health clinics' (Murdoch, 2008).

While Marthakal homelands are regularly occupied, Galiwin'ku felt the effects of two cyclones in 2015, at the same time as a new subdivision was being completed. The development had been built in return for a mandatory 40-year lease to the government over the town without the payment of rents.[18] However, some Yolngu expressed their concern at the length of time the project took, as well as problems of access to the area. One Balanda resident pointed out how the building construction was at odds with similar construction work being carried out in Palmerston, Darwin. By February 2011, it had become clear that planning for Galiwin'ku housing had been done in reverse compared to that for the new subdivision on the mainland, creating significant issues for prospective

18 Four housing precinct leases have been confirmed in Maningrida, Gunbalanya, Galiwin'ku and Wadeye, a whole of township lease in Nguiu for 99 years, and for 80 years in three Groote Eylandt communities.

residents.[19] While around 20 dwellings had been completed in the Galiwin'ku suburb, there was no access to sewerage, water, lighting and roads. In contrast, the new subdivision at Palmerston[20] had demarcated sites with road access, lighting, waterworks, nature strips and bus stops before house building began. The new housing on Galiwin'ku was initially referred to as Palmerston, but its name was changed to Humpty Doo, in part because of the lack of bus access. Given that families were split between Galiwin'ku and the new subdivision, bus access between them became a key issue to ensure that Yolngu could look after growing families and the elderly.

All housing on Galiwin'ku was surveyed and divided according to 'new builds' and existing housing scheduled for repair. Families who were to receive new houses (decided by the Local Housing Reference Group) had to agree which members would be entitled to them, in turn altering the dynamics of kinship and residency patterns.[21] In the past, repairs to houses depended on which departments owned them (e.g. the education department or the council). With financial backing from the state through the Strategic Indigenous Housing and Infrastructure Program and the National Action Plan, new houses built in the mid-2000s comprised single-storey dwellings, as well as some duplexes of four units made of steel frames, with steel cladding, steel roofs and timber floors. Each unit's floor area was 200 square feet (18.5 square metres) and each one had a carport.[22] Yet, on an island where the wet season lasts only a few months, and the number of cars owned is fewer than one per dwelling, carports have tended to be used for sitting in the shade.

For Yolngu, the financial and material aspects of housing are not their primary concern. Rather, it is the need to ensure continuities of care and provision for their relatives. As one Christian widow noted, 'the house of love' takes many forms. Yet, a commitment to provide for all the family can also be a source of frustration. This widow was proud of her double house (comprising four rooms on one side and four on the other), having worked hard over many years to maintain one-half of it for herself, her daughter and her grandchildren. Yet, she was also frustrated that she could not persuade her relatives' children living in the other half of the

19 I am grateful to Kaye Thurlow for her analysis of these systems.

20 Palmerston is a satellite city of Darwin created for its commuters and comprises 18 suburbs.

21 Tenancy agreements are made with Territory Housing and administered by the shire.

22 For a detailed analysis of modes of provision in urban Aboriginal and Torres Strait social housing elsewhere, see Milligan, Phillips, Easthope, Liu and Memmott (2011).

long house to do the same.[23] The house was large, but the sloping ground in front meant that it was difficult to grow plants, which she enjoyed. A Balanda friend had bought seeds from Darwin to try to improve the grass around it, but the poor soil meant that roots were weak and the rains washed away the grass seed. An extensive, unfenced sandy area at the back of her house provided a short cut for walkers travelling between the main road and the street behind the house. While all new housing designs are fenced off, in part to demarcate the house boundary and keep dogs in and cattle out, this woman's older, mission-built house provided no such privacy.

The option of moving to a new home would seem attractive; however, the choice of who should leave their existing home for the new area presented emotional, spiritual and practical challenges, prompting this woman and other families to think seriously about a range of relational issues and obligations, including those of looking after the deceased. I asked this widow if she would like to move to the new residential area. She replied that even if she had the option to leave, she would have to stay where she was; she wanted the shire to build her a new house on the other side of her husband's grave that was prominently marked by ritual flags in the sandy area some metres behind the house. She said she could not leave the home as she had to look after his grave, even though it was not her choice that he had been buried there.

Neoliberalism, Moral Generosity and Intercultural Relations

Neoliberalism expects those in its sights to rise to the challenges that the system sets, yet it does so without reference to culture or to an end point of its own target setting. In a neoliberal framework, homes are moveable, like targets; job expectations and figures change; and percentages are indicators, not absolutes. Thus, it is not surprising that the sentiment of resilience becomes just as, if not more, important than accomplishment. In the Yolngu case described above, to ignore the spiritual dimensions of power and powerlessness (*märr* and *märrmiriw*), as well as the

23 Reference to the 'house of love' is part of a Christian discourse circulating on Galiwin'ku. This Christian woman explained how money also divides 'the house of love'; at one time, the cost of getting a new Basics Card was the equivalent of half of their pay going on a flight/taxi fare to get to the bank.

sentiments of love, moral duty and care that they engender, would be to impoverish an understanding of the 'good life'. These sentiments and obligations are embodied through the protection of family members who look after their deceased loved ones by singing, dancing and tending for the grave.

Despite neoliberal rhetorics of advancement, I have tried to illustrate how difference generated by neoliberalism contains within its own ideology a process of symbolic violence (see Bourdieu, 1984). As well as presenting intercultural challenges to understanding, cultural intermediaries have provided a conduit through well-established relationships in various roles as missionaries, politicians or non-government organisations, either alongside or together with government aspirations for mobilising local productivity. Nevertheless, they have played a key part in translating the conditions of precarity, as well as filtering national global challenges around economic sustainability into locally meaningful conditions of production. A concern for intermediaries in the past has been the ability to address tensions effectively, and in ongoing dialogue, when they are produced by the very complexities of a value system and its concepts that do not align neatly with Eurocentric aspirations to wealth, power, productivity and notions of individualism. The effect is to create uncertain futures. Precarity, though, is not only the condition of working within neoliberal parameters, it is also the effect of capital and its emergences through the experiences of being human. As I have argued, for Yolngu, targets are not their main priority; rather, care in relationships exemplifies how 'giving-on-and-with' (Glissant, 1997, p. 192) others enfolds Yolngu into the set of obligations of return. It is clear from the examples presented here that the 'good life' needs to be considered a dialectical relation between intercultural and customary facets that influence macro-economic demands, as well as the micro-pressures of family, ritual and inter-clan relations. Kinship and cultural specificities influence what interdependency means with one another as well as with outsiders. Whatever economic systems are employed, there are differing degrees of humanising and dehumanising processes, some an effect of those systems and others that generate recognition of the difficulties in trying to effect and maintain stable regional (and global) economies (see Muehlebach, 2013, p. 298; Roy, 2012). I have tried to illustrate how the Yolngu moral economy operates from linguistically and culturally appropriate strategies to address the good life. Service providers are daily confronted with intercultural dilemmas relating to cultural difference, which Yolngu must also deal with in terms of changing policies and practices. Therefore, it is imperative that the appropriate translation of concepts, values and employment outcomes are implemented to generate the maximum potential for 'allocative power' to effect positive cycles of integration between Balanda and Yolngu in all spheres of interaction, not just in jobs or housing. As I have argued, these practices of moral generosity, relative power dynamics, educational literacy and culturally appropriate ways of working build 'up a reservoir of knowledge and aspiration that, given appropriate direction, could lead us to a better economy' (Hart, 2013, p. 21). Yet, care is also needed to ensure that cultural blindness, relational insensitivity, linguistic indifference and neoliberal agendas do not mute the relation–identity principle (cf. Deutsch, 1998) and lead to further fragmentation of senses of self and empowerment.

References

Adler, R. B. & Elmhorst, J. M. (2008). *Communicating at work: Principles and practices for business and the professions*. New York, NY: McGraw-Hill.

Altman, J. C. (2009). Contestations over development. In J. Altman & D. Martin (Eds), *Power, culture and economy: Indigenous Australians mining* (pp. 1–15). Canberra, ACT: ANU E Press. doi.org/10.26530/OAPEN_459470

Altman, J. C. (2010). What future for remote Indigenous Australia? Economic hybridity and the neoliberal turn. In J. C. Altman & M. Hinkson (Eds), *Culture crisis: Anthropology and politics in Aboriginal Australia* (pp. 259–80). Sydney, NSW: UNSW Press.

Altman, J. C. (2014). Submission by Emeritus Professor Jon Altman, CAEPR. In E. Klein (Ed.), *Academic perspectives on The Forrest review: Creating parity* (pp. 3–4) (CAEPR Topical Issue No. 2). Retrieved from caepr.cass.anu.edu.au/sites/default/files/docs/Topical_Issue-2_2014_CAEPR_Collaboration_Forrest_Review_0.pdf

Altman, J. C. (2015, 11 March). Homelands under the hammer, again, from the aspiring PM for Indigenous policy. *Crikey*. Retrieved from www.crikey.com.au/2015/03/11/homelands-under-the-hammer-again-from-the-aspiring-pm-for-indigenous-policy/

Altman, J. C., Biddle, N. & Hunter, B. H. (2008). *How realistic are the prospects for 'closing the gaps' in socioeconomic outcomes for Indigenous Australians?* (CAEPR Discussion Paper No. 287). Retrieved from caepr.cass.anu.edu.au/sites/default/files/docs/2008_DP287_0.pdf

Altman, J. C. & Hinkson, M. (Eds). (2010). *Culture crisis: Anthropology and politics in Aboriginal Australia.* Sydney, NSW: UNSW Press.

Austin-Broos, D. (2003). Places, practices and things: The articulation of Arrernte kinship with welfare and work. *American Ethnologist, 30*(1), 118–35. doi.org/10.1525/ae.2003.30.1.118

Australian Bureau of Statistics (ABS). (2011). *Census quickstats.* Retrieved from www.censusdata.abs.gov.au/census_services/getproduct/census/2011/quickstat/UCL715001?opendocument&navpos=220

Australian Government. (2015). *Closing the gap.* Retrieved from www.dpmc.gov.au/sites/default/files/publications/Closing_the_Gap_2015_Report.pdf

Bourdieu, P. (1984). *Distinction.* London, England: Routledge and Kegan Paul.

Bray, J., Gray, R., Hand, M., Bradbury, K., Eastman, B., Eastman, C. & Katz, I. (2012). *Evaluating new income management in the Northern Territory: First evaluation report.* Canberra, ACT: Department of Families, Housing, Community Services and Indigenous Affairs.

Christie, M. (2010). The task of the translator. *Learning Communities International Journal of Learning in Social Contexts Australia, 2,* 67–74.

Derrida, J. (1968). *Différance.* Project Lamar. Retrieved from projectlamar.com/media/Derrida-Differance.pdf

Deutsch, H. (1998). Identity and general similarity. *Philosophical Perspectives, 12,* 177–200. doi.org/10.1111/0029-4624.32.s12.8

Fischer, E. F. (2014). *The good life: Aspiration, dignity and the anthropology of wellbeing.* Stanford, CA: Stanford University Press.

Glissant, E. (1997). *Poetics of relation* (B. Wing, Trans.). Ann Arbour, MI: The University of Michigan Press.

Hart, K. (2013). *Manifesto for a human economy.* Retrieved from thememorybank.co.uk/2013/01/20/object-methods-and-principles-of-human-economy/

Hart, K. (2015). Introduction. In K. Hart (Ed.), *Economy for and against democracy* (pp. 1–18). New York, NY: Berghahn.

Hunter, B. (2014). *Indigenous employment and businesses: whose business is it to employ Indigenous workers?* (CAEPR Working Paper No. 95). Retrieved from caepr.cass.anu.edu.au/sites/default/files/docs/CAEPR_Working_Paper_95_0.pdf

Kim, S.-Y., Kim, J. & Lim, T.-S. (2013). The impact of relational holism on conflict management styles in colleagueship and friendship: A cross-cultural study. *Studies in Communication Sciences, 13*(1), 56–66. doi.org/10.1016/j.scoms.2013.04.001

Lahn, J. (2014). Submission by Dr Julie Lahn, research fellow, CAEPR. In E. Klein (Ed.), *Academic perspectives on The Forrest review: Creating parity* (pp. 1–3) (CAEPR Topical Issue No. 2). Retrieved from caepr.cass.anu.edu.au/sites/default/files/docs/Topical_Issue-2_2014_CAEPR_Collaboration_Forrest_Review_0.pdf

Lawrence, T. (2013, 23 January). Nova Peris, the Prime Minister and Trish Crossin. *Independent Australia.* Retrieved from independentaustralia.net/politics/politics-display/nova-peris-the-prime-minister-and-trish-crossin,4905

MacDonald, G. (2000). Economies and personhood: Demand sharing among the Wiradjuri of New South Wales. In G. W. Wenzel, G. Hovelsrud-Borda & N. Kishigami (Eds), *The social economy of sharing: Resource allocation and modern hunter-gatherers* (pp. 87–111). Osaka, Japan: National Museum of Ethnology.

Milligan, V., Phillips, R., Easthope, H., Liu, E. & Memmott, P. (2011). *Urban social housing for Aboriginal people and Torres Strait Islanders: Respecting culture and adapting services* (AHURI Final Report No. 172). Retrieved from www.ahuri.edu.au/__data/assets/pdf_file/0014/2075/AHURI_Final_Report_No172_Urban_social_housing_for_Aboriginal_people_and_Torres_Strait_Islanders_respecting_culture_and_adapting_services.pdf

Morris, M. W., Williams, K. Y., Leung, K., Larrick, R., Mendoza, M. T., Bhatnagar, D. ... Hu, J.-C. (1998). Conflict management style: Accounting for cross-cultural differences. *Journal of International Business Studies, 29*, 729–47. doi.org/10.1057/palgrave.jibs.8490050

Muehlebach, A. (2013). On precariousness and the ethical imagination: The year 2012 in sociocultural anthropology. *American Anthropologist, 115*(2), 297–311. doi.org/10.1111/aman.12011

Murdoch, L. (2008, 27 September). The homelands' ancient ties. *Sydney Morning Herald*. Retrieved from www.smh.com.au/national/the-homelands-ancient-ties-20080926-4ovi.html

Myers, F. & Peterson, N. (2016). The origins and history of outstations as Aboriginal life projects. In F. Myers & N. Peterson (Eds), *Experiments in self-determination: Histories of the outstation movement in Australia* (pp. 1–22). Canberra, ACT: ANU Press. doi.org/10.22459/ESD.01.2016.01

National Aborigines Week. (1985, September). *Galiwin'ku News*. Galiwin'ku Adult Education Centre.

Northern Territory Government. (2009). *Outstations policy. Our home, our homeland: Community Engagement Report*. NT Australia: Socom + DodsonLane. Retrieved from apo.org.au/system/files/14480/apo-nid14480-35086.pdf

Peterson, N. (2005). What can the pre-colonial and frontier economies tell us about engagement with the real economy? Indigenous life projects and the conditions for development. In D. Austin-Broos & G. MacDonald (Eds), *Culture, economy and governance in Aboriginal Australia* (pp. 7–18). Sydney, NSW: Sydney University Press.

Roy, A. (2012). Ethical subjects: Market rule in an age of poverty. *Public Culture, 24*(1), 105–08. doi.org/10.1215/08992363-1443574

Schwarz, C. (2006). Christianity, identity, power, and employment in an Aboriginal settlement. *Ethnology, 45*(1), 71–86. doi.org/10.2307/4617565

Tang, R. F. Y. & Kirkbride, P. S. (1986). Developing conflict management skills in Hong Kong: An analysis of some cross-cultural implications. *Management Learning, 17*(3), 287–301. doi.org/10.1177/135050768601700315

Thiele, K. (2008). *The thought of becoming: Gille Deleuze's poetics of life*. Zurich, Switzerland: Diaphanes.

Ting-Toomey, S. (1988). Intercultural communication styles: A face-negotiation theory. In Y. Y. Kim & W. B. Gudykunst (Eds), *Theories in intercultural communication* (pp. 213–35). Newbury, CA: Sage.

Trouillot, M-R. (2003). *Global transformations: Anthropology and the modern world*. New York, NY: Palgrave MacMillan. doi.org/10.1007/978-1-137-04144-9

Trudgen, R. (2000). *Why warriors lie down and die*. Darwin, NT: Aboriginal Resource Services Inc.

Trudgen, R. (2014). *Getting Yolngu into business*. Why Warriors Pty Ltd. Retrieved from www.whywarriors.com.au/2014/07/getting-yolnu-into-business/

Watt, R. (1988). *Field study to Yirrkala*. Batchelor, NT: RATE Productions.

Yap, M. & Biddle, N. (2012). *Unpaid work, unpaid care, unpaid assistance and volunteering* (Paper 4, CAEPR Indigenous Populations Project: 2011 Census Papers). Retrieved from caepr.cass.anu.edu.au/sites/default/files/docs/PopProject_2011_Census_Paper04_FinalWeb_1.pdf

8

'The Main Thing Is to Have Enough Food': Kuninjku Precarity and Neoliberal Reason

Jon Altman

> Being able to get to your country and being able to live here too, that's the good life. Sometimes going bush, sometimes living here; the main thing is to have enough food. When you have enough food to eat, that's good.

These opening lines are drawn from a series of interviews conducted in Kuninjku, a dialect of the pan-dialectical language Bininj Kunwok (Garde, 2013) during a week in February 2015.[1] The focus of my questioning was on what constitutes the 'good life' today, in the immediate past and, potentially, in the future. The question was posed to John, my friend of nearly 40 years, in his language by Murray Garde, expert linguist and accredited translator. I asked the question sitting on the ground outside John's decrepit government-supplied home at the remote township of Maningrida in Australia's Northern Territory.

1 I made this methodological decision because my Kuninjku is too limited to be immune from potential misrepresentation or error and I was keen to have Murray Garde's expert assistance. Interviews were conducted with a cross-section of Kuninjku speakers, mainly old and middle-aged, but including some young people, mainly male, but also females. The interviews were conducted in the township of Maningrida during the wet season when most Kuninjku are living there rather than at their small homelands in the hinterland.

John's response can be multiply interpreted, but there are two key messages. One is about mobility and maintaining connection to one's country. John continues:

> What makes me happy is when I go back to my home out bush and I can go out hunting and I can live like the old people from olden times. That makes me happy when I am in my camp, I can paint, I can drink tea and walk around my camp and the sun goes down. Good, happy. In Maningrida, sometimes happy, sometimes not. I only think about my country. I get sad when I think about my home out bush and I can't get out there. This place here is for white people, but it gives us access to Balanda [Western] food and to health services at the clinic. We can go out bush but the problem is when we get sick or when we have no [Western] food out there. So it pushes us to come and live here to get Balanda food and health services, but we still want to live out bush. It is a contradiction that frustrates us.

The other key message indexed by John's reflections is about what might be referred to in Australian English as 'getting a good feed', or what we might think of as 'food sovereignty' (Li, 2015). John talks about food in two ways: Balanda (or Western) food, which is purchased from the store; and bush tucker, which is hunted, fished or gathered:

> I am worried about my country and those old people buried there or when they used to go collecting food … [he lists all kinds of bush food]. I think about those old people and the food we used to eat.

In the middle of this interview, Peter, a white man (or Balanda) who lives in Maningrida and has worked for years with the Maningrida Progress Association, which runs a local store selling Balanda food, arrives with a large fish (a barramundi) he has caught for John.

> 'Why did he give you that fish?' I ask.
>
> 'For supper, because we have no food,' says Kay, John's wife.
>
> 'He must have caught it on my country,' says John.
>
> Ngarritj, John's grandson, says, 'Peter goes hunting at Bulkay and he gives them fish.'

Later, I ask the same question of Peter, who tells me that he delivered the fish to John's camp because Kay had asked for it. She had told him they were hungry; it was caught near Maningrida in salt water, not in the fresh water at Bulkay.

Just prior to Peter's arrival, I had been showing John my book *Hunter-Gatherers Today: An Aboriginal Economy in North Australia* (Altman, 1987), based on my anthropological fieldwork in 1979 and 1980 at Mumeka outstation on John's country. The book features a photograph of a young John on the front cover holding bush food—a goanna, magpie geese, a barramundi and a catfish—from a hunt he and I undertook at Bulkay. I had asked John:

> 'If I was to write a book about what people do every day [today] in Maningrida, what would I write?'
>
> He replied: 'I don't know. I am going to try to tell everyone to go back to our outstation.'
>
> 'What about bush tucker?'
>
> 'Before bush tucker.'

Earlier, Japhat, another Kuninjku man, had commented:

> We have a lot of bush tucker out bush. Before, a long time, the old people thought a lot about bush tucker, but the new generation they think about the foods that white people have brought, sugar, bakky [tobacco]. The white people's food has changed our thinking. We don't think about our bush foods as much.

***

In this chapter, I want to ask why the struggle 'to get a feed' (in colloquial Australian) and remain connected to one's country can be so difficult for someone like John Mawurndjul, who is among Australia's foremost contemporary artists, living in one of the richest countries in the world.

On several occasions recently, and with increasing frequency in the last decade, I have known Kuninjku people to be hungry and without food in Maningrida. Sometimes, prior to sitting down for a meeting or social gathering, they have asked me to buy them food, an unusual request in my nearly four decades of acquaintance. Such requests have been made reluctantly and with a degree of shame; they are in marked contrast to the high visibility and ready availability of food out bush and offers of bush tucker made to me on my visits to outstations.

There are two issues here I seek to analyse. Living in Maningrida today, mainly on welfare, what people are short of is food sourced from the store. This is because their income is low and this food is expensive. When they live in the hinterland they have access to abundant bush food, although they often lack access to Western foods. However, they increasingly find it difficult to live at their outstations, even though this is the stated preference of many of their senior people, like John, who recognise, with some sadness and frustration, that this is not an aspiration necessarily shared by young people, the so-called new generation.

My introduction so far has focused on Kuninjku perspectives and agency, something that Kuninjku themselves emphasise. However, this is only a small part of a bigger story in a context in which the role of the Australian settler state and its ever-changing policy approaches to Aboriginal development looms large in the structuring and restructuring of people's livelihood options.

I wish to deploy the historical technique of the *longue durée* to give a degree of priority to historical structures over events. John came in from the bush, where he was being reared as a member of a hunter-gatherer group, to Maningrida in 1963. I first met him 16 years later in 1979. During the following 37 years, 1979–2016, I have visited him in Arnhem Land regularly, and he in turn has visited me in Canberra on several occasions. In that time, the livelihood fortunes of Kuninjku people have fluctuated quite dramatically, always heavily structured by relations with the state. What I aim to do here, then, is to trace a series of social experiments that have been conducted on Aboriginal people residing in remote Australia and examine their effects, as experienced by the subjects of those experiments.

I begin by providing a contextualising background on the Maningrida region. I then give a brief account of two historical periods that preceded my initial engagement in this region, which I term 'precolonial' and 'colonial'. I then focus on two periods, the first underway by the 1970s, which I term 'postcolonial', and the second, clearly manifest from about 2005 to the present, which I term 'neo-colonial', the latter being my priority.

Each of these phases has greatly influenced the nature of the Kuninjku livelihood and domestic economy and their transformation in ways that have not necessarily followed the Western development pathways imagined and promised by state officials. While the materialist and structural nature of my analysis dovetails with Wolfe's theorisation (1999, 2015)—that the logic of settler society and late capitalism is to have unimpeded access to the land and its resources—for a time, in the postcolonial period, it appeared that Kuninjku might be able to resist the destruction and elimination of their native society. In the contemporary neo-colonial context, this process of elimination, proposed to occur through beneficial integration of Kuninjku into the mainstream, has re-emerged. It is my contention that, for people like the Kuninjku, any form of forced integration constitutes a form of structural (Farmer, 2005) and economic violence (Peck, 2010).

This chapter is written at a moment when the democratically elected Australian Government is unwilling to support the rights of Indigenous Australians to live differently—indeed, in which there is a dogged and bipartisan national policy focus on 'Aboriginal advancement to integration' (Schapper, 1970). In this context, the complex politics of constitutional recognition of Indigenous peoples has stalled; there are policy proposals to defund and close down small Indigenous communities, usually with populations of less than 100, even where land rights or native title have been legally recognised; ongoing debates about the possible amendment of racial discrimination law to allow racial vilification as a libertarian right to free speech; and ongoing special discriminatory laws that target Indigenous people.

The dominant policy framework, agreed upon by all Australian governments since 2008, is the supposedly humane but ultimately developmental and modernist Closing the Gap strategy, which has clear aims to eliminate statistical disparities between Indigenous and other Australians. The Australian Government's Indigenous Advancement Strategy is quite explicit in its aim to alter the norms and values of Indigenous peoples to match those of mainstream Australians, and to deliver supposedly equalising outcomes to Indigenous people, including the Kuninjku, measured by Western statistics (Council of Australian Governments, 2011).

The Maningrida Region: Synoptic Background

The township of Maningrida looms large in the lives of Kuninjku people today and so I want to provide a brief summary of its establishment, its peoples and the region. Maningrida was originally called Manayingkarirra (from the phrase *Mane djang karirra*, meaning 'the place where the Dreaming changed shape'), a camping place on a river, now called the Liverpool River, on the lands of the Dekurridji clan. In 1949, a trading post was established by what was then the Native Affairs Branch of the Northern Territory Administration as a policy experiment to repatriate 'tribal' people who had walked to Darwin, 500 kilometres away. It was abandoned in 1950.

In 1957, Maningrida was re-occupied by state officials and established as a Welfare Branch government settlement to create a regional colonial presence deep within what was then the Arnhem Land Aboriginal Reserve, and, again, to help to keep Aboriginal people out of Darwin. Government policy at that time embraced assimilation—the quest to transform Aboriginal people into mainstream subjects. Maningrida slowly developed over the 1960s into a township where Aboriginal people, still wards of the state, could be trained for assimilation through education and work and the adoption of Western ways of living.

Since 1957, Maningrida has had both Balanda (non-Indigenous) and Bininj (Aboriginal) populations. It is a place of dual ethnicity, with power legally vested with Balanda as agents of the colonial state. In the early 1970s, policy shifted dramatically from imposed assimilation, which had failed, to decolonising self-determination, which was initially viewed by all with great optimism as a means to empower Aboriginal people and to overcome earlier development failures. However, this was a constrained self-determination, with state authority still reigning supreme, as symbolised by the coat of arms fixed to the wall of 'Her Majesty's' Maningrida police station and the flags of Australia and the Northern Territory flying outside the West Arnhem Shire office.

The Maningrida region covers about 10,000 square kilometres of tropical savannah. It has a current Aboriginal population of about 3,000 and a non-Aboriginal population of about 300, although the accuracy of available statistics, even from the five-yearly official census, are of dubious veracity. I conceptualise this region geopolitically as comprising two spaces:

a township or service centre of about 300 houses, shops, a school, a police station and other service facilities; and a hinterland where 100 houses are scattered across about 35 locations called outstations. I try to avoid using the term 'community' when talking about Maningrida because it is made up of diverse residential clusterings (or 'communities') defined by languages, lineages, political alliances, land ownership in the hinterland and territorial orientations. Occupational affiliations mainly define the Balanda groupings—teachers, nurses, those employed in various Aboriginal organisations and so on—and their residential clustering.

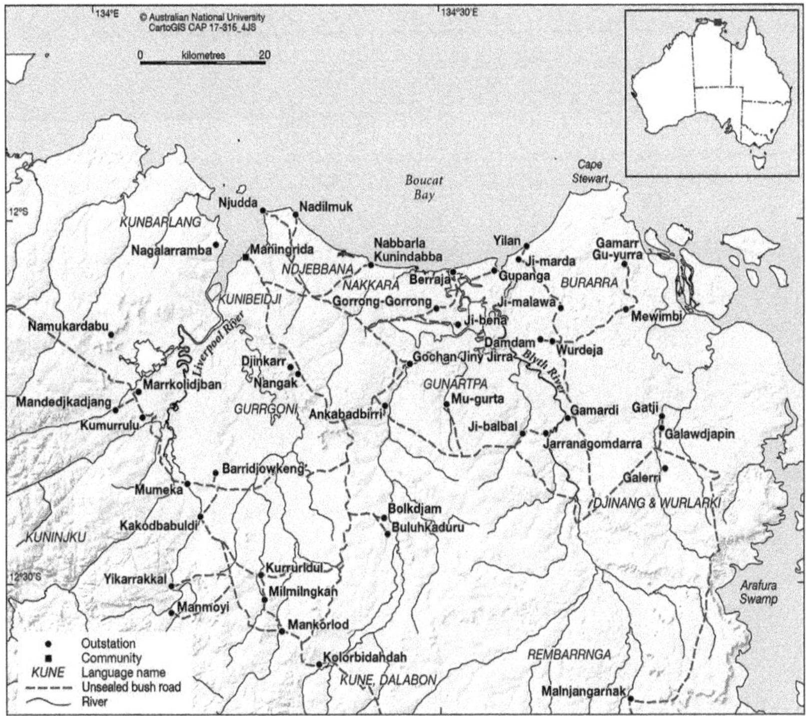

Figure 8.1: Map of the Maningrida Region

Source: CartoGIS, College of Asia and the Pacific, The Australian National University.

Figure 8.1 summarises the location of the region in tropical north Australia; the spatial relationship between Maningrida and far smaller outstations averaging populations rarely over 25 persons; and the main geographic distribution of regional languages (shown capitalised in the map), of which the Kuninjku dialect is just one. Maningrida today is a multilingual township, with speakers of all regional languages resident since its establishment. Associated with language diversity, there is also political diversity and contestation; Maningrida is located on the land of the Dekurridji, whose ownership was only legally recognised after the passage of land rights law in 1976. Historically, other more demographically powerful groups with superior cross-cultural skills had been politically dominant at Maningrida. Today, the Dekurridji and their affines and close allies have recouped some local authority, which remains very much subordinate to that of the state. No social field in this region is either typical or static; they vary in size, regional mobility, adherence to customary law and place of residence. The main integrating regional institutions are Aboriginal ritual cult, mortuary and social exchange ceremonies, Christian fellowship (for those who participate) and Australian Rules football.

My focus on the Kuninjku in this chapter mainly reflects my long-term research relationship with this group. I have been working with them since 1979; yet, attempting to define even them as a community or social field is challenging. There are about 300 Kuninjku, so defined because they speak a dialect of the pan-dialectical Bininj Kunwok language, whose speakers reside in the Kakadu–West Arnhem region (Evans, 2003; Garde, 2013). The Kuninjku community I work with is located at the eastern extremity of this language bloc and is mainly composed of members of six intermarrying clans defined by patrilineal descent. Kuninjku in general 'marry' each other in accord with customary marriage rules, which emphasise clan and moiety exogamy as a core principle. They also sometimes marry their immediate neighbours, especially members of other Bininj Kunwok dialect groups to the west. They are associated with 10 outstations and use territories they own under land rights law for livelihood and spiritual sustenance.

Key distinguishing features of this 'community' include Kuninjku people's relatively recent contact with the colonial state, remnants of the community only moving to Maningrida in 1963; their eagerness to decentralise in the 1970s—Kuninjku were among the first in north Australia to do so; their poor adaptation to settlement life; and their practice, like other groups but more so, of moving continually between township and hinterland, and between outstations. However, in the last decade or so, a number of Kuninjku families have been settled in Maningrida almost continuously for employment, children's education and access to health services. The future permanence of such residential choice is difficult to assess given historical shifts from outstations to town and vice versa.

When Kuninjku are in Maningrida they reside in four residential clusters they call 'bottom camp', 'side camp', 'shelter' and 'new sub', the last a recent 'suburban' addition to the township, consisting of 100 houses constructed for Aboriginal residents since 2009. In total, the Kuninjku camps consist of 10 houses in various states of disrepair and four 'temporary' tin sheds (in use for over a decade), which they refer to as 'chicken houses'. These residential clusters are spread across the township but are oriented towards Kuninjku country to the south-west. The defining sociological feature of these clusters is that residents predominantly share hunted game and store-purchased foods, as well as cash, with each other on the basis of kinship ties. There is also an emerging Kuninjku camp at a place called 'the Fifteen Mile' just outside Darwin, where Kuninjku rent two very basic shelters from the Department of Housing and Community Development. The main emerging reason for visiting Darwin is access to kidney dialysis treatment, another being access to alcohol, which is hard to find in Maningrida. The interviews recorded for this chapter were conducted at or near each of these camps.

Hunter-Gatherers Primed for Developmental Assimilation

Until the late 1950s, and even into the early 1960s, Kuninjku people lived as hunter-gatherers in what was effectively an un-colonised part of the Arnhem Land Reserve, policed at the border by the Australian state to prohibit entry by Europeans. Some of my research collaborators today were born in the bush between the 1920s and 1950s and spent their early life intentionally at a distance from colonial authority and other Balandas at the frontier.

Given the focus here on access to food as an idiomatic expression of the good life, it is of interest that Kuninjku are related to people to the west who had migrated to the mission at Oenpelli, and who had participated in a research experiment of hunter-gatherer living conducted by the 1948 Arnhem Land expedition (see Thomas & Neale, 2011). Without rehearsing too much detail, information collected by McCarthy and McArthur (1960) at Fish Creek (or Kunnanj) in October 1948 provided the ethnographic evidence for Sahlins's (1972) theorisation of the 'original affluent society' in his *Stone Age Economics*. This theorisation continues to have some influence today (Gammage, 2011). Sahlins (1972) also theorised that people like the Kuninjku engaged in a particular form of domestic moral economy—'a domestic mode of production' that was largely self-sufficient, sustainable and based on the moral imperative to share in a generalised manner with kin and co-residents.

I have taken issue with elements of Sahlins's depiction of 'original affluence', mainly because my fieldwork experience and primary data collection suggest that while there was seasonal surplus, there was also a degree of seasonal precarity involved in living off the land. Even today, with access to bought food and modern technology, making a living out in the bush during the wet seasons is difficult because of seasonal flooding and inaccessibility of wildlife (Altman, 1987, 2011). Moreover, some forms of bush food collection were, and continue to be, arduous in terms of work effort. However, there is no doubt that as hunter-gatherers, Kuninjku people had a sustainable mode of production. As Hamish, one of my Kuninjku interlocutors, put it: 'The old people had the true power to be self-sufficient. They worked hard producing food to survive, yams, all kinds of food they carried and shared … with others'.

While Kuninjku had occasional contact with the colonial state, explorers, pastoralists and missionaries in the period prior to World War II, patrol reports document populations still living in the bush as hunter-gatherers from the 1930s to the 1960s (Altman, 2016). All this changed in 1957 with the establishment of a government settlement at Maningrida, followed by the blazing of a bush vehicular track from Oenpelli mission to Maningrida through Kuninjku country in 1963. After 1963, most Kuninjku moved to live in Maningrida although many continued seasonal visitations back to their country for hunting and ceremonies.

The Kuninjku hunting economy more or less disappeared when they lived in Maningrida. State colonial domination sought to centralise and sedentarise these mobile hunter-gatherers to prepare and equip them for integration as citizens into the settler society. This initial social engineering project of improvement was grounded in an explicit policy of assimilation, articulated in 1961:

> All aborigines and part-aborigines are expected eventually to attain the same manner of living as other Australians and to live as members of a single Australian community enjoying the same rights and privileges, accepting the same responsibilities, observing the same customs and influenced by the same beliefs, hopes and loyalties as other Australians. (Commonwealth of Australia, 1961)

Economic thinking was deeply influenced by the post-war modernisation paradigm of the time. For many reasons, that grand project of socio-economic convergence between Indigenous and other Australians failed at Maningrida, as it failed more broadly, especially in remote Australia.

Life at Maningrida represented a radical change from bush living. For a start, Kuninjku were living on other people's country, that of the Dekurridji. They were also living with many other Aboriginal people from the region, as well as Europeans, in a sedentary small township setting. Most importantly, even though Kuninjku, like other Aboriginal people in Australia, were granted voting rights in 1962, at Maningrida they were categorised as wards of the state and subject to the supreme colonial authority of a superintendent sanctioned by Australian law. A radical shift in livelihoods saw people becoming waged labourers on below-award training allowances, or else engaged in one form or another of training for late modernity, including 'domestic duties'. Kuninjku, like others, had access to very rudimentary housing, primary education and basic health services in Maningrida; for a time, they ate in the settlement's communal dining hall as it was deemed the best way to deliver Western food.

Kuninjku adapted very badly to settlement life and the state project of assimilation mainly because they remained strongly committed to their own values regime and notions of autonomy and authority. Consequently, their lot at the settlement, which was notionally established for their betterment and to prepare them for integration into modernity, was precarious. State officials were quick to identify what was then termed 'the Gunwinggu problem', which simply reflected Kuninjku unwillingness to respond to the official solution: *imagined* assimilation. I say 'imagined' because, as history has subsequently demonstrated, settlements like Maningrida lacked the economic base to engage viably with market capitalism. Part of the solution envisioned by the authorities was for Kuninjku minors to attend school and for their parents to actively engage in make-work or commercially fraught projects heavily subsidised by the state. For many reasons, including bullying by other Aboriginal kids and unimaginative curricula and teaching methods, Kuninjku kids avoided school more than others, while their parents engaged in poorly paid employment reluctantly and sporadically (Altman, 2016).

Maningrida failed as a project of assimilation for two main reasons. First, counter to capitalist logic, the settlement was established as a coastal trading post and then, later, as an *entrepôt* without any assessment of the commodities that might flow from the hinterland. As it turned out, there were very few of any commercial value. Second, and again counter to capitalist logic, a series of state-subsidised projects were established, including forestry, cattle and buffalo raising, dairy, market gardens, orchards, flower propagation, fishing and fish processing, a piggery and chicken raising, without any realistic appraisal of commercial viability or comparative advantage. All failed. Interestingly, the production and marketing of Aboriginal art, which was not supported back then as a state enterprise, has subsequently proven to be the only sustainable commodity export from the region.

Unsurprisingly, as a group regarded by other Aboriginal people at Maningrida as myall (or wild and primitive), living marginalised and impoverished in the township did not suit Kuninjku. They experienced 'structural violence' (Farmer, 2005) and economic deprivation. As John put it: 'Sometimes we Kuninjku kids were hungry and sick, so we didn't like being here [in Maningrida]'. Many yearned to return to live on their ancestral lands. By the late 1960s, they had taken steps to achieve this aim by purchasing two second-hand cheap vehicles; and there was a growing administrative sympathy on the part of some enlightened local non-Indigenous officials for this aspiration given the evident failure of Kuninjku to adapt to urbanised and sedentarised life.

Decentralisation and Postcolonial Economic Hybridity

Kuninjku were able to reconstitute a significantly transformed hunter-gatherer economy in the early 1970s after decentralisation back to their land. This transformation was underpinned by access to welfare and to domestic and global art markets for which Kuninjku art was adapted and commoditised for sale. Out of the failure of the assimilation experiment and a form of precarity living in Maningrida came a period of postcolonial possibility supported by a policy explicitly termed self-determination—that is, 'Aboriginal communities deciding the pace and nature of their future development as significant components within a diverse Australia' (Australian Human Rights Commission, 2008).

A new set of government programs was established that supported plural forms of livelihood. Kuninjku people were able to engage productively with these new institutional arrangements and establish what I have termed a hybrid or plural form of livelihood that matched their priorities to remain interconnected to their immediate social community, connected to their ancestral lands and engaged ceremonially with that land in accordance with tradition. All this required a highly flexible mode of living and of making a living—a hybrid economy, which was created and maintained with the crucial assistance of a regional resource agency, the Bawinanga Aboriginal Corporation (BAC).

Two transformative policy shifts facilitated the Kuninjku reconnection to their community lands in the early 1970s. First, belated recognition of Kuninjku as Australian citizens saw them empowered to find their own solution. Their emerging rights included access to welfare paid to individuals, initially as family allowances and pensions. Deploying their enduring kin-based relations of production allowed the pooling of funds to underwrite their livelihoods as hunters, fishers and harvesters with store-purchased, everyday commodities and important Western equipment, such as vehicles and guns. Second, the progressive Whitlam Government committed to land rights law that legally recognised land ownership by Aboriginal people living on gazetted reserves like Arnhem Land. Recognising an associated escalation in movement back onto country, the government supported the establishment and funding of specially incorporated outstation resource agencies. It also incrementally introduced full entitlement to welfare to 'unemployed' outstation residents, which, because people were rarely work- or income-tested, meant payments effectively operated as a basic income scheme. Added to this was a rapid expansion, from the late 1980s, of funded participation in the community-controlled Community Development Employment Projects (CDEP) scheme. This was a crucially important institution because it allowed earning of extra cash without income testing and accommodated highly flexible living arrangements.

The 30-year period from about 1975–2005 saw a remarkable transformation in the Kuninjku economy and ways of living. Engaging with the new institutions born of an increased tolerance of difference, Kuninjku crafted an unusual hybrid form of economy based on a relatively high harvesting of wildlife for sustenance, successful engagement with market capitalism through the production and sale of art, and creative use of state income support. This form of economy was based on a virtuous cycle: unconditional income support at outstations underwrote hunting activity, arts production generated discretionary income that could be invested in vehicles that enhanced access to game on country, which, in turn, generated considerable bush tucker that offset the need for store-purchased foods and also provided greater access to the natural products needed for arts production.

This economic system had many elements that suited Kuninjku. It was flexible and so could accommodate their extraordinarily high levels of residential mobility, often associated with intensified ceremonial participation and sociality, and it was anarchic, so eliminated relations of domination in the workplace, which are anathema to Kuninjku values. It was an economy predicated on an arguably serendipitous understanding of what Westerners might define as the Ricardian (after David Ricardo) principle of comparative advantage and a growing division of labour by specialisation (rather than just by gender). The customary skills that Kuninjku had managed to retain during their time in Maningrida in the 1960s could now be deployed to self-provision and to produce commodities in the form of fine art for export. Over time, new specialisations emerged, for example, in the production of textile art, land and resource management and and the performance of ritual services in the Aboriginal domain.

By 2005, the Kuninjku, who had been the most marginalised and impoverished 'community' in the 1960s, were the most successful regionally; Kuninjku artists were travelling internationally for exhibitions and fêted as Australian cultural ambassadors. They produced the majority by value of exports from the region in the form of art. Their enhanced regional status saw them increasingly take up residence in Maningrida, where their ownership of high-status four-wheel drive vehicles not only made their economic success highly visible, but also allowed a high degree of movement between Maningrida and outstations in the hinterland. Some Kuninjku lived and sought to make a living and get food mainly in Maningrida; others lived mainly at outstations; many lived across the two.

From the early 1970s, Kuninjku had found their own solution to what the authorities had dubbed 'the Gunwinggu problem' and to what Kuninjku had found an utterly unacceptable way of living, regimented by white authority (Altman, 2016). However, this form of apparent economic justice was not the product of Kuninjku agency or serendipity alone. It was also highly dependent on funded programs that supported Kuninjku desires to live differently. Of crucial importance was BAC, established in 1979 as an outstation resource agency, and Maningrida Arts and Culture (MAC), established in 1973 to assist with the marketing of art, which became a business unit within the far larger BAC.

I cannot describe here in any detail the evolution and life cycles of these two organisations that played an instrumental role in the emergence of Kuninjku success. I just note that BAC was incorporated as a special institution of the self-determination era to provide services and support to its members, including those Kuninjku who were mainly outstation residents in its early years. BAC grew rapidly from humble beginnings to become a significant regional organisation. It transformed into a major employer from 1989, when it became host of the nation's largest CDEP scheme of some 600 participants. It used access to this multimillion dollar program to develop into a profitable regional development agency. Politically, BAC developed a reputation as a progressive organisation that advocated for land rights, appropriate forms of economic development, outstations support and regional self-determination for its members and their families. From the Kuninjku perspective, and very concretely, BAC assisted with income support and services out bush, the latter including delivery of Western food supplies; access to guns and gun licences; access to vehicles (via assistance to saved money in 'truck' accounts) and assistance with their purchase; and assistance with vehicle registration, repair and servicing.

MAC, as a business arm of BAC, became very effective in marketing art, and especially Kuninjku art. By 2004, there were about 100 Kuninjku artists (out of an estimated population of 300) selling art via MAC and responsible for nearly 60 per cent of turnover; by 2007–08, as MAC's turnover peaked, close to AUD1 million per annum was being paid to Kuninjku artists.

In terms of an overarching framework, one can analyse the postcolonial transformation of the Kuninjku way of life by deploying Fraser's (2009) three dimensions of social justice: recognition, redistribution and representation. BAC advocated for recognition of Kuninjku difference through political representation; it administered CDEP scheme income support effectively and provided other important services, such as managed savings accounts for the purchase of vehicles as member-tailored forms of redistribution.

The Aboriginal and Torres Strait Islander Commission (ATSIC), a democratically elected institution established by the Australian Government in 1990 (and abolished in 2004), advocated strongly at the national political level, and at international forums, for recognition of the right of Indigenous people like the Kuninjku to live on their traditional lands and to live differently (ATSIC, 1995). Coincidentally, ATSIC also administered and championed the CDEP scheme, its largest program; ran the Community Housing and Infrastructure program, which provided limited financial support to outstation resource agencies for housing and infrastructure; and, under its cultural policy, assisted art centres like MAC.

For a period of over 30 years, these institutional arrangements delivered helpful support that allowed Kuninjku to actively pursue meaningful livelihood opportunities. However, this tolerance of difference came at a cost, as they missed out on some citizenship entitlements when residing at outstations or Maningrida; housing was overcrowded and rudimentary; medical services were limited; and educational opportunities were extremely narrow, delivered only in English and often totally absent at outstations. Yet, by the early twenty-first century, Kuninjku had found their own form of hybrid livelihood, increasingly living between town and country and benefiting from the political representation for this mode of living provided by BAC. Nevertheless, Kuninjku were highly dependent on both the state and their regional organisation, which left them vulnerable to dramatic policy shifts.

Neo-Colonial Intervention for Neoliberal Assimilation

Over the past decade, the Kuninjku community has become entangled in national welfare and Indigenous policy-reform processes and a global economic downturn that clearly demonstrate this vulnerability and underline their inability to influence state power and policy unilateralism. This powerlessness has seen the rapid erosion of the transformative gains of the previous 30 years. Today, Kuninjku are caught up in a broader reconceptualisation of the 'Aboriginal problem' that has gained considerable following among the political, bureaucratic and corporate elites, and increasingly in public perception as well.

A second wave of colonisation and new forms of state experimentation has emerged once again in the name of improvement. Underpinning this second wave of domination, which appears unaware of the disasters of the past, has been a generalised view that the nature of the transformation of remote-living Aboriginal people has been a development failure. This failure is blamed on excess dependence on welfare, permissiveness allowed from the advent of the self-determination era and subsequent associated social and community dysfunction (Pearson, 2000; Sutton, 2009).

This dominant view has justified a paternalistic and discriminatory intervention in the Northern Territory since 2007 that has quite explicitly sought to alter the norms and values of Indigenous people to accord with Western ones. A policy discourse has emerged that seeks a fundamental shift of Aboriginal world views away from a relational focus on family, community and attachment to land, to those of the imagined neoliberal subject focused on individualism and material accumulation, and on heightened engagement with the free market.

This recolonising project imposes centralisation in Maningrida, once again, in line with state-enforced engagement with standard forms of Western education, employment and enterprise, irrespective of the absence of conventional labour markets or market opportunity. Despite the developmental rhetoric and neoliberal reasoning of governments in their seeking to 'develop the north' (Australian Government, 2015), this new project to deliver 'advancement' for Aboriginal people through integration is occurring at a time of great global uncertainty about the future of late capitalism in general, and conventional forms of paid work in particular. It is also influenced by a mood of selective austerity, as evident in welfare reform arguments that hold that the (rich) Australian state cannot afford the cost of servicing small, dispersed Aboriginal communities as it must repay high national debt (largely generated by excessive middle-class welfare and tax concessions for the rich).

Consequently, in the present, we see a process of recolonisation with associated radically altered institutional arrangements. The social contract that had emerged to underwrite the Kuninjku hybrid economy has been shattered, and a new Kuninjku precarity has re-emerged, reminiscent of the 1960s.

I choose 2004 as the starting point for this latest project of improvement inspired by neoliberal values (although I realise that this shift has earlier origins in a longstanding conservative ambivalence towards land rights and notions of Indigenous difference), as it was in 2004 that ATSIC was abolished and a new form of mainstreaming was introduced. ATSIC's suite of programs, including those beneficial to groups like the Kuninjku, were dispersed to mainstream agencies, and with them the political apparatus that had promoted difference and diversity was dismantled.

I will not recount this recent complex history of policy change and associated political disputation here in detail; this has been done elsewhere (e.g. Altman, 2014; Rowse, 2012; Sullivan, 2011). My synoptic analysis instead looks to summarise features of relevance to the Kuninjku, who have been inadvertently caught up in these dramatic policy shifts and the abolition of the institutions that underpinned their livelihood.

In her research on Indigenous people and crime, Anthony (2013) described the ruse of recognition:

> The Janus-face of sentencers shows a face of leniency that basks in its humanity and morality in recognising a wronged group and its cultural peculiarities *and* a face of penalty that glares at difference with condemnation to rationalise its exclusion of a risk group. (p. 27)

Since 2004, this Janus-face has been very evident in what I term 'the ruse of tolerance' as policy has shifted to eliminate the right to be different, with disastrous consequences for groups like the Kuninjku and their own transformative project.

The new governmental approach has three elements. First, there has been a broad discursive shift away from viewing remote Indigenous communities as disadvantaged to viewing them as dysfunctional. This shift has been most clearly seen in the Northern Territory with the National Emergency Response, known as the 'Intervention', first instigated in June 2007, a project that refers to failed states, laments disorder and seeks to recolonise remote Indigenous communities and spaces to reconnect Indigenous citizens to the mainstream (Dillon & Westbury, 2007). This project was implemented unilaterally, punitively and paternalistically by the Australian Government, aided and abetted by right-wing think tanks, opportunistic bureaucrats and some influential Indigenous actors.

Second, in line with trends in other rich Western countries, Australia has embarked on a project of welfare reform that has redefined citizenship not just in terms of rights, but also in terms of 'balancing' responsibilities, including the responsibility of individuals to use welfare in a manner that enhances productive engagement with mainstream education and the labour market (see Bielefeld, 2014, pp. 722–23). Such views have been given moral authority by the influential writings of Indigenous political actors like Noel Pearson (2000, 2009). At the same time, there has been a shift in welfare policy influenced by neoliberal thinking, which sees marginalisation as a product of individual failing rather than of politico-structural factors, including discrimination and racism (see Bourgois, 2003; Standing, 2014).

Third, there has been the promotion of a utopian myth that a market capitalist solution is possible in remote Indigenous Australia—all that is needed is the promotion in Arnhem Land of the free market ideas of Friedrich Hayek, Milton Friedman and Hernando de Soto and all economic and social problems will be solved! Wiegratz (2010) referred to this as the promotion of 'fake capitalism'. Alternatively, following Cahill (2014), one might interpret this emerging state project, in close alliance with the capitalist plutocracy, as seeking to embed neoliberalism throughout Indigenous Australia in class, ideological and institutional forms. However, this is not a neoliberalism based on the free market but, rather, one that is ideologically conflicted and dependent on state intervention to first morally restructure Indigenous subjects using behavioural carrots and sticks.

The problem with the 'new' approach is that it is based on blind faith and continues to ignore any inconvenient evidence that it might not work. Nowhere is this clearer than in Arnhem Land, where major resource extraction projects like the Ranger uranium mine and Gove bauxite mine are facing either closure—the Ranger mine in 2020—or major downgrading, as happened at Gove, after 45 years of operation, with the closure of a massive alumina processing plant. Despite the evidence that mining is not sustainable, developmental ideology encapsulating current policy rhetoric to 'develop the north' (Australian Government, 2015) persists.

From the Kuninjku perspective, this radical shift in policy is bewildering—an imposed, imagined new solution to deep structural challenges that were being slowly and productively addressed in collaboration with BAC. Suddenly, Kuninjku, like other Indigenous peoples in remote Australia, are reclassified as undeserving poor who need to be managed with new technologies of surveillance (especially to manage individual expenditures via electronic debit cards), and their behaviour punished and rewarded as subjects of experiments deploying Western behavioural economics.

When in Maningrida, Kuninjku are vulnerable to charges of child neglect, especially with heightened surveillance by roving social workers; they are liable to lose welfare income or be fined for high levels of school absenteeism; they live in overcrowded housing that appears disorderly; and are disengaged from mainstream forms of paid employment because their preferred alternative life way, developed over the last few decades, has prepared them poorly for the few regimented jobs that might be available. What is most concerning is that with such paternalistic governmentality, the postcolonial possibilities of the previous three decades have been demolished in the name of improvement.

Structurally, this has occurred because local political and economic institutions that were of fundamental importance to the operation of the Kuninjku hybrid economy have either disappeared or been drastically weakened. In the name of creating so-called real jobs, which are neither regionally available nor desired, the CDEP scheme has been abolished and replaced by a work for the dole program that requires Kuninjku to work 25 hours a week for their welfare entitlement, week in, week out, year in, year out. The new institution, first called the Remote Jobs and Communities Program and then renamed the Community Development Programme, has proven more successful in penalising participants for non-compliance—largely a result of its demanding requirements—than in finding employment for the 950 people registered as unemployed in the region.

For Kuninjku, this new scheme, having replaced the income security provided by the CDEP scheme, means less income and comes with the constant risk of being in breach of activity requirements (like attending scheduled meetings, training or some designated activity). There is also the risk that extra earnings will see the application of the social security income taper, as more earned income results simultaneously in less welfare income. While the program is administered by BAC, there are now multiple external, rather than just one, community forms of accountability and much time wasting and bureaucratic engagement—meta work that interferes with productive work in the hybrid economy. Moreover, Kuninjku occupations such as hunter, fisher, artist and ceremony specialist are not recognised as legitimate forms of 'employment' or 'activity'.

The story of BAC's declining fortunes is complex, and politically fraught. From 2004, BAC opposed destructive reform of the CDEP scheme. In 2007, it vigorously opposed the Northern Territory Intervention, including a unilateral Australian Government decision to transfer responsibility for outstations to the Northern Territory Government. BAC then underwrote a High Court challenge by key Maningrida traditional owners to the compulsory leasing of their land by the Australian Government for five years. The High Court found against the plaintiffs and BAC had to wear costs (since forgiven) of AUD1 million. Up until 2009, BAC robustly managed to represent the livelihood interests of its members. However, in 2010, new senior management attempted to comply with the government's developmental agenda without proper business planning, with dire consequences. Two years later, BAC went into special administration, insolvent and AUD10 million in debt. Only in July 2014 did BAC emerge, much diminished, from special administration, with debts of AUD3.5 million, to be repaid over five years, and a 'threatening shelved' liability to government of AUD6.5 million.

Unsurprisingly, since 2010, BAC's capacity to deliver a distinctive mix of social, cultural and commercial enterprises to its members has been largely curtailed and reoriented to the commercial. One wonders whether it will ever be able to deliver again on its diverse aims to promote the interests of its members. Some might argue that this diminished role suits the agenda of recent and current federal governments.

From a Kuninjku perspective, the decline of BAC's fortunes has been disastrous, in part because BAC's capacity to service the outstations and their vehicles has all but disappeared. A rapid change in management personnel at BAC has also seen a loss of corporate capacity to locally understand the intricate workings of the hybrid economy. Since the change in the corporation's senior management, social relations between management and Kuninjku have not settled; indeed, they have become severely strained.

MAC represents the clearest point of articulation between the regional economy and market capitalism. Its financial viability, of great relevance to Kuninjku incomes, has declined markedly in recent years. After the global financial crisis, sales of Aboriginal art nationally are estimated to have plummeted by 50 per cent (Office of the Registrar of Indigenous Corporations, 2012). Combined with the negligence of the special administrators that saw no application submitted for government cultural support when most needed, artists' incomes have declined markedly; in 2014, the gross earnings of Kuninjku artists were around 20 per cent of what they were five years earlier. In this respect, it is instructive to note the differential treatment in Australia of those vulnerable to global economic shocks; there have been no industry rescue packages for struggling Kuninjku artists, unlike for many other Australians experiencing technological unemployment. Today, MAC is slowly recovering but it will be some time before it can reach its peak turnover, in 2008–09, of over AUD2.6 million.

Let me summarise this livelihood disaster, which can be largely attributed to institutional changes driven by the Australian Government, as well as to risky engagement with market capitalism, using two frameworks. First, in terms of the hybrid economy (Altman, 2010), each of its three interlinked sectors—the market, the state and the customary—has shrunk; people earn less arts income from the market and, with the demise of CDEP scheme income support, Kuninjku receive less in transfer payments from the state. There is also a decline in the contributions to their diet from hunting, fishing and wild food gathering. This is partly because people have less access to vehicles to get onto country and less services support to live on country. There are other factors too, including acute difficulty in gaining access to vehicles and firearms, processes that were once facilitated by BAC. Conversely, with a heightened police presence in Maningrida in the wake of the Northern Territory Intervention, unlicensed guns and unregistered vehicles are being confiscated at unprecedented rates; people are losing their very means of hunting and arts production, and their ability to inhabit their traditional country.

Second, in terms of Fraser's (2009) social justice framework, an earlier 'recognition' or tolerance of difference has been replaced by intolerance, even at times by some BAC staff who lack local cultural understandings or corporate history, and increasingly prioritise the financial performance of the organisation. The prospects for the recognition of difference have declined as national and regional representative organisations (i.e. ATSIC and BAC) have been abolished or fundamentally altered and depoliticised.

The bottom line is that, in 2017, after a decade of progressively intensified state intervention to improve livelihoods, the Kuninjku are living more precariously than at any time since I started working with them in 1979, and probably since they moved out of Maningrida in the early 1970s. The structural and economic violence (Farmer, 2005; Peck, 2010) experienced at that time—a result of the exercise of colonial authority and stigma from other Aboriginal groups in Maningrida—is now not only being repeated, but also supplemented by forms of 'bureaucratic torture' (Lavie, 2014) unimagined in the past. All this is occurring in the name of improvement based on neoliberal reason and the elusive promise of forms of conventional development that the state and market capitalism, despite all the rhetoric, are incapable of delivering.

Kuninjku Push Back

Kuninjku responses to these circumstances have been mixed: some Kuninjku have retreated from engagement with capitalism, others are using enhanced ceremonial participation as a symbol of defiance and as a means to maintain a semblance of their regional status, itself based on difference. A handful have found work: two as rangers, a few as screen printers, one in night patrol, one at the school. It is a turbulent time for Kuninjku and the institutions that championed their difference; the Australian state and its agents are determined to recalibrate Kuninjku, their norms and values, and their institutions, away from the support of difference towards the promotion of sameness.

Kuninjku see all this very clearly; they lament the fact that today they are more impoverished than in the past, as I noted at the start, barely having enough welfare to purchase expensive store-sourced food, increasingly stuck in town and unsupported when at outstations in the bush. To some extent, their analysis, which I will report briefly, is similar to mine and rendered in terms of the social sciences binary of structure and agency. However, Kuninjku give more self-critical attention to their role in creating this situation over external structuring forces than I might, although there are some variations in interpretations about causes among my interlocutors.

On structure, Kuninjku see that both government policy and BAC have changed. As Kuninjku have few Western negotiating skills, especially an absence of English literacy beyond the most basic level, they had become heavily dependent on BAC to mediate on their behalf with the Australian state. Consequently, the distinction between government and BAC and the effect of changes of government policy on BAC become entangled and, at times, a little confused. For example, Ivan said:

> [In 1979] BAC came and all that time it was good with BAC. We worked with BAC, but then the government rules changed and BAC started to change too. Then the government came and they made BAC do what the government wanted and then they didn't want to work with us anymore. This was after Ian Munro time [after 2009]. BAC used to make roads for us and so on, but the government policies changed. BAC's policies changed and they didn't want to support us anymore. Why the government rules changed … and why the government came and made Bawinanga do what the government wanted and then they didn't want to work with us anymore. They got tired of us Bininj. They weren't interested in us anymore?
>
> There has been a process of a loss of enthusiasm from BAC. In the beginning the Balanda were enthusiastic about helping people out bush. Then BAC got very big, more Balanda, and their thinking changed and they lost interest in Bininj. Today there are different Balanda and they are not interested in us and delivering the services to us in the bush. They are interested in their own affairs and they have their own ideas. BAC are supposed to follow our instructions and wishes, but they follow their own agenda. They don't take an interest in what we are saying.

John put things more succinctly: 'I have still got the same law, but the government keeps changing their rules'.

Kuninjku people are feeling acutely what Povinelli (2011) has termed 'the economies of abandonment'. They are deeply concerned about the 'new generation' stuck in Maningrida, developing a taste for Western foods from the store. As Hamish said: 'Today people of this generation are not really standing properly on the ground. They don't tread upon the ground with the same confidence'. Likewise, Samuel said:

> [BAC] have changed. They are only concerned about Maningrida. I don't know if they will ever do a tucker run again. Some of us are used to eating bush tucker. We are the last generation to eat bush tucker but the children today they are not used to eating bush food.

Samuel's sister, Kay, put it this way: 'The young people are tired. The Balanda food has spoilt them'. John added: 'If you stay here in Maningrida you don't learn anything about your country and how to gather food from it. You only think about chicken and Balanda food'.

What worries people most is the constant pressure for the new generation to move to Maningrida, transform into Balandas and forego Kuninjku ways. As John said:

> The government wants us to stay here in Maningrida. They want us to come and live in houses here. They make the houses here to attract us … When people are themselves free to be Bininj they are happy, happy! When they come to Maningrida to live they become like Balanda. 'Hey you blackfella, you have got everything you need in Maningrida, come in here and live here.' But we have got our own country, our outstations too. So I am still pulled between the two.

Kuninjku are pushing back against this latest state assault in two interlinked ways: by maintaining a moral code of sharing with family and by escalating their participation in a transforming ceremonial life. These are big topics that I can only address briefly here.

Sharing remains a fundamental feature of life for Kuninjku people. They continue to participate in such practices, mainly with their kin, and they value sharing behaviour highly. As one of my interlocutors, Hamish, put it: 'We must never refuse any request from family. We must give to them every time'. Sharing game and cash unsolicited, and asking for game properly, especially in ceremonial contexts, are forms of behaviour that are regarded as demonstrating the very best of Kuninjku relational norms and values.

However, even here there is concern about transformational changes associated with living in town. John drew out the differences:

> Balanda values are different in relation to sharing. The old people who lived out bush ate bush tucker, yams and all kinds of tubers and plant foods … [he names them] and you can be an Aboriginal person there sharing it freely. But sometimes Bininj change their thinking and move towards Balanda law or Balanda thinking. They become different; some are living out bush and some are living in Maningrida worried about food. You change when you come to live in Maningrida.

Hamish elaborated:

> In the old days it was very hard to deny a request for food. They had to put the food they hunted out in the open. You couldn't hide your resources. Now you can hide food and money and get away with not sharing. We like people to initiate the sharing but if they don't then we go and ask. We feel they should offer. Some people don't offer. Everyone is different. Some people are more generous than others.

It is in this context that ceremony has taken on added value because it is usually performed away from Maningrida and people can still gain some access to transport from BAC to go to outstations for ceremonial purposes, where Bininj values and hunting for bush tucker dominate. Ceremony in turn has changed and diversified. There are still the old rituals, like Kunabibi, used to discipline initiates through seclusion in bush camps over many months. However, there are also new ceremonies like Yiwarrudj, or Christian fellowship, and funerals that increasingly mix Kuninjku song cycles with English gospel; these ceremonies, which are replacing earlier mortuary ones, can last for weeks on end.

All of these ceremonies constitute work for Kuninjku, as articulated in their language. Such work, though, is inseparable from sociality. It includes work at ceremonies performing song and dance, paid with both Western food and bush tucker; organising and managing ceremonies; garnering resources by soliciting anywhere and from anyone, but especially kin, for assistance to sustain people at ceremonies; and at ceremony-linked hunting, as opportunities arise and are intensified, often using vehicles provided for ceremonial transportation. Conversely, ceremony provides an opportunity to escape Maningrida and Balanda surveillance and supervision, provided one can persuade employers or government officials at Centrelink that this is all legitimate 'cultural practice' in accordance with bureaucratic guidelines.

Ceremonies also have a strong integrative function. They link Kuninjku and other regional groups together to celebrate tradition and to mourn the dead and bury them with proper decorum on their country. Moreover, ceremony allows Kuninjku to assert their difference and their identity, and to make strong public statements about their exclusive spatial domains; increasingly, signs are posted on access roads warning that ceremony is in progress and that any trespassing, even by state authorities like the police, will not be tolerated.

Yiwarrudj, or Christian fellowship, is especially important in bringing the young together with the old, dancing in front of ghetto-blasters for hours on end. These constitute important ceremonies of hope. Fundamentalism is creeping in, too, as Glenn told us: 'Jesus is coming back and will take the Christians up to the sky and the non-believers will be left behind'. Many Kuninjku traditionalists worry about the emerging tensions between new Christian fellowship and their authentic ceremonies. However, beyond praying to Jesus, what hope is there for the future, for the 'good life' that all my interlocutors increasingly see as something in the past?

Reviving Postcolonial Possibilities

'How can things be made better?' I ask. John and Kay answer:

> It won't get better, can't fix it. Might be change is needed. Country is there, the country is good, but the people are the problem. I don't know what is wrong with them. People want to move around, I'm telling you the right way. Sometimes people want to live here [Maningrida] sometimes they want to go back. Maybe things will get better and change or maybe not. I don't think so.

I would like to finish this chapter on a hopeful note but, like my interlocutors John and Kay, I find it difficult at this moment to be optimistic. It is not that long ago that when I visited we had shared a life way that allowed Kuninjku to move productively, with a high degree of fluidity and assuredness, between capitalist and non-capitalist economic forms. Indeed, through their active agency, Kuninjku people had creatively refigured a form of moral economy that, while heavily transformed, was still dominated by relationships of reciprocity within the Kuninjku community (and beyond) and displayed a high degree of egalitarianism and a sharing ethic characteristic of hunter-gatherer societies (Sahlins, 1972). Using dichotomies that are familiar to anthropologists, one might depict the Kuninjku as having creatively combined gift and commodity economies (Gregory, 1982), maintaining forms of gift exchange with family to push back against white domination while engaging with forms of commodity and labour exchange. When able to do this, life was far better for Kuninjku—people were not hungry and they could access the bush foods they value.

This fluid form of economy was based on a combination of distinct Kuninjku cultural logic alongside limited market capitalist opportunity. However, in recent years it has clashed with a dominant neoliberal logic that is looking to transform Kuninjku norms and values and preferences to those of mainstream Australians. This state project looks to effectively eliminate people like the Kuninjku by deploying subtle forms of what Lavie (2014) has termed bureaucratic torture and what Peck (2010) has referred to as economic violence. The high dependence of Kuninjku people on basic state support to activate the customary and market sectors of the hybrid economy make them extremely vulnerable to the project to impose a new form of moral economy on them. This raises important questions about the morality of a state apparatus that is willing to crush any resistance to this project of improvement with harsh financial penalties. Market capitalism imposes a moral logic that undermines any semblance of Kuninjku economic autonomy: when demand for art declines Kuninjku suffer, and when incomes decline there is no commensurate decline in the price of basic commodities. Indeed, it seems that as income decreases, people purchase cheaper foods that are less nutritious and do them physical harm.

This pessimistic assessment is not made lightly; it is based on observation of the extraordinary bureaucratic hurdles that Kuninjku need to negotiate on an almost daily basis to bridge cultural and linguistic divides in the absence of effective mediation. I have watched as Kuninjku have gone to the police to try and negotiate the complex processes of getting a gun licence or renewing a driving licence; I have seen vehicles impounded in the remote bush by police for being unregistered and their drivers, responding to requests from kin to go shopping or hunting, fined exorbitant amounts or face imprisonment.

Kuninjku people enjoy land rights and resource rights in remote Arnhem Land but these do not readily translate into the economic right to make a reasonable living on their country. In particular, having failed to reform land rights law to individualise communal lands, the Australian Government is now looking to individualise what is often communal labour through a new work for the dole regime under which Kuninjku people regularly lose access to welfare because they fail to meet some official deadline, often unaware of its existence or of other requirements, which change regularly.

In an uneven contest of values, the state champions individualism and ways of living calibrated to the standards of the Australian mainstream only, while Kuninjku prioritise relational ideals and ways of being. Kuninjku refuse to acquiesce meekly to the domination of the powerful irrespective of the suffering inflicted in the process. From their perspective, the state is losing legitimacy as it fails to deliver any improvement. Under such circumstances, the economic right of Kuninjku people to a livelihood encompassing a diversity of values is surely worth considering, especially at a time when there is global uncertainty about the future prospects of late capitalism.

The recent policy shift, which I have called neo-colonial, and which constitutes a second wave of colonisation 60 years after the first, is exposing Kuninjku people to welfare reform based on a fictitious notion of free market opportunity in remote Arnhem Land. It is unjust. This can be demonstrated very clearly with the three tests that Standing (2014, pp. 123–24) proposed for assessing whether reforms are socially just. The 'security difference principle' requires a reform to improve the security of the most insecure in society; the 'paternalism test principle' requires that any new controls not be imposed on some groups that are not imposed on others; and the 'dignified work principle' requires all types of productive work to be recognised and respected, not just labour in subordinated make-work activity. Each of these principles is broken in the Kuninjku case: people's income is highly insecure and declining; Kuninjku are subjected to paternalistic controls over welfare and expenditure that other Australians rarely experience; and their forms of work in the customary realm are neither recognised nor respected, even when they contribute to Kuninjku wellbeing.

At the international level, Australia has conjoined the United Nations Declaration on the Rights of Indigenous Peoples, which specifically calls for the recognition and respect of Indigenous rights of self-determination, yet pluralism in Australia is presently at a dead end. How to improve the prospects of the Kuninjku, a very insecure group in Australian society, so that they might be positioned to resist the tyranny of a new social engineering experiment doing them economic harm is a pressing question.

Fraser (2009) suggests that intractable issues of social justice will increasingly need to defer to a higher supranational power or 'inter-mestic' politics. Ultimately, judicial activism at the international, rather than domestic, level might provide the only means to ensure difference recognition for groups like the Kuninjku. How the Kuninjku might garner the political means to appeal to domestic and international publics is, at present, an almost insurmountable challenge. Perhaps the starting point is a politics of embarrassment. How can postcolonial possibilities enjoyed just a decade ago be revived to put an end to the economic violence currently being wrought? How is it that in rich Australia, first peoples like the Kuninjku, with property rights in vast tracts of land and natural resources, struggle to enjoy the fundamental human right to have enough food to eat?

Acknowledgements

The fieldwork on which this chapter is based was supported by the UK Economic and Social Research Council (ESRC). In writing this chapter, I would like to thank all my Kuninjku friends and interlocutors, especially as recorded here, John Mawurndjul, Kay Linjiwanga, Samuel Namunjdja, Janet Marawarr, Japhed Namunjdja and Ivan Namirrki. I would like to especially acknowledge my close friend Hamish Karrkarrhba who recently passed away prematurely aged just 50 years before the publication of this chapter. I hope that what I describe and analyse here accurately represents their perspectives and circumstances. I would like to thank a number of academic colleagues, especially Chris Gregory (who accompanied me on one field visit), Murray Garde (who accompanied me on another and assisted me enormously in recording interviews in Kuninjku and translating and transcribing them) and Melinda Hinkson, as well as other members of the research team with whom I interacted intensively at workshops in Manchester in 2011, Canberra in 2012, Edinburgh in 2014 and Manchester again in 2015.

References

Aboriginal and Torres Strait Islander Commission (ATSIC). (1995). *Recognition, rights and reform: A report to government on native title social justice measures*. Canberra, ACT: ATSIC.

Altman, J. C. (1987). *Hunter-gatherers today: An Aboriginal economy in north Australia*. Canberra, ACT: Australian Institute of Aboriginal Studies.

Altman, J. C. (2010). What future for remote Indigenous Australia: Economic hybridity and the neoliberal turn. In J. C. Altman and M. Hinkson (Eds), *Culture crisis: Anthropology and politics in Aboriginal Australia* (pp. 259–80). Sydney, NSW: UNSW Press.

Altman, J. C. (2011). From Kunnanj, Fish Creek to Mumeka, Mann River: Hunter-gatherer tradition and transformation in Western Arnhem Land, 1948–2009. In M. Thomas & M. Neale (Eds), *Exploring the legacy of the 1948 Arnhem Land expedition* (pp. 113–34). Canberra, ACT: ANU E Press. doi.org/10.26530/oapen_459230

Altman, J. C. (2014). Indigenous policy: Canberra consensus on a neoliberal project of improvement. In C. Miller & L. Orchard (Eds), *Australian public policy: Progressive ideas in the neoliberal ascendancy* (pp. 115–32). Bristol, England: Policy Press. doi.org/10.2307/j.ctt1ggjk39.13

Altman, J. C. (2016). Imagining Mumeka: Bureaucratic and Kuninjku perspectives. In N. Peterson and F. Myers (Eds), *Experiments in self-determination: Histories of the outstation movement in Australia* (pp. 279–300). Canberra, ACT: ANU Press. doi.org/10.22459/esd.01.2016.14

Anthony, T. (2013). *Indigenous people, crime and punishment.* Milton Park, Abingdon: Routledge. doi.org/10.4324/9780203640296

Australian Government. (2015). *Our north, our future: White paper on developing northern Australia.* Canberra: Commonwealth of Australia.

Australian Human Rights Commission. (2008). *Face the facts: Questions and answers about Aboriginal and Torres Strait Islander Peoples.* Retrieved from www.humanrights.gov.au/publications/2008-face-facts-chapter-1

Bielefeld, S. (2014). Compulsory income management and Indigenous peoples—exploring counter narratives amongst colonial constructions of 'vulnerability'. *Sydney Law Review, 36*, 695–726. doi.org/10.1080/10383441.2014.979421

Bourgois, P. (2003). *In search of respect: Selling crack in El Barrio* (2nd ed.). New York, NY: Cambridge University Press. doi.org/10.1017/cbo9780511808562

Cahill, D. (2014). *The end of laissez-faire? On the durability of embedded neoliberalism*. Cheltenham, England: Edward Elgar. doi.org/10.4337/9781781000281

Commonwealth of Australia. (1961, 20 April). *Parliamentary Debates, House of Representatives* (p. 1051). Canberra, ACT: Australian Government Publishing Service.

Council of Australian Governments. (2011). *National Indigenous reform agreement (closing the gap)*. Canberra, ACT: Council of Australian Governments.

Dillon, M. & Westbury, N. (2007). *Beyond humbug: Transforming government engagement with Indigenous Australia.* West Lakes, SA: Seaview Press.

Evans, N. (2003). *Bininj gun-wok: A pan-dialectical grammar of Mayali, Kuninjku and Kune* (2 vols.). Canberra, ACT: Pacific Linguistics.

Farmer, P. (2005). *Pathologies of power: Health, human rights and the new war on the poor.* Berkley, CA: University of California Press.

Fraser, N. (2009). *Scales of justice: Reimagining political space in a globalizing world.* New York, NY: Columbia University Press.

Gammage, B. (2011). *The biggest estate on Earth: How Aborigines made Australia.* Sydney, NSW: Allen & Unwin.

Garde, M. (2013). *Culture, interaction and person reference in an Australian language.* Amsterdam, Netherlands: John Benjamin. doi.org/10.1075/clu.11

Gregory, C. A. (1982). *Gifts and commodities.* London, England: Academic Press.

Lavie, S. (2014). *Wrapped in the flag of Israel: Mizrahi single mothers and bureaucratic torture.* New York, NY: Berghahn.

Li, T. M. (2015). Can there be food sovereignty here? *Journal of Peasant Studies, 42*(1), 205–11. doi.org/10.1080/03066150.2014.938058

McCarthy, F. D. & McArthur, M. (1960). The food quest and the time factor in Aboriginal economic life. In C. P. Mountford (Ed.), *Records of the American-Australian scientific expedition to Arnhem Land. Vol. 2: Anthropology and Nutrition* (pp. 145–94). Melbourne, VIC: Melbourne University Press.

Office of the Registrar of Indigenous Corporations. (2012). *At the heart of art: A snapshot of Aboriginal and Torres Strait Islander corporations in the visual arts sector.* Canberra, ACT: ORIC.

Pearson, N. (2000). *Our right to take responsibility.* Cairns, QLD: Noel Pearson and Associates.

Pearson, N. (2009). *Up from the mission: Selected writings.* Melbourne, VIC: Black Inc.

Peck, J. (2010). *Constructions of neoliberal reason.* Oxford, England: Oxford University Press. doi.org/10.1093/acprof:oso/9780199580576.001.0001

Povinelli, E. (2011). *Economies of abandonment: Social belonging and endurance in late liberalism.* Durham, NC: Duke University Press.

Rowse, T. (2012). *Rethinking social justice: From 'peoples' to 'populations'.* Canberra, ACT: Aboriginal Studies Press.

Sahlins, M. (1972). *Stone age economics.* Chicago, IL: Aldine and Atherton.

Schapper, H. (1970). *Aboriginal advancement to integration: Conditions and plans for Western Australia.* Canberra, ACT: Australian National University Press.

Standing, G. (2014). *A precariat charter: From denizens to citizens.* London, England: Bloomsbury Academic.

Sullivan. P. (2011). *Belonging together: Dealing with the politics of disenchantment in Australian Indigenous policy.* Canberra, ACT: Aboriginal Studies Press.

Sutton, P. (2009). *The politics of suffering Indigenous Australia and the end of the liberal consensus.* Melbourne, VIC: Melbourne University Press.

Thomas, M. & Neale, M. (Eds). (2011). *Exploring the legacy of the 1948 Arnhem Land expedition*. Canberra, ACT: ANU E Press. Retrieved from press.anu.edu.au/publications/exploring-legacy-1948-arnhem-land-expedition

Wiegratz, J. (2010). Fake capitalism? The dynamics of neoliberal moral restructuring and pseudo-development: The case of Uganda. *Review of African Political Economy*, *37*(124), 123–37.

Wolfe, P. (1999). *Settler colonialism and the transformation of anthropology: The politics and poetics of an tthnographic event*. London, England: Cassell.

Wolfe, P. (2015). *Traces of history: Elementary structures of race*. London, England: Verso.

9

The Rise of the Poverty-Stricken Millionaire: The Quest for the Good Life in Sargipalpara

Chris Gregory

Bless me, O goddess Lakshmi, with children and grandchildren, stores of grain, elephants, horses, cows and chariots, good health and longevity,

Let illness, debt, poverty, evil, cowardice, sorrow, untimely death and the mental anguish that burns the mind forever be destroyed. (Vedic chant)

bap bera kansa tama, beta bera thenga-tuma.

Brass and copper at the time of father, but only a stick and a hollowed-out gourd at the time of son. (Halbi proverb)

'Dwell in My House, O Lakshmi'

The micro-economic history of the neighbourhood of Sargipalpara I present in this chapter can be read as a classic illustration of the ancient saying that 'as it is in the microcosm, so it is in the macrocosm (and vice versa)'. Just as Indian politicians and businessmen at the state and national levels in India have embraced the right-wing ideology of the Bharatiya Janata Party (BJP) on free market global capitalism and profited immensely from it, so too have local councillors and businessmen in the market town of Kondagaon and its neighbourhoods, such as Sargipalpara, enthusiastically welcomed the new economic order and successfully exploited the opportunities this has presented. This 'ant's-eye' perspective on the Bastar plateau—from its north-eastern corner—contradicts the popular 'bird's-eye' view of Bastar, which sees it as part of the 'red corridor' along the central spine of India said to be controlled by Maoist revolutionaries, the 'Naxalites'. Things always look different from the ground, and so it is for the residents of Sargipalpara for whom the north Bastar plateau presents itself as a 'parallel state' (Sundar, 2016) divided neatly between the hilly, drier, mainly millet-growing, Naxalite-controlled zone to the west, and the relatively flatter, wetter, mainly rice-growing areas in the BJP-controlled zone to the east. Kondagaon is the centre of a booming market economy in the east that stands in stark contrast to the Naxalite-controlled western zone, where many villages still have no electricity and where the Naxalites deliberately keep roads in a state of disrepair to make it hard for the government's counterinsurgency forces to pursue them. To the extent that trends in voting patterns are a measure of the quest for the good life, then the people of Sargipalpara are enthusiastic participants in a brave new world championed by the BJP. The local councillors of Sargipalpara sing the praises of the BJP with a fervour that borders on the religious as they point to the new houses, new cars and new motorbikes that now populate their neighbourhood.

The changes in material wealth have indeed been dramatic. The rapid commercial growth of Kondagaon has absorbed former small farming hamlets like Sargipalpara into its orbit and transformed them into city suburbs. The rapidly growing population of Kondagaon, fed by high local birthrates and rural–urban and interstate migration into Bastar, has sent urban land prices booming. Sargipalpara is now a desirable address for the emerging elite, whose new two- and three-storey mansions present a striking contrast to the mudbrick, thatched huts of the indigenous inhabitants, a few of whom have been able to imitate this rise, to varying degrees of success, with flash houses of their own. The new prosperity in north Bastar, then, has introduced new forms of inequality, one quite spectacularly evident in the modern mansion standing beside its traditional mudbrick neighbour. This phenomenon can be found all over India, and the world at large. Perhaps the world's most stunning example is to be found in Mumbai, where Mukesh Ambami, India's richest man and recent entrant into Forbes's list of top 10 billionaires, built the world's most expensive house in the world after Buckingham Palace, a 27-storey skyscraper requiring 600 servants to maintain it. Sargipalpara is not Mumbai; however, the changing skylines and recent history of both places have been shaped by the same dominant global values, the unequal economic consequences of which are quite literally there for all to see.

While extreme economic inequality presents itself materially as a visual contrast of the most obvious kind, other economic consequences are less visible. One such example is the paradoxical rise of what I call the 'poverty-stricken millionaire'—the poor, urban householder who suddenly finds that their previously worthless residential land is now worth millions. The rise of this paradoxical new economic class cautions against any simple-minded approach to understanding the growing inequalities in the world today and poses questions about the values that inform the thoughts and actions of this new class. At state are notions of wealth and competing conceptions of it—that of the global political economy and, conversely, of the domestic moral economy of Sargipalpara.

Piketty's (2014) bestseller gets to the heart of the matter from a global political-economy perspective. He showed that the composition of wealth in market value terms has changed dramatically over the past three hundred years. Data on the metamorphosis of capital in France over the period 1700–2010, for example, shows that agricultural land constituted about 60 per cent of all wealth in 1700 but fell to less than 1 per cent by 1970. By contrast, the share of capital wealth in the form of urban-housing land maintained the same relative value (about 15 per cent) from 1700–1970, but then rose rapidly to account for some 60 per cent of all capital in 2010. In other words, France was transformed from an agrarian capitalist economy to an industrial economy, and then to one in which urban-residential land is now the dominant form of wealth, an artefact of the rapidly rising relative price of urban land fuelled by the boom in the financial sector that followed the era of deregulation that began when Nixon floated the dollar in August 1971. India's economic history over the past 300 years has been very different; however, the same market forces have created the same patterns in the relative prices of rural and urban land over the past three decades. The phenomenon of the 'land-rich, dirt-poor' householder has emerged everywhere, but the domestic values that inform their quest for the good life are everywhere different because familial values and religious values are everywhere different.

The indigenous Halbi-speaking residents of Sargipalpara have a concept of wealth that is much broader than the narrow political-economy perspective in which the exchange value of commodities is deemed to be the only value that matters. This indigenous conception of wealth is elaborated in a 31,000-line oral epic about the goddess Lakshmi sung at rice-harvest time by women priestesses called *gurumai*. Lakshmi is the all-India goddess of wealth and prosperity and, as the popular iconography illustrates, she is always associated with material wealth of some kind, be it grain, gold, cattle or the merchant's ledgers. She is also associated with water, elephants and lotuses. It suffices to note that these objects symbolise wealth of a 'spiritual' form. As the words of the epic make very clear, the spiritual values are very much of a this-worldly human kind. Lakshmi—who is rice personified in Bastar—brings wealth and happiness to those with whom she dwells. The ritual focus is on persuading Lakshmi to dwell in one's house today rather than living in nirvana tomorrow. Lakshmi is a fickle goddess who takes offence at bad conduct and leaves as soon as this happens. When she goes, her elder sister Alakshmi, the goddess of poverty and misery, takes her place. At harvest time every year, rice in the form of Lakshmi is ritually harvested and wedded to Narayan. During her journey from the rice field to the wedding venue she passes through the streets of Sargipalpara, stopping at houses along the way so that female household heads can ritually invite her to enter. The epic myth, and its ritual enactment, is an explication of the values of a domestic moral economy of a kind that makes no distinction between the realms of kinship, economy and religion. The 31,000 lines of the epic can be seen as an elaborate allegorical development of the two lines from the Vedic chant above, which capture the essence of the idea of the two notions of wealth involved: the objective material form and the human form. Material wealth includes domestic wealth in the form of food, clothing and shelter; productive wealth in the form of servants, seed, cattle, horses and elephants; and mercantile wealth in the form of gold, money, credit and the like. By contrast, human wealth includes familial wealth in the form progeny and harmonious relations with kin; social wealth in the form of fame, friends and social acceptance; and personal wealth in the form of good health and longevity.

Like all allegories, the epic tale admits of multiple interpretations, but the basic values as expressed in this particular version of the tale are clear and reflect the gender and cultural status of the singers. Lakshmi, an egalitarian goddess, is only concerned with right conduct and will dwell with anyone, whatever their caste. It is interesting to note that the egalitarian values that pervade the epic are of a social and cultural kind rather than an economic kind. Indeed, the epic notes the fact that some people are 'haves' and others are 'have-nots', but makes no moral judgement about it. A discussion of the values that underpin the epic is beyond the scope of this essay; suffice to say that it articulates what Ramanujan (1991) called a 'counter system' because it gives 'an alternative set of values and attitudes, theories of action other than the official one' (p. 33). The epic is unusual in that it is not a story of war and conquest. Nobody is killed. The only violence is domestic violence, when Narayan beats his newly wed wife Lakshmi. While I am yet to meet anyone in Sargipalpara who would not prefer more money to less, it is domestic-political relations within households and between households that primarily concern most people, especially women. This is a 'kinship-intensive' world where second and third cousins live cheek by jowl and where cross-cousin marriage has resulted in people being related in multiple ways. Human wealth, in the senses outlined above, is a central concern. The Maoist insurgency movement is, for the most part, something remote happening in the hills in the rural areas to the west; it is not part of people's everyday urban lives in Sargipalpara. The trans-cultural moral values the epic articulates give people food for thought as they practise the difficult art of trying to live together well in a world where history is forever throwing up new dilemmas and paradoxes, the emergence of the poverty-stricken millionaire being the latest.

In the micro-economic history of Sargipalpara that follows—one that reflects my 30 years of familiarity with the place—I illustrate, in general terms, how the paradox of the poverty-stricken millionaire has arisen and discuss, in more particular terms, how the indigenous subalterns manage their quest for the good life in terms of local conceptions of material and human wealth. I end with a case study of one poverty-stricken millionaire's quest for the good life. In my struggle to comprehend the mass of confusing data I have collected over the years, I am guided by Mauss's (2007) sage advice:

> Note the differences between moral environments; court morality and popular morality. Women's morality is not men's; the morality of the old is not the morality of the young, and sexual morality is not general morality'. (pp. 156–57)

The Emergence of the New Elite of Kondagaon

In the early 1900s, Kondagaon was a small farming village beside a creek next to the main road south to Jagdalpur, the capital of the then Princely State of Bastar in east-central India. Its residents grew rice, millet and vegetables, which they traded for other commodities in the Sunday market; some earned a few extra rupees by selling chai, snacks and other products to the passing traffic. Sargipalpara, another farming village, lay a couple of kilometres upstream and about half a kilometre back from the main road.

When I arrived in Kondagaon in 1982 to commence fieldwork on the periodic marketing system, it was a small market town with a population of 17,279 people, some 25 per cent of whom were relatively recent migrants; its Sunday market was the local regional centre of a large network of periodic markets on the north Bastar plateau; and its roadside shops and houses were spread ribbon-like two kilometres up and down National Highway 30. My wife and I found a place to stay in Sargipalpara, a neighbourhood ward of the expanding town of Kondagaon, the administrative centre of a regional district of the same name. Our house, a new, mudbrick, four-room dwelling with a tiled roof, was one of the first to be built in the neighbourhood on land that a Hindi-speaking migrant had purchased a few years before from a local Halbi-speaking farmer.

Between 1982 and 2006, I made 12 return visits to Kondagaon. Throughout this period the region remained, for the most part, a sleepy backwater where rice farmers eked out a precarious existence on rainfed-irrigation paddy fields. It seemed as if the effects of the 1991 neoliberal economic policies that transformed the Gangetic plain and other parts of India were never going to be felt on the Bastar plateau. Therefore, I was shocked by the changes I observed in 2013 when I returned after an absence of seven years. The region, which has long attracted migrants from near and far within India because of its relatively abundant agricultural lands and its forests rich in game, minor forest products and timber of various useful kinds, was now attracting a new breed of immigrant. The mango trees along the main highway—those that had not been pulled out in the highway upgrade—advertised their arrival; competing agribusiness companies had covered the trunks of the trees with multicoloured foolscap-size cloth advertisements for new hybrid varieties of maize. The rice farms in the villages beside NH30 were flush with new maize crops irrigated by tube wells, the highway forming the main street of Kondagaon had been widened and commercial activity was flourishing as never before as the invisible hand of the neoliberal economic multiplier worked its magic.

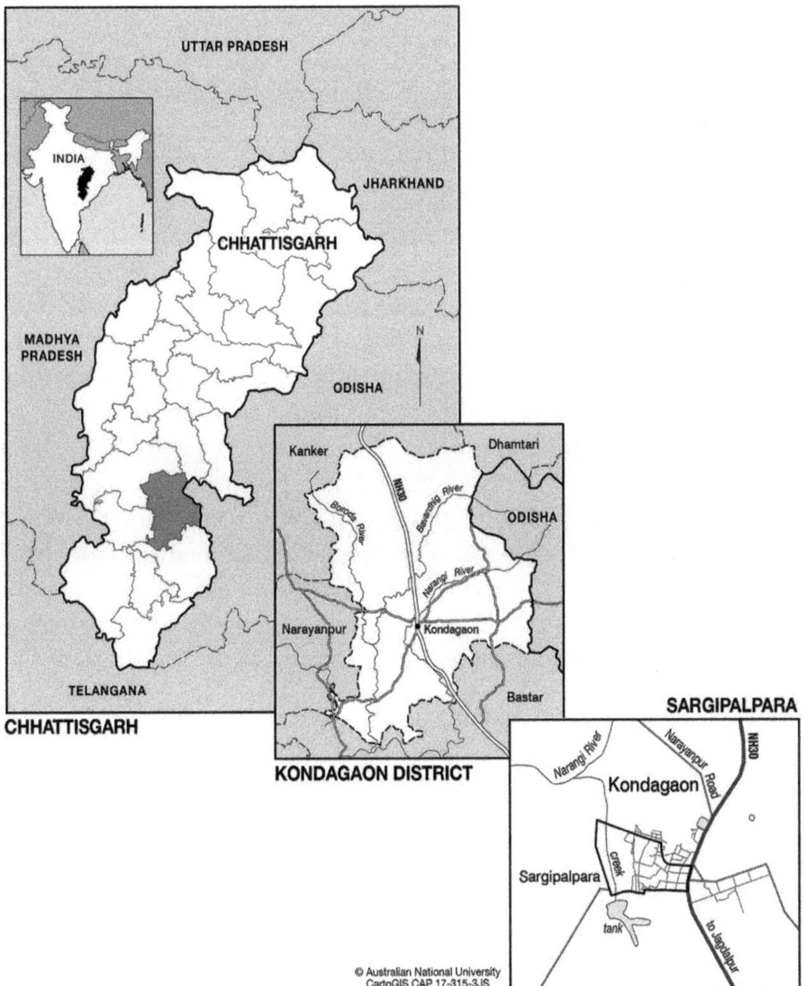

Figure 9.1: Map of Sargipalpara Ward, Kondagaon, India

Source: CartoGIS, College of Asia and the Pacific, The Australian National University.

The good life led by these new agents of change—mostly single men—is there for all to see. They dress in shirts with a logo that identifies their company; stay in Kondagaon's brand-new, air-conditioned, four-star hotel; work hard during the day competing with one another to strike new business deals; and relax in the evening with wine and whatever local women they are able to procure. These newcomers to Bastar, some of who bring their families and settle in the town, are the latest in a long line of migrants whose quest for the good life has brought them to Bastar. Some, the landless dirt-poor who scrounge a living working as domestic servants, day labourers and petty traders, have come from neighbouring states to escape rural poverty. Others, such as the mercantile elite from the Marwari-speaking region of Rajasthan, who began arriving in large numbers in the 1960s and 1970s, continue to prosper. The sons of migrants I studied in my 1980s research (Gregory, 1997) are shrewdly exploiting the new economic opportunities opening up; they claim their status as Kondagaon's cultural elite by building mansions in the now desirable residential area of Sargipalpara, marrying off their daughters to high-status families from their own caste from different parts of India and celebrating with expensive weddings fit for royalty. Yet, not all migrants have come for money. Some, such as the Hindu refugees from the Bangladesh Liberation War of 1971, were resettled in Bastar under a Government of India program; their quest for the good life has been a battle to re-create a moral community torn apart by the deadly violence of war. Then there are the Naxalites, the Maoist revolutionaries, whose quest for the good life stands in violent, polar opposition to the neoliberal entrepreneurs, whose conception of the good life is defined by the profits from the new hybrid seeds they are introducing and the natural resources, such as timber and iron ore, they are extracting.

When I first arrived in Bastar, the Naxalites were a distant rumble of unrest in the deep south; over the years they have slowly moved north and today inhabit the so-called red corridor that runs down the central spine of India. Their arrival, as the law of social physics would predict, has excited an equal and opposite counterinsurgency reaction. The north Bastar plateau is now a parallel state, where the land to the west of the north–south-running NH30 is ruled by the Naxalites and the region to the east by the ruling ultraconservative BJP. The border is marked at regular intervals by camps of counterinsurgency militia who, afraid of being shot, live like prisoners behind tall razor wire topped fences under the watchful eye of armed guards in towers. Kondagaon, like most towns and cities in Bastar, is very much under the control of the BJP Government. As such, everyday life in Kondagaon goes on as if the guerrilla war between these combatants does not exist, until an atrocity—such as the attack on a convoy of Indian National Congress leaders in the Darbha Valley in south Bastar on 25 May 2013, which killed 27 people—interrupts everyday life. I was in Kondagaon when this happened. The government declared a statewide curfew. All commercial and administrative activity ceased completely. An eerie silence followed that lasted 24 hours. Business as usual picked up again the next day as if nothing had happened. That, at least, is how things appeared; of course, what goes on behind the scenes is another matter, but that is something that people in Kondagaon never talk about—and do not want to talk about. Those locals who do talk about politics are enthusiastic supporters of the new economic order.

'You have been coming here for 30 years *dada*', a native Halbi-speaking BJP municipal councillor said to me in 2013. He continued:

> You have seen the changes. We are rich now. We have nice houses, TV, sewing machines, beds, cupboards. Look at this *pakka* (modern) house we are standing in. Our chief minister is a great man. He has made us rich. Look at that sewing machine. He gave me one too. He has given many things away.

The councillor's monologue became more animated with every sentence. It was like a rousing political speech, and his fervour was contagious. 'Yes, yes', shouted two other men in the room, both of who were affines, or kinsmen, of the councillor: 'Raman Singhji, the Chief Minister, is a great man'. It is indeed true that the material conditions of many households in Sargipalpara have improved dramatically, but in a very uneven way. The *pakka* house that we were standing in was the only one belonging to a local in the immediate, crowded neighbourhood.

The past 100 years, then, has utterly transformed Kondagaon from a small, remote, roadside farming village into a rapidly growing, commercial and administrative centre that is now very much part of the Indian national polity and global economy, with all the social tensions that implies. Migration from all parts of India has turned it into a microcosmic exemplar of India's macrocosmic cultural diversity: while Hindi is the lingua franca, native speakers of Tamil, Telegu, Malayam, Bengali, Oriya, Marathi and every other major language of India, can be heard; while Hinduism is the dominant religion, the temples of its many and varied sects, as well as the mosques, churches and places of worship of every other religion in India can be seen; and hardly a week goes by in the annual cycle without the performance of the ritual of some religion somewhere in the town. Kondagaon's current (2011) population of 30,717 has members of all the major castes of India, but they live cheek by jowl in neighbourhoods whose rapid economic development has created a complex mixture of rich household and poor, high caste and low.

Ethnography is only possible when it takes a particular point of view; mine is that of the people who became my neighbours during my first field trip in 1982, members of the Halbi-speaking Ganda community, whose ancestors first settled in Sargipalpara an unknown number of generations ago, but certainly more than six. These people are members of the dirt-poor subaltern class of Kondagaon who have been both victims and patients of the rapid economic changes since the 1980s: victims in the sense that many are the landless sons and daughters of fathers who, in their selfish quest for the good life, sold their ancestral farmlands to outsiders to profit from the rapidly rising prices; patients in the sense that some are the passive recipients of new-found wealth as the owners of *kacca* (mudbrick) urban houses on land that (in 2014) is worth INR700 per square foot, a veritable fortune in a town where a kilogram of rice costs INR25. These are the poverty-stricken millionaires, the members of the new 'dirt-poor but land-rich' class.

The Indigenous Subalterns of Sargipalpara

The distinction between the elite and the subaltern is not a matter of academic debate in Sargipalpara. The starkness of the contrast is there for all to see as soon as one enters the neighbourhood. The elite live in large, newly constructed, brightly coloured, two-storey mansions surrounded by lush, well-watered gardens growing behind high walls and secure, elaborately designed, wrought-iron gates. By contrast, the subalterns live in small, old, tumble-down, white-washed, mudbrick, roadside shacks behind narrow, dusty pavements. This visual contrast is the outward and visible sign of an ever-widening gulf between the rich and poor in Kondagaon; underlying it are inward and invisible cultural values and social relationships whose form and colour can only be grasped by entering the houses and listening to the voices of the inhabitants. For these voices to make sense, it is necessary to zero in on the human geography of Sargipalpara, and to reconstruct the history of valuation of the four different categories of land that lie within its boundaries.

The official census statistic is a useful starting point not just for its quantitative data but for the qualitative data provided in the official language used to classify the data. The latter is very important because it embodies the values used to inform government policy. The 2011 population of Sargipalpara of 2,062 people lived in 472 houses, an average of 4.36 per household. The household data are grouped firstly into castes and then into four official super categories called 'General' (G), 'Other Backward Castes' (OBC), 'Scheduled Castes' (SC) and 'Scheduled Tribe' (ST). The G category contained 109 households made up of Brahmans (30), Muslims (16), Thakur (16) and 47 households from a variety of other castes. The OBC category contained 141 households, with the Kosta (66) and Raut (21) being numerically dominant. The SC category contained 106 households, most of which belonged to the Ganda caste (87), while the ST category contained 116 households, 94 of which belonged to the Gond tribe. These official categories have important affirmative action implications for those so classified, which makes the tribe/caste distinction a hotly debated issue of identity politics in Bastar. To transcend the terms of debate these official government categories trap one in, it is necessary to subdivide caste data by language if we are to identify the subaltern and pose new questions for investigation.

Representatives of almost every major language group in India can be found in Sargipalpara; however, Halbi is the mother tongue of the original settlers of Sargipalpara and Hindi the lingua franca of everyone. If the data on official caste category is subdivided vertically by language—Halbi speakers versus non-Halbi speakers—then we get the classification shown in Table 9.1, which can be read in two ways.

Table 9.1: Sargipalpara: Classification of Households by Official Caste and Unofficial Class

Official classification	Subalterns (mainly Halbi speakers*)	Elite (mainly non-Halbi speakers^)	Total	%
Official caste (G + OBC + SC)	231	125	356	75
Official tribe (ST)	116	–	116	25
Total number of households	347	125	472	100
%	74	26	100	

* This includes some speakers of other Bastar languages such as Gondi, Kosti, Bastari and Bhatri.

^ These include speakers of 11 Indo-Aryan languages—Oriya, Marathi, Bengali, Awadhi, Bhojpuri, Gujarati, Marwari, Panjabi, Nepali, Sindhi and Chhattisgarhi—and three Dravidian languages—Telegu, Malayalam and Tamil.

Source: Fieldwork data.

Reading *down* the rows gives the official picture of the social structure of Sargipalpara: 75 per cent of the population are officially classified as members of a 'caste' and 25 per cent as members of a 'tribe'. Reading *across* the columns gives us a different take on the official picture: 74 per cent of houses consist of Halbi speakers and the remaining 26 per cent non-Halbi speakers. The elite in Sargipalpara come almost exclusively from this latter group. The Halbi speakers constitute the bulk of the subalterns. The terms of the official debate defined by the distinction between 'tribes' and 'castes' poses the question of the cultural, political and economic status of the 25 per cent of households officially classified as ST. The terms of the debate defined by mother tongue pose the question of the cultural, political and economic status of the 75 per cent of households, the subalterns who live in *kacca* houses. It is the latter group I propose to investigate, but official data are of little help here. Their history is unwritten although recoverable by genealogical analysis and the collection of data on their oral traditions.

What unites these subaltern households vis-a-vis the elite is that they are the descendants of people who have been settled in Bastar for an unknown number of generations, but definitely more than six. Most of the elite, by contrast, have been in Bastar for two to three generations, but definitely not more than five generations. This, at least, is what the genealogies that I have collected reveal, an objective fact readily confirmed by the stories people tell. The sharp distinction, visually observable at the macro-level between elite and subaltern, becomes rather more complex as one zooms in on the multi-levelled divisions and subdivisions between the 347 subaltern households.

The first division is between those householders whose ancestors settled in Sargipalpara as farmers over four or five generations ago and those landless day labourers and petty traders who have recently arrived from neighbouring towns and villages on the Bastar plateau. The latter are the poorest of the poor. Many have come from villages where population growth and limited supplies of land have rendered them landless. They have been attracted to Kondagaon for the employment opportunities it provides and to Sargipalpara because relatives from whom they could seek assistance with accommodation and food live there.

The descendants of the original settlers constitute the bulk of the 'poverty-stricken millionaires' whose urban household plots have skyrocketed in value. These households are subdivided into two distinctive cultural subgroups based on relative wealth and caste status. The Kosta caste (66 houses) are the wealthiest. Their caste community (*samaj*) is the strongest and, in their own eyes and the eyes of many others in Sargipalpara, they are the most entrepreneurial. The superficial evidence for this is the number of *pakka* houses owned by members of this caste and the lavishness of the weddings they hold. On my last visit, in 2013, I attended a wedding of a daughter of a relatively wealthy Kosta man who has the largest *pakka* house owned by a Halbi speaker. The wedding was the talk of the town because he was the first Bastarian in Sargipalpara to include a car in his daughter's dowry. Many of his fellow caste members expressed great dismay about this because of the pressure its puts on them to follow suit.

The Ganda (Weaver) Sub-Lineages

The 83 houses of the less well-off and so-called lower status Ganda people are my central focus. This people also have their subdivisions, based on clan status and wealth, as Table 9.2 illustrates. The Korram clan, which consists of three sub-lineages comprising 48 households, is the only landowning clan. The other clans, consisting of some 35 households, have no farmland. The Baghel sub-lineages, as the village names of Sambalpur and Umgaon suggest, are relatively recent immigrants from these villages. They are the poor relatives but have many affinal links with the Korrams. They live together in a densely packed southern section of Sargipalpara the locals sometimes refer to as Baghelpara.

Table 9.2: Socioeconomic Differentiation of the Ganda (Weaver) Community of Sargipalpara

Lineage	Location within Sargipalpara	Households (no.)	Landholding (acres)
Original settlers			
Korram I	Eastern section	11	1.0
Korram II	Northern section	10	5.5
Korram III	Western section	27	9.0
Total		48	15.5
Migrants			
Baghel Sambalpur	Southern section	20	–
Baghel Umgaon	Southern section	5	–
Others	Southern section	10	–
Total		35	–
Grand Total		**83**	**15.5**

Source: Fieldwork data.

The Korrams, then, are descendants of the original settlers, and settlement of the houses of the sub-lineages reveals the microhistorical geography of this part of Sargipalpara. Figure 9.2 shows the settlement patterns of the clans and sub-lineages of the Ganda community. It only covers part of the neighbourhood officially classified as Sargipalpara, and omits the 50 or so houses of the elite that are scattered around and between the Ganda houses. The households of the Korram I sub-lineage are coloured red and are clustered to the east; the households of the Korram II sub-lineage are coloured blue and clustered to the north; the households of the Korram III sub-lineage are coloured green and are clustered to the west; and the recent arrivals, the Baghels, are densely clustered to the south.

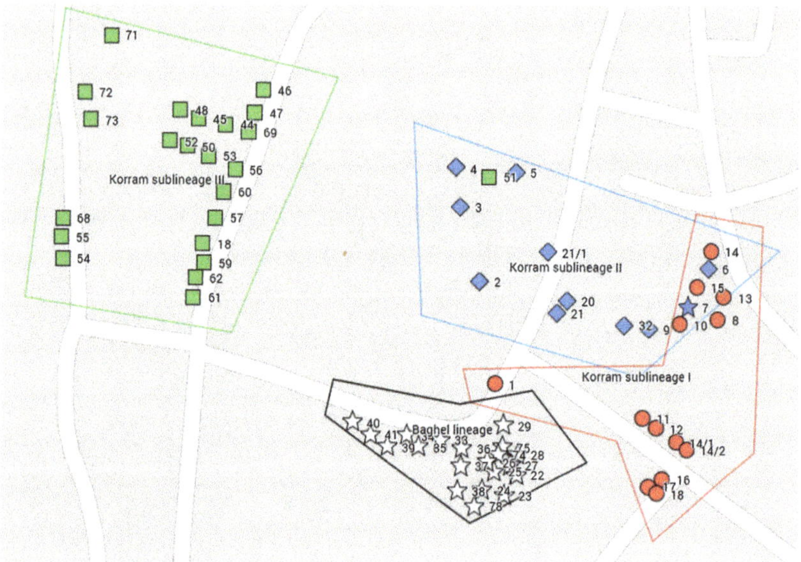

Figure 9.2: Map of Settlement Patterns of the Clans and Sub-Lineages of the Ganda Community of Sargipalpara

Source: Google Maps and fieldwork data.

The genealogical links between the three sub-lineages of the Korram clan have been forgotten, but kin within each sub-lineage are related as cousins to the third or fourth degree. My data show that some 17 per cent of marriages were internal to Sargipalpara, 59 per cent with Ganda spouses from neighbouring villages, and 24 per cent were inter-caste marriages, most of which involved Ganda women and immigrant men. Eighteen of the 83 Ganda households in 2011 were headed by women who were either widows or divorcees.

Kinship relatedness, then, is very dense and all householders are integral parts of a very complex web of ever-changing relationships of consanguinity and affinity that bind people together. The patrilineal superstructures that unite households, although invisible to outsiders, are relatively stable, as they evolve slowly over time. Figure 9.3 shows the genealogical ties that bind the 10 households of the Korram II sub-lineage together.

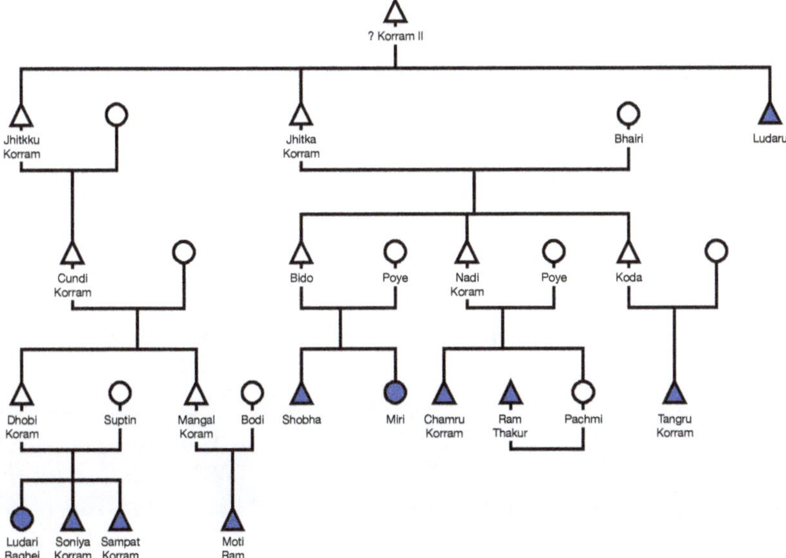

Figure 9.3: Genealogical Relationships Between the Households of the Korram II Sub-Lineage

Key: Triangle = male; circle = female; horizontal link below = marriage; horizontal link above = siblings; vertical link = descent.

Source: Fieldwork data.

Of particular interest is household number 20 (H20), which is known as 'Chamru's household', even though Chamru died in 1999. This household is exceptional; however, it is precisely because of this that it can provide insights into the history of Sargipalpara as a whole. This household, which is the largest both in numbers of people and traditional landholdings, exemplifies the dirt-poor, land-rich paradox in Sargipalpara in its most extreme form. The origin of this paradox lies in the way the local agrarian economy of Sargipalpara has been turned upside down. It is necessary to briefly examine the history of this inversion.

Indigenous Conceptions of Land Classification and Valuation in Sargipalpara

In the days when the residents of Sargipalpara were farmers, the value of land reflected its productivity as farmland. Land in Bastar is classified into four classes. At one extreme is the relatively highly productive, low-lying riverbed land on clayey loam called *gabhar.* This top-quality land is used exclusively for rice growing. At the other extreme is the relatively unproductive fourth-grade land called *marhan*, found on coarse sandy soil in the higher, wooded areas, suitable only for growing low-yielding, dry-grain crops like millet. These are the areas where farmers build their houses. Between these two extremes, Halbi speakers identify two intermediate categories: *mal,* second-grade, slightly higher land, suitable for growing rice but at a lower yield; and *tikra,* sloping, sandy, third-grade land best suited for millet.

Sargipalpara, whose boundaries are illustrated in Figure 9.1, contains all four categories of land. The creek travels through the low-lying lands to the west, the area where the best quality land lies. As one walks eastward towards Chamru's household, the elevation of the land slowly increases from a low of 580 metres at the creek bed to 600 metres (where the residential area begins), and the rice-yield ratio (kilos of rice harvested to kilos planted) falls gradually, from 30:1 on the top-quality *gabhar* land, to 20:1 on the second-grade *mal* land, and 10:1 on the third-grade *tikra* land. Relative land values have been directly correlated with these ratios on the relatively rare occasions when it has been sold (inheritance is the normal mode of transfer).

The commercial development of Kondagaon stimulated an active market in land. The top-quality *gabhar* farmland was still much sought after and its price rose rapidly in absolute terms over the years, but not as much as the fourth-grade upland *marhan*, which was in excess demand as urban household land. In 2015, *gabhar* sold for around INR130 per square foot while *marhan* sold for about seven times that amount, as Table 9.3 shows. Ganda householders have been active sellers in this market, which is why only 18 households of the 83 have any farmland left today. Twelve of the farmland-owning households have holdings of one acre or less, most of it of the second or third quality; the other six households, with holdings of 3 acres or less, again have holdings of mostly the lower quality type. Chamru's household still owns about 2.5 acres of farmland and was one of the largest owners of fourth-grade *marhan* land. However, as the urbanisation of Kondagaon turned this land into top-quality household land, much of this, too, has been sold. Two parts of the large plot on which the present house stands have recently been carved off and sold to buyers who have erected large *pakka* houses.

Table 9.3: Sargipalpara Land: Contemporary Market Values Versus Traditional Productive Values

Halbi land classes	Use value of land	Productive value (rice seed to yield ratio)	Market value (per square foot in 2015)
Gabhar			
Top-quality, low-lying creek bed land (580 metre elevation)	High-yield, late variety rice	>30:1	<Rs130
Marhan			
Low-quality, higher creek bank land (600 metre elevation)	Low-yield, early variety rice; millet; housing	<10:1	>Rs700

Source: Fieldwork data.

A close examination of the Google map of Sargipalpara reveals the presence of modern agri-business too. Farming in Bastar is, for the most part, based on rain-fed irrigation, but the dam that has been constructed has created the potential for a limited amount of irrigated farming of hybrid maize in the dry season. The six large, contiguous rectangular plots—something never seen in peasant farming systems because of the tendency of land to be divided and dispersed as it is inherited down a patriline—is owned by the new business elite. The visual division between elite and subaltern in the residential quarter is now being reproduced on the farmland.

The preceding discussion has revealed that life in Sargipalpara is simply complex. It is simple because economic changes have created a new and obvious stratification between the new elite and the original subalterns. It is complex because a household such as Chamru's is embedded in a multilayered domestic moral economy that opposes its members as land-rich, dirt-poor subaltern descendants of original settlers against recent arrivals who are dirt-poor; low-caste Ganda people originals against the higher status Kosta; members of the Korram clan against their affines in the recently settled Baghel clan; and members of the Korram II sub-lineage against other Korram sub-lineages. Chamru's household is a classic example of what Polanyi (1944, Chapter 4) describes as 'socially embedded'. The economic basis of their economy—peasant proprietorship in parcels of farmland of different quality—has, for the most part, gone, sold to high bidders. For them, the economy has become a superstructure whose workings they do not understand, but whose power they feel; it has dealt them a bittersweet blow by turning them into poverty-stricken millionaires. This has provided opportunities for some members of the household, misery for others, and difficulties for all because the complex, polyvalent, multilayered domestic moral economy in which they are socially embedded provides no simple answers to the moral dilemmas they face. The original subalterns of Sargipalpara live in precarious times, but it is a precarity shaped uniquely by the historical geography of the land they have settled on.

The Story of One Poverty-Stricken Millionaire Householder's Quest for the Good Life

We are now in a position to consider one poverty-stricken millionaire householder's quest for the good life in Sargipalpara. Given the complexity of the sociocultural and economic structure of the domestic moral economy in Kondagaon, it is useful to recapitulate the argument about the socioeconomic embeddedness of the household before delving into even greater complexity. Chamru's household is one of 10 households of lineage II of the Korram clan, the original landowning settlers who stand opposed, as members of the Ganda (weaver) community, to other landless members of the Ganda caste who have migrated to Sargipalpara from neighbouring villages over the past generation or so. The 83 houses that belong to the Ganda caste are part of the 347 houses that constitute the subaltern class of Sargipalpara. The 264 'other castes' category includes about 66 households of the Kosta (silk weaver) caste who, like the Ganda, were original settlers; the rest are, for the most part, landless migrants from nearby villagers. In other words, around 30–35 per cent of subaltern houses are in the 'land-rich, dirt-poor' category. Considered a class, this group is betwixt and between the dirt-poor group and the relatively rich, elite group that numbers some 125 households.

Figure 9.4 captures the embeddedness of Chamru's household; it is clear that as one moves up the hierarchy, the values that govern relationships between the houses change from the domestic and familial to the national and political, in which class becomes an issue. Economic and religious values permeate every level, but the links between the religious and the familial come to the fore as one moves into the household level. The domestic moral politics of Chamru's household illustrate this.

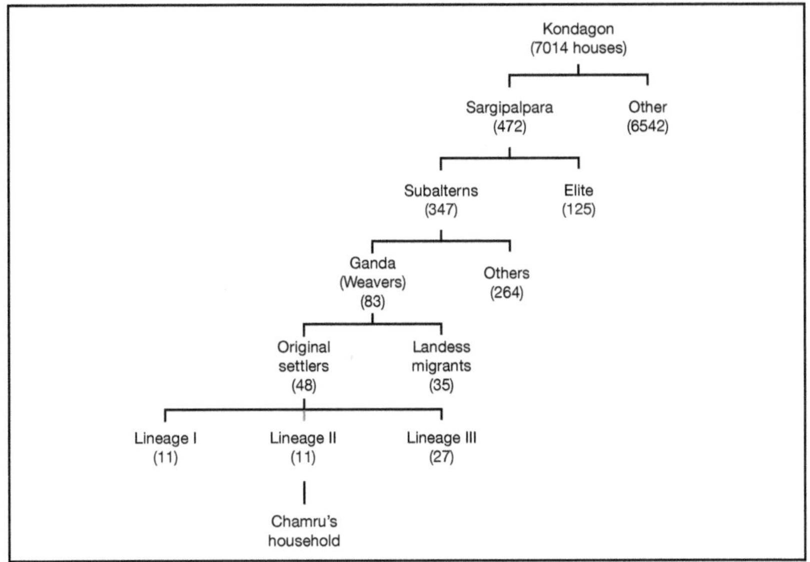

Figure 9.4: The Social Embeddedness of Chamru's Household

Source: Fieldwork data.

Figure 9.5 shows the structure of Chamru's household, H20, as it was in 2013. This household, now headed by Chamru's widow and fifth wife, is exceptional for a number of reasons. First, numbering 21 people, it is the largest household in Sargipalpara by far, given that the average size is around five people per household. Second, Chamru had seven surviving daughters, a son by his fifth wife and a son by his third wife. Three of these daughters have in-marrying husbands and children living in the house. In-marrying husbands are called *lamsena* in Halbi; they are the butt of jokes because tradition demands that wives move to their husband's places after their wedding. The *lamsena* arrangement is classically resorted to when the parents of the groom cannot afford to pay for the wedding. The betrothed boy moves into his bride-to-be's household as a servant on the understanding that the cost of the eventual wedding will be paid for by the bride's father. Third, the household is located on a relatively large 15,600 square foot urban plot that had a market value in 2015 of INR11,000,000 (USD175,000), a fortune by local standards. This household, then, is a wealthy joint family but one that does not fit the classic model of the Indian joint family united by a male head, his sons and their wives. Like all joint families, this one will inevitably divide; how it does so remains to be seen. Nevertheless, we can gain some insight into the values that will inform people by examining the history of the family, focusing on Chamru's quest for the good life and on its consequences.

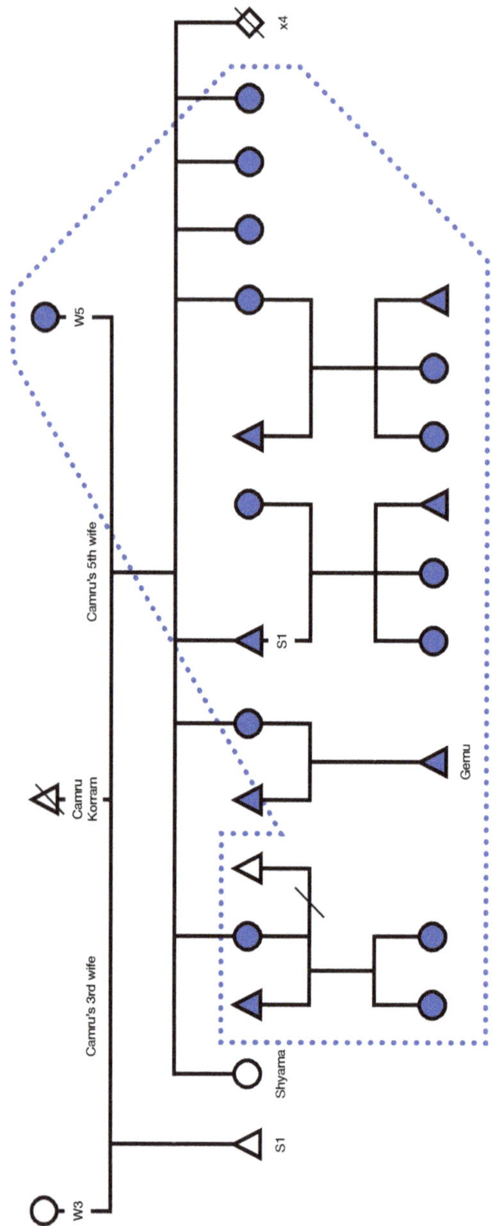

Figure 9.5: The Kinship Relationship Between Members of Chamru's Household

Key: Triangle = male; circle = female; horizontal link below = marriage; horizontal link above = siblings; vertical link = descent; slash = deceased or divorced.

Source: Fieldwork data.

To the extent that wealth is measured in terms of progeny and familial respect, Chamru has been an undoubted success. Not only has he produced nine surviving children, but he continues to live on in the memory of his kinsfolk as a respected *duma*—an ancestral spirit who possesses mediums and who is consulted for advice on domestic-political matters. For women like Gurumai Sukdai, a respected singer of the Lakshmi Jagar epic and mother of three daughters, progeny is the most important form of wealth. Nay more, the fact that Chamru had seven daughters is his most important achievement, for girls are, as the epic she sings makes clear, the embodiment of Lakshmi and of the auspiciousness she personifies. However, to the extent that wealth is measured by personal wealth (in the sense of a long and healthy life), social wealth (in the sense of fame) and material wealth (in the sense of an abundance of possessions), then Chamru's career has been much more chequered. He achieved great fame and fortune twice, but squandered it twice and died relatively young. Gurumai Sukdai gave me a long and detailed account of his life. In the following paragraphs I give a potted summary of her account along with the occasional quote.

As the descendant of an original settler to Sargipalpara, Chamru inherited farmland, weaving as a hereditary caste occupation and a religious specialists' role as spirit medium (*siraha*). By the time Chamru reached manhood, machine-produced cloth had long destroyed the hand-loom trade in Sargipalpara; however, he was able to successfully exploit the economic opportunities that his landholdings and his renown as a spirit medium presented. He was fortunate enough to be part of a patriline that produced four sons in his father's generation, but only two males in his own generation. As such, he inherited a relatively large portfolio of land of different qualities, including a substantial amount of the low-quality *marhan*, whose subsequent market value as residential land was to soar. Chamru never went to school but was a successful farmer who, through hard work and careful marriages, managed to increase his landholdings.

The steady growth of Kondagaon brought with it migrants from neighbouring states, many of them single men looking for wives and for business opportunities. One of these migrants persuaded Chamru to give him his sister in marriage and to go into business with him making bricks at Bailadila in south Bastar, where the establishment of an iron ore mine provided opportunities for a quick profit. Chamru mortgaged his farmland, pawned his wife's jewellery and headed off to Bailadila. As Gurumai put it:

> In this way his by now extensive landholdings passed from his direct control but he retained ownership. They had so much rice the eyes could not see it all. They had lots of land and lots of grain but in those days the price of farmland was very low. They had workers but their earning fell as a result of this and they were in big trouble. Such was his greed to make money on the brick contract that he did not save anything, not a single grain of rice. He lost everything. There was much wealth in his father's time but now there was nothing. We say *bap bera kansa tama, beta bera thenga-tuma*, which translates as 'brass and copper at the time of father, but only a stick and a hollowed-out gourd at the time of son'. His life was like that.

By this time, Chamru had married his fifth wife, who produced 13 children, only nine of whom survived. They lived in great poverty and suffered a lot. According to Gurumai, their fortunes began to change after his wife decided to plant a tulsi shrub and to host a performance of the Lakshmi Jagar epic. Such performances involve the singing and ritual enactment of the 31,000 lines of the oral epic. This must be done at harvest-season time every year for three years; it lasts for nine days in the first year; 11 days in the second year; 13 days in the final year; and always finishes on a Thursday, called *Lachimbar* (Lakshmi's Day) in Halbi.

A crucial factor in the family's economic turnaround was Chamru's growing fame as a spirit medium. His spiritual ancestor possessed him when he was a teenager. His grandfather had great renown as a spirit medium and apocryphal tales had long circulated of his grandfather's miraculous powers. He died relatively young and his duties were taken over, first by Chamru's father and then his father's brother, both of whom also died relatively young. Chamru was only a teenager when his powers as a medium were revealed; however, it was only after he returned from Bailadila that he began to be consulted on a regular basis. This was not entered into as a business, although his growing fame as a medium had accidental material side benefits. As Gurumai Sukdai noted:

> There was an altar at Chamru's house. People from faraway would come to be cured. Chamru was highly respected and lots of worshipping (*puja*) and religious activity happened in his house. People would come on Tuesday and Saturday to consult the spirit (*dev*) who possessed him. People were grateful for getting cured and as a sign of appreciation they would leave a gift. He was regarded as a very trusted spirit.

This accidental wealth enabled him to free his mortgaged land and to begin again as a farmer. His growing family, previously a hindrance because they represented mouths to feed, now became an asset through the labour they performed in the house and on the farm:

> As the children grew up they worked here earning money washing pots and doing housework. A Hindi-speaking outsider named Kori moved into the house, taking Chamru's eldest daughter as his wife. He helped Chamru free his mortgaged land and repaired his house. The family became very wealthy, even more so than many of his neighbours from the Kosta community. The family employed workers on their farmland and wealth in the form of brass and copper pots and pans. They had lots of money, many good rice plots and a large household plot. But Chamru became greedy and lost it all. All that remained was his house. He lost everything because his deity ceased to possess him because of his drunkenness and greed. He began to practise witchcraft on his patients. He would tell people that he was curing them but he was actually practising witchcraft. When people suspected this, they became frightened and stopped coming. He was a physically fit man but he died in the prime of his life. They performed his mortuary ritual and his eldest son Hari, from his second wife, shaved his head and performed the duties of chief mourner. The deity did not possess anybody else after his death.

Chamru's rise and fall as a spirit medium is a classic illustration of the fickle nature of fame. The gossip and rumour that circulates about someone's outstanding power and elevates them above the rest of the pack is the very same gossip and rumour that brings them undone when something happens to lead people to question the assumptions they hold about the person in question. It matters not whether the assumption is true or false; it is the fact of the assumption that matters. The rumour that he was practising witchcraft, which was no doubt fuelled by his alleged drunken behaviour, spread and brought him down. Such is the morality of the domestic moral economy; when the court of public opinion judges someone's behaviour as immoral the consequences can be very serious. This informal system of public morality, which is neighbourhood- and community-based, sits alongside two formal, more narrowly caste-based systems of morality and social control. The first is grounded in local religious beliefs and practices and centres around the ancestral spirits (*duma*) and the mediums (*siraha*) they possess. In this sense, Chamru, as ancestral spirit, continues to play a role in the social life of the living. Gurumai's account of his apotheosis is as follows:

Chamru's younger brother Shobha had two sons. The youngest, Lachman, was miraculously cured of a severe disability after he was possessed by Chamru's spirit *(duma)* and became a *siraha*. Lachman was fit and healthy as a child but as he grew up his body became deformed. He stopped wearing clothes. He was naked like a cow. He couldn't stand to have clothes on his body. He was unable to walk and even unable to wash his body after defecation. His mother had to do this for him. He would just wrap himself in a shawl and sit. When Chamru died the community performed a sacrifice ritual called *jatra*. This went on for four days. *Sirahas* from many villages were invited. After three to four days they performed the *dev bharto* ritual to see if anyone from Chamru's clan would become possessed. To everyone's surprise Chamru's deity possessed Lachman and he stood up straight. He was cured of his disability and he returned to normal life. He got married and is now the father of a son. Lachman is now a renowned *siraha* who is possessed by many different spirits. It takes more than five men to hold Lachman when he is possessed by a very powerful female deity like Kankalinmata. Another is Telanginmata. When this female deity possesses him, she makes a hole in his tongue, dresses up in female clothes (*nath*, *choli* and *lahanga*) fastens bells to her feet, puts a red mark on her forehead and dances vigorously. Other deities who possess him include Gouriyamata and Butiyadev. Ancestral spirits (*duma*) of dead *siraha* possess him too. These include Chamru's spirit as well as those of Chamru's father and Chamru's father's brother. Another is Curlin, a deity who flies through the air, enters the body of pregnant women, and causes them delivery problems that kill them during childbirth. When this *dev* comes nobody stays nearby because she tickles him or her and kills them. Another great female deity of Bastar who possesses him, is Mata Mawli. *Siraha*s in this lineage all die in the prime of their life.

The second form of male social control is of a more secular kind. The final stage of Gurumai's story tells of Chamru's son's succession to his father's role as both medium and caste leader (*naik*).

Now the deity possesses Chamru's eldest son, who is also the *naik*. Ganda people from many villages gathered and installed Chamru's eldest son Hari as their caste leader (*naik*). They arranged for the musicians and sacrificed two goats. They appointed Hari as *naik* and Nandlal as *paik*. The *naik* and *paik* are always from the same clan and the job of the *paik* is to assist the *naik*. They are selected on the basis of their ability to do the job and, upon the death of a leader, a younger brother or family member of the deceased will be selected if they are deemed suitable. Whenever a caste meeting (*samaj*) is to be held the *paik* goes to the house of every member and informs them about the date, day and time of meeting. The job of the *naik* is to arrange for the reintegration of outcasts. For example, if the

> gods have caused problems for someone, or if someone hits someone else with a shoe—be it in a domestic argument between husband and wife or some other fight—then the *naik* must arrange for their purification and reintegration. He brings water from Bare Dongar [the former capital of Bastar in precolonial times] and stores it in his house. He arranges for the caste community (*samaj*) to gather, sits the affected person down, and sprinkles them with the holy water. From then on, the affected person may mix with other members of their caste, who will now accept water from the hand of the previously outcast person. A deity possesses Hari so that, like his father Chamru, he is both *naik* and *siraha.*

Chamru may not have achieved lasting wealth and fame when judged at the neighbourhood and community level, but at the lower level domestic moral economy of Sargipalpara's three Korram clan lineages, his life was a very successful one. He acquired wealth in the form of progeny and fame, both as caste leader and medium. The rising price of urban land in Sargipalpara has given the household new-found wealth for the third time. Chamru only fails on the score of a long life, but that seems to be the price one has to pay to be a respected medium in Sargipalpara. Chamru's son now takes on this dubious status. He also assumes the mantle as poverty-stricken millionaire, but whereas his father built up the large joint family that now occupies H20, his son will have to negotiate its division and dissolution.

Conclusion

The preceding account of the recent micro-economic history of Sargipalpara has focused on the objective economic facts of land prices and class and one woman's perspective on the life of a man of renown. My interlocutor, Gurumai Sukdai, as the singer of two oral epics, is a woman of renown herself. I have collected her autobiography and her biography as told by her youngest daughter, Babita. I finish with a very brief extract from the latter to illustrate Mauss's point that a woman's morality is not that of men's:

> Mum learned to be become a *gurumai* from my father's mother. Before that she used to go to make bricks. She used to make clay roof tiles. She used to sell rice and she also used to travel to the periodic markets. She also knows how to lay bricks with a builder. She did all these different jobs and raised her children. She also made bricks and built a house. She ate rice in one break and gruel in another and built a big house.

> Her middle daughter used to go to work with mum and helped her. The youngest one [the narrator] went to school. She studied until seventh grade. After this she left school and, under her own volition, went to a temple and got married. Before the marriage her husband did not drink. Later on, he learnt to drink. He also learnt to how to gamble. Hanging about with his friends, he learned every bad habit and forgot about home. Forgetting about home made it very difficult [for the narrator] to clothe and feed the family. The children, too, feel very sad. When working, he works like a bull, but he doesn't know to eat. Even when explained he does not understand. After mum and my sisters saw my condition they were sad and they brought food, soap, oil and clothes for me. Of the three sisters, the greatest sadness and misfortune has befallen me. My fate is the worst of all. Their destiny was to find a good husband. My destiny was to find a bad husband. The way my husband lives has made my life like that of a widow.

Sadly, Babita did not become a widow. Unlike the goddess Lakshmi, who merely gets beaten-up by her husband, her husband murdered her in a drunken rage, and it was left to her elderly mother to raise her four young children. Such events enable one to appreciate why the activities of the Naxalites and the BJP are a distant concern and why domestic morality is a principal cause of concern for women. The enemy lies within for these women in urban areas. For those lucky ones like Gurumai Sukdai who have a small urban plot, the values of the global political economy can be a blessing as well as a curse. Her household, while of the land-rich, dirt-poor kind, is not of the 'millionaire' variety like Chamru's. Nevertheless, she has exploited the opportunities the urbanisation of Sargipalpara has offered by dividing her house into three small apartments and renting two of them out.

References

Gregory, C. A. (1997). *Savage money: The anthropology and politics of commodity exchange.* London, England: Harwood. doi.org/10.4324/9780203986639

Mauss, M. (2007). *Manual of ethnography*. London, England: Berghahn.

Piketty, T. (2014). *Capital in the twenty-first century*. Cambridge, MA: Harvard University Press. doi.org/10.4159/9780674369542

Polanyi, K. (1944). *The great transformation: The political and economic origins of our time.* New York, NY: Rinehart.

Ramanujan, A. K. (1991). Towards a counter-system: Woman's tales. In A. Appadurai, F. J. Korom & M. A. Millls (Eds), *Gender, genre, and power in South Asian expressive traditions* (pp. 33–55). Philadelphia, PA: University of Pennsylvania Press.

Sundar, N. (2016). *The burning forest: India's war in Bastar*. New Delhi, India: Juggernaut Publication.

www.ingramcontent.com/pod-product-compliance
Lightning Source LLC
Chambersburg PA
CBHW040142270326
41928CB00023B/3319

* 9 7 8 1 7 6 0 4 6 2 0 0 0 *